Crisis in Soviet Agriculture

Stefan Hedlund

CROOM HELM
London & Sydney

ST. MARTIN'S PRESS
New York

For my parents

© 1984 Stefan Hedlund
Croom Helm Ltd, Provident House, Burrell Row,
Beckenham, Kent BR3 1AT

Croom Helm Australia Pty Ltd,
G.P.O. Box 5097, Sydney,
NSW 2001, Australia

British Library Cataloguing in Publication Data

Hedlund, Stefan
    Crisis in Soviet agriculture.
    1. Agriculture—Economic aspects—Soviet Union
    I. Title
    338.1'0947   HD1992
    ISBN 0-7099-1281-1

All rights reserved. For information, write:
St. Martin's Press, Inc., 175 Fifth Avenue,
New York, NY 10010
Printed in Great Britain
First published in the United States of America in 1984

Library of Congress Cataloging in Publication Data

Hedlund, Stefan, 1953-
    Crisis in Soviet agriculture.

    Includes bibliographical references and index.
    1. Agriculture and state—Soviet Union.
2. Agriculture—Economic aspects—Soviet Union.
3. Agriculture—Soviet Union.   I. Title.
HD1993.H43   1984   338.1'847   83-42998
ISBN 0-312-17401-2

Printed and bound in Great Britain

CONTENTS

FIGURES AND TABLES

Figures

Tables

ACKNOWLEDGEMENTS

This study is the result on the one hand of a long-standing interest in the workings of the Soviet economy, and on the other in problems that arise in the relations between state and peasantry in economic development. The development of Soviet collective agriculture seemed a reasonable compromise between these two interests.

The actual shape that the study has taken was greatly influenced by Alec Nove, whose inspirational remarks and helpful comments at an early stage of the work, as well as on the final draft, are warmly acknowledged. Much of the research for the study has taken place at the Institute for Soviet and East European Studies in Glasgow, and the helpful assistance of their library staff is also hereby acknowledged.

The actual writing of the book, however, has taken place at the Department of Economics, Lund University, where it was also presented as a doctoral dissertation in June 1983. During that time I benefited greatly from helpful comments from a large number of people, most of whom were participants at the Departmental International Seminar. Lena Ekelund, Carl-Hampus Lyttkens, Magnus Persson, Tore Sjökvist, Stig Tegle and Åsa Weibull all read various versions of the manuscript. Göte Hansson, Bengt Höglund and Ingemar Ståhl provided valuable comments in particular on the critical final draft. Amongst people outwith my own department, I owe a large debt to Lars Edgren, Kristian Gerner, Lennart Jörberg and Harald Ståhlberg for insightful comments on the historical parts of the study, and on the correspondence — or lack of such — between my ideas and actual Soviet reality.

Above all, however, the gratitude to my supervisor, Mats Lundahl, should be acknowledged. His stern supervision has — in a truly Stalinist fashion — prevented me from leaving the narrow path leading to the completion of this book. At the same time he has also shown the good judgement to supply me with just enough encouragement, at the right times, to save me from sharing the fate of Stalin's collectivised peasantry.

Last but not least, I am indebted to Alan Harkess who has adjusted my own very personal view of how English should be written, to Pia Åkerman who has over-fulfilled the plan several times in typing the manuscript, and to Erling Pettersson who has provided the electronic wizardry of word processing.

To all of these, and to others who have helped at various points in

Acknowledgements

time, goes my warmly felt gratitude. Maybe it will not be necessary to indicate responsibility for any remaining errors and omissions?

GLOSSARY

In a study of this nature, the use of a number of Russian terms and expressions is unavoidable, simply because translations would either lose the exact denotation of the original, or be contrary to standard practice of reference. Such words have, when first encountered, been explained either in the text or in a footnote. On some occasions explanations have been repeated in later chapters. To assist the reader further, this glossary provides explanations of the most important terms used in the present study.

Agitprop: Acronym for agitation and propaganda. Separate department in the party organisation.

Apparatchik: A full-time employee of the party *apparat*, or bureaucracy. Sometimes also used with reference to people in the state hierarchy.

Artel: A producer's collective. Normally used with reference to the form of agricultural co-operation that later developed into the *kolkhoz*, but originally also covering artisans' co-operatives.

Barschina: The most common form of serfdom in pre-1861 Russia. Roughly equivalent to day labour.

Bezdorozhe: Literally 'roadlessness'. Depicts the time of year when the bulk of the road network is turned into impassable mud.

Beznaryadnoe zveno: The 'unassigned link'. A small group of peasants that work together under self-determination, and who are remunerated according to the results of their efforts.

Buro torgovlya: State organisations that exist in some of the permanent urban markets, and which accept produce from the peasants for sale on commission basis.

Chernozem: Black earth. By far the best soils in the Soviet Union.

Dogovor: Contract or agreement.

Edinolichnik: Private peasant in the true sense of the word, i.e. one who does not belong to a state or collective farm. Very few of these remain.

Edinonachalie: One-man management. Highly important principle in Soviet administrative theory. Denotes the very personal nature of responsibility of the Soviet official or manager.

Gosbank: Acronym for *Gosudarstvennyi bank*, the state bank.

Glossary

Gosplan: Acronym for *Gosudarstvennaya planovaya komissiya*, the state plan commission.

Kadastr: Land survey.

Khozraschet: Acronym for *khozyaistvennyi raschet*, economic calculation. Aimed at a higher reliance on the use of 'profits' as plan indicators.

Kolkhoz: Acronym for *kollektivnoe khozyaistvo*, collective farm.

Kolkhoznik: A male member of the kolkhoz.

Kolkhoznitsa: A female member of the kolkhoz.

Kolkhoztsentr: The central body of the kolkhoz organisation.

Kombed: Acronym for *komitet bednota*, a committee of poor peasants.

Kommuna: Commune. One of the first forms of Soviet agricultural co-operation, and also that which was most 'communistic'.

Kompleksnost: Indicates the (lack of) co-ordination in production, which is necessary in order to provide, for example, integrated systems of machinery.

Komsomol: Acronym for *kommunisticheskii soyuz molodezhi*, the Communist youth organisation.

Kontraktatsiya: A system of contracted deliveries to the state of agricultural produce at previously fixed prices.

Kraikom: Acryonym for *krainyi komitet*, party committee at the *krai* (regional) level. The krai is a very large administrative unit that only exists in some republics.

Kulak: Fist. Used with reference to better-off peasants who in various ways exploited their neighbours.

Lichnoe podsobnoe khozyaistvo: private subsidiary farming. Refers to the private plots in collective and state farms. The Soviets deny that they are private, and prefer the expression 'personal'.

Minselkhozmash: Acronym for *Ministerstvo selskokhozyaistvennykh mashin*, the Ministry for Agricultural Machinery.

Narkomzem: Acronym for *Narodnyi kommissariat zemli*, People's Commissariat of Agriculture, during Stalin.

Nedelimyi fond: Indivisible fund. Used for investment purposes.

Nomenklatura: Appointment list containing those positions that cannot be filled without party approval.

Obkom: Acronym for *Oblastnoi komitet*, party committee at *oblast* level.

Oblast: Administrative unit above the *raion*.

Obrok: Form of serfdom that was based on quit-rents instead of labour services.

Orgotdel: Acronym for *organisatsionnyi otdel*, department in charge of matters regarding the party organisation.

Otdel: Department.

Otstoyaschii: Backward. Used with reference to financially weak kolkhozy.

Politotdel: Acronym for *politicheskii otdel*, political department. Introduced by Stalin with the Machine Tractor Stations in 1933, in order to strengthen party control over agriculture.

Pravo kontrolya: Right of control.

Pribil: Profit.

Prodnalog: Acronym for *prodovolstvennyi nalog*, tax-in-kind. Introduced by Lenin in 1921 as the starting signal of the New Economic Policy (NEP).

Prodrazverstka: Policy introduced during War Communism, the basic principle of which was forceful extraction of produce from the peasantry.

Raiispolkom: Acronym for *raionnyi ispolnitelnyi komitet*, executive committee of the local soviet.

Raikom: Acronym for *raionnyi komitet*, district party committee.

Raion: Administrative unit at district level.

Razkulachivanie: Dekulakisation. Official term for the process whereby the top layer of the Soviet peasantry was deported during the collectivisation campaign.

Rentabelnost: Profitability.

Samizdat: Illegal network for the publication of pamphlets and books in uncensored form, normally typewritten and mimeographed.

Sebestoimost: Non-labour cost.

Selkhozkhimiya: State organisation with responsibility for the supply of agricultural chemicals.

Selkhoztekhnika: State organisation with responsibility for the supply of agricultural machinery.

Sovkhoz: Acronym for *sovetskoe khozyaistvo*, state farm.

Starosta: Village elder.

Tekuschestvo: Turnover of Soviet officials.

Toz: Acronym for *tovarichestvo po obschestvennoi obrabotki zemli*, association for the common cultivation of land.

Travopole: Crop rotation pattern that includes grasses.

Troika: Committee of three, originally with reference to a team of three horses.

Tsentrosoyuz: Central body of the consumer co-operative organisation.

Upolnomochennyi: Plenipotentiary. Person with complete authority vested in him to carry out specific tasks.

Glossary

Zagotovki: Requisitions of agricultural produce.
Zakupki: Procurements of agricultural produce.

1 INTRODUCTION

This is a book about Soviet agriculture. It is not, however, a book about agricultural production as such. It is a book about the institutions and decision-making processes that determine this production. Consequently, we shall not be concerned with agronomic detail, but rather with the institutional framework of the agricultural sector. Furthermore, as the title implies, the purpose of our study will be to deal with the present crisis in Soviet agriculture, and this may need some elucidation.

A major problem facing Soviet agriculture is that of low productivity, which is due partly to adverse natural conditions and partly to a low level of mechanisation and an underdeveloped infrastructure. There is nothing new about these problems, however, and they hardly merit the term 'crisis'. Consequently we shall not be concerned with international comparisons of agricultural output, nor with long-run measures aimed at improving the overall framework. Our understanding of 'crisis' is rather to be found in a growing gap between demand and supply of agricultural produce in the Soviet Union, and in the consequent pressures on the government to 'do something' in order to alleviate the food shortages.

On the demand side, it is important to state at the outset that there is no crisis in food supply in terms of impending starvation. The problem lies in the population's *expectations* of continued improvements in living standards. The importance in eastern bloc countries of secure food supplies at low prices takes on an importance that for a Westerner might be hard to comprehend. By providing food and other basic necessities at low prices, the state to some extent compensates its population for the loss of a broad range of political rights. In the Soviet case the government is coming under increasing pressure by demands not so much for *more food* as for an *improved diet*, above all in terms of an increased meat consumption. This, then, is one side of the crisis – the future ability of the Soviet regime to buy legitimacy by fulfilling popular expectations for improvements in food supply.

The main focus of our presentation will thus be on the supply side, and on the possibility of achieving major increases in agricultural output in the *short run*. In pursuing this ambition, we shall make extensive use of historical experience. It will be an underlying assumption of the study that many of the problems that face modern Soviet agriculture

1

follow directly from past agricultural policy. We shall thus start with an investigation of how the present institutional framework emerged, and what attempts have been made to change it.

The present situation will then be analysed in terms of a game between the different actors involved, viewed against the background of historical experience. Finally, in the context of a discussion of possible changes, it will be argued that the only viable solution to the crisis is one that attempts to alter the institutional framework and the decision-making processes, i.e. it will have political implications.

The 'Crisis in Soviet Agriculture', as we see it, is thus a combination of two factors. On the one hand, the population's expectations for improvements in food supply exceed the present capacity of production and ability to import, and on the other, the only way to achieve major additions in output in the short run is by making political concessions in terms of reform. The reason that the situation is becoming critical at this point is, first, that the gap between demand and supply is taking on unprecedented proportions; and, secondly, while in the past there were possibilities of short-term additions to output by means of sheer expansion, this road is now closed, and a solution must be found in improved yields.

To describe the present situation we are going to use the metaphor of comparing Soviet agriculture to a chain that is composed of many different links, some weaker and some stronger. As the chain is exposed to an ever increasing strain, some of the weaker links will eventually have to yield, and it will be our endeavour to find out where the break might occur. Let us start by setting out the background to the crisis.

A Crisis Develops

During the latter half of the 1970s, the Soviet Union witnessed mounting problems in its agricultural sector. Farms failed to meet plans, and meat production especially performed inadequately. To cope with the situation, imports, mainly of grains, were allowed to rise substantially.[1] The US, which was the main supplier, found that increasingly vociferous domestic opinion demanded the use of the 'food weapon' in order to exert pressure on the Soviets. Finally the Carter administration resorted to grain embargoes to demonstrate its displeasure at Soviet intervention in Afghanistan.[2] Although the effectiveness of these embargoes is debatable, especially since other nations — notably Argentina — stepped in to cover deficits, the situation is obviously disturbing to the Soviet leadership and the US stance has repeatedly been denounced as 'highly uncommercial'. Against the background of the threat of more concerted action at a future critical point, there are indications that there is a strong desire to reduce the dependence on food imports not only for hard currency reasons.

One element of the crisis is thus external, but the most important one is domestic, and at the beginning of the 1980s the situation has deteriorated even further. Four consecutive harvests have been clear failures, particularly in 1981 and 1982 when statistics on the grain harvest were actually withheld.[3] Food is becoming increasingly difficult to obtain, and meat has been rationed for some years.[4] Against this background, it is obvious that something must be done, and in May 1982 a special Central Committee plenum was held to discuss a new 'Food Programme' for the 1980s.[5] Brezhnev's speech at that plenum gives valuable information both on the Soviet view of the present problems and on the future course of policy. Let us use this speech to set the stage for our analysis.[6]

A New Agricultural Programme

The starting point for Brezhnev's account of Soviet agricultural performance is the May 1965 plenum of the Central Committee. A new agricultural strategy was outlined that was to come to grips with the problems that had mounted during the last years of Khrushchev's rule. According to Brezhnev this strategy has performed well.

Since 1965 the areas under irrigation and drainage have both increased by 1.7 times. Available draught power has increased threefold, which also applies to the supply of mineral fertiliser. As a result, labour productivity has trebled and gross output in value terms has increased by 50 per cent, from 83 billion roubles in 1961-5 (annual average) to 124 billion in 1976-80. Comparable figures for the US and the Common Market countries are given as 29 and 31 per cent respectively.

In spite of a population increase of 35 million during the period, *per capita* output has increased by 28 per cent. *Per capita* consumption of meat has increased by 41 per cent to reach 58 kg, that of vegetables by 35 per cent to 97 kg, etc. Data on increases in the production of various agricultural products are given in Table 1.1, and in this light it would not appear that there is a mounting crisis. Where then does the problem lie? From the sheer volume of recent writings in the Soviet Press, and from the mere fact that a separate plenum was held on the issue, we can infer that the Soviets are worried, and these worries focus on three points. First, largely due to rapid increases in wages with no corresponding increases in prices, demand expands at a faster pace than supply; secondly, rapid urbanisation has left fewer people as actual producers on the land, which has greatly increased the strain on the transport and distribution system; and thirdly, increases in agricultural *productivity* have not been satisfactory. (The latter point is an obvious indication that the Soviets are finding themselves in a position where a shift has to be made from a policy of expansion to one of improved yields.) Apart from the points above, it is also mentioned *en passant* that there are problems in the fields of procurement, storage, transport, processing and trading in agricultural produce, which obviously largely stem from the infrastructural problem.

Table 1.1: Agricultural Production (million tons; eggs: million pieces, annual averages)

	1961-5	1976-80
Grain	130.3	205.0
Vegetables	16.9	26.3
Meat	9.3	14.8
Milk	64.7	92.7
Eggs	28.7	63.1

Source: *Pravda*, 25 May 1982.

To combat the problems, the Food Programme suggests measures much along the same lines as those applied during the past 17 years — only more. The share of the nation's resources that goes into agriculture is to increase substantially. State procurement prices for most agricultural products are to go up, at an estimated annual cost of 16 billion roubles. State contributions to rural development, such as housing, schools, cultural activities, etc. are to increase at a further cost of 3.3 billion, and debt amounting to 9.7 billion is to be written off.

As a result of these increases in inputs, available draught power is to increase by 1.6 times, the supply of mineral fertiliser by 1.7 times, and the areas under irrigation and drainage are each to be expanded by 23-5 million hectares. The plan targets for output during the 12th plan (1986-90) are set at 250-5 million tons of grain, 20-20.5 million tons of meat and 37-9 million tons of vegetables.

A Credible Cure?

Given the performance during 1976-80 (see Table 1.1) these targets are ambitious indeed, and the question arises whether they are realistic. Will the Food Programme be capable of alleviating the present difficulties? Brezhnev presents a fairly bright picture of past performance, but unfortunately reality is considerably more sombre. The growing gap between demand and production is serious. Over the period indicated, wages have doubled, while most consumer prices have remained unchanged. The resultant increase in demand has been further aggravated by the shift towards more meat consumption. Since conversion ratios from feed to grain are very unfavourable, and since grains constitute the bulk of the feed balance, this has greatly increased the strain on grain production.

To close the gap between demand and supply would mean either curbing the former, via price increases, or boosting the latter, via increased imports or increased production. Price increases are neither mentioned in the Food Programme, nor likely to occur, given the importance of low food prices. Increased imports, on the other hand, are unlikely, partly because of statements in the Food Programme, and partly because of sheer logistics. Ports, storage and transport facilities are already overstrained. The problem must thus be solved via increases in production, and this is yet again where the main problem lies.

Agricultural investment has been increasing continuously throughout the Brezhnev era, and further increases from the present record level can hardly be possible for much longer.[7] The opportunity costs in industry will simply be too high. Furthermore, the rate of return to investment has been falling throughout the 1970s,[8] largely due to factors that lie outside agriculture proper. Deficient quality, faulty specifications, lack of spare parts, etc. are some of the most frequent complaints in the Soviet press, and we will return to these problems at length in Chapter 6. The important point for our purpose is that merely increasing investment will not help. A tell-tale sign that the Soviet leaders are also aware of the fact that the solution does not lie in more inputs is the repeated emphasis that is placed on the importance of a better utilisation of existing resources.

Another aspect of our problem is the relation between production and use. The countries of the Common Market have together almost the same population as the Soviet Union. They have also approximately the same volume of disposable grain (production plus net imports).[9] Yet there is a substantial difference in living standards. The difference between production and use must consequently be much larger in the Soviet Union than in the Common Market countries. The first part of this difference lies in reported yields. In the West it is common practice to report *barn yields*, i.e. production that has actually been harvested and stored. In the Soviet Union it is practice to report *bunker yields*, i.e. what is delivered from the combine. The difference is made up of moisture and foreign matter content. The magnitude of this difference will vary depending on the weather situation at harvest time. If the weather is dry the difference will not be great, but in a wet harvest a considerable portion will be water and soil. It is common practice in the West to deduct between 5 and 10 per cent from Soviet figures to obtain comparable data.[10]

A further explanation of the difference between production and use concerns waste. Due to a lack of covered trucks and many drivers not taking enough trouble to avoid spilling, a large part of the harvest will be lost in transit to the elevators.[11] Part of these losses will be covered by the conversion to barn yields, but not all, since it is common practice not to store grain on the farms, but first to take it to the elevators and then back to the farm.[12] Even more serious, however, are losses due to insufficient or substandard storage facilities. Each year a large part of the harvest is simply left to rot in the fields or in poorly constructed elevators, due either to a lack of storage or to lack of transport. Some Soviet sources put these losses as high as 20 per cent of total output.[13]

An important cause of these losses is obviously insufficient investment in agricultural infrastructure. The main thrust of our argument, however, will be aimed at showing that imbalanced and wasteful utilisation of existing resources makes this problem vastly more serious than it need be.

It thus appears that the problems are not of a kind that can be eradicated by simply increasing the input of resources into agriculture. Yet this is precisely the aim of the 'new' programme – increased investment and increased procurement prices. Consequently there is a considerable risk that it will not in any substantive way get to grips with the real problems. Good money will end up chasing bad. More land can be brought under cultivation through massive investment in drainage and irrigation. Labour productivity can be increased through large increases in the supply of machinery. The fertility of land can be increased through further increases in the supply of mineral fertiliser, etc. Increases in agricultural output can no doubt be achieved in this way, but only at a high opportunity cost in terms of reductions in the input of resources into other sectors of the economy. Industrial growth rates are not only below their past impressive heights, but also below present plans and decreasing.[14] The real problems are the falling rate of return on investment, the falling productivity of labour, etc., which are not solved by substantial increases in resources.

One part of the Food Programme that is encouraging is the increased emphasis on improved rural living standards. The flight to the cities is becoming an increasingly serious problem,[15] especially since it tends to be young, educated people that leave. The bias in population structure between urban and rural areas is widening. Young people who are sent away to receive specialist training have a marked tendency not to return. This problem is obviously a consequence of the large gap between urban and rural living standards. Consumer goods that are in short supply in the cities are usually impossible to get in the village shops. Housing standards are inferior, access roads are frequently poor, electrification of the entire country has only recently been completed and power cuts are frequent.[16] The consequences of this continuous drain on the most productive parts of the labour force are obviously serious, and it is good that attention is being paid to the problem. It would hardly be realistic, however, to expect any beneficial short-run effects from measures aimed at closing the rural-urban differential. At best, the trend will be slowed down, and in the longer run may be reversed.

Hence, the three main pillars of our argument thus far are (a) that the present crisis in Soviet agriculture should be seen in terms of the political implications for the regime of a failure to close the widening gap between consumption and production of agricultural produce, (b) that this cannot be achieved by reducing real wages, and (c) that continued increases in investment and in procurement prices will have smaller and smaller effects and thus prove to be more and more costly.

The purpose of our study shall thus be to look for possible improvements in the utilisation of *given* resources, which after all are massive, and our approach will be to look for conflicts in the incentive structure that guides decision making. Furthermore, since our understanding of the crisis is one of a food crisis, we shall only deal with food-producing *kolkhozy*, and since we are interested in elements of crisis, the study will have a heavy bias towards unsuccessful farms. First, however, let us set out the background against which the argument will be presented.

The Agricultural Sector

The performance of Soviet agriculture today is causing a greater and greater strain to be placed on the rest of the economy. Its one-time role of supplying resources for the industrialisation drive — if it ever was the case – belongs to the past,[17] and it is now a net recipient of substantial resources, in terms of capital investment and subsidies, as well as written-off debt.

One indication that the role of agriculture in the industrialisation process has been weak is the slow transfer of the population from rural to urban status. Figures in Table 1.2 show that the Soviet pattern deviates considerably from that of other industrialised nations. Japan especially shows a marked relationship between rapid industrialisation and rapid population transfer. We can thus see that the share of the Soviet labour force that is engaged in agriculture is unusually high, and due to the considerable importance that will be placed on the labour problem in subsequent chapters, we shall digress briefly to discuss its component parts.

Table 1.2: Share of the Rural Labour Force in Total (per cent)

	1950	1975
US	12.3	3.8
Japan	50.1	12.5
Germany	22.7	6.4
Soviet Union	48.0	23.7

Source: Manevich (1981), p. 56.

Labour Force

As of 1 January 1980, the Soviet population was 264.5 million, out of which 98.2 – or 37 per cent – resided in rural areas.[18] The total labour force amounts to over 124 million, about half of which is female. Out of these about 110 million are found in the 'national economy' and the remainder in collective farms. People belonging to collective farms (we will return to these distinctions below) are accounted for separately, since they are not as such employed by the state. In order to estimate the agricultural labour force, we have to add people employed in state farms (11.9 million) and in inter-farm enterprises (0.4 million). This gives us a figure of 26.1 million, or about 24 per cent of the total labour force.[19] Here, however, the considerable input of labour on peasant private plots is not included.[20] If this were done, the figure might well be brought up to around 30 per cent of the total labour force, which is extremely high compared with other industrialised nations.

The most important point for our purpose lies in precisely this fact.

In spite of massive investment, it has not been possible to achieve noteworthy reductions in the agricultural labour force. On the contrary, we find that participation rates among women and the elderly are increasing, particularly on the private plots, and that the number of urban dwellers who are helping out with the harvest is also increasing rapidly. Once again we must conclude that the problem does not lie in a lack of resources: it must be sought in a wasteful utilisation of given resources.

Let us now proceed with our description of the agricultural sector, first to outline its institutional framework, and then to examine its performance in terms of output.

Institutions

On the surface, Soviet agricultural production takes place under three different modes of production. There are state farms, or *sovkhozy* (*sovetskoe khozyaistvo*), where everything is owned by the state and where everybody is a state employee, there are collective farms, or *kolkhozy* (*kollektivnoe khozyaistvo*), where everything but land (and minor property of the individual households) is owned collectively and which are formally autonomous units, and finally there are the private plots (*lichnoe podsobnoe khozyaistvo*), small parcels of land, to which all peasant households as well as a number of state employees are entitled.

In Soviet practice the first two modes of production are distinct. Sovkhozy form part of the so-called national economy, as state enterprises, whereas kolkhozy are independent entities, entering into contractual agreements with the state on a strictly voluntary basis. Lip-service is also paid to this distinction in the practice of issuing *directives* to the former and *recommendations* to the latter. For our purposes, however, the two are identical, and we shall briefly substantiate this point. Table 1.3 summarises some main indicators. It can be seen from the table that there are now about as many state farms as there are collective farms. The latter were originally far more numerous, exceeding 250,000, but through a process of amalgamations and of converting unsuccessful kolkhozy into sovkhozy, the gap has narrowed substantially and is still shrinking. The average state farm is larger than the average collective farm.[21] It has more land, more capital equipment and more livestock. Again, however, the differences are narrowing. On the other hand, the average collective farm tends to have higher labour productivity, largely due to a greater supply of effort.[22]

A major historical difference between the two types of organisation lay in the form of pay. Sovkhoz workers were state employees, and were accordingly paid a fixed monthly salary, whereas kolkhoz pay was a residual after all other expenditure had been met. Since 1966, however, the latter pay a guaranteed minimum for work done which is related to pay in the former. Another difference concerned investment. While kolkhozy were forced to finance investment out of revenue, sovkhozy received allocations from the state budget for such purposes. At present, a system of full cost accounting (*khozraschet*) is increasingly adopted by sovkhozy, which in essence means that they too will have to meet all their costs out of revenue. A third difference, finally, concerns the private plots. Originally these were found only in the kolkhozy, as a concession to peasants who were being forcibly collectivised. Over time this privilege has been extended to broad groups of state employees as well, in rural and urban areas, albeit on a smaller scale than those found in the kolkhozy.

Table 1.3: Kolkhoz-Sovkhoz Comparisons, 1965-80

	Kolkhozy				Sovkhozy			
	1965	1970	1975	1980	1965	1970	1975	1980
Number of farms (000)	36.3	33.0	28.5	25.9	11.7	15.0	18.1	21.1
Households (mill.)	15.4	14.4	13.5	12.8				
Work-force (mill.)	18.6	16.7	15.2	13.3	8.2	8.9	10.3	11.6
Gross output (bill. roub.)	35.5	42.3	42.0	41.8	20.6	29.5	35.3	44.5
Capital assets[a] (bill. roub.)	42.3	60.0	91.7	109.8				
Sown area (mill. hectares)	105.1	99.1	98.2	95.2	89.1	91.7	107.3	111.8
Livestock (mill. head)	38.3	41.7	47.6	47.9	24.5	29.1	35.6	40.1
Tractors (000)	756	942	1,064	1,057	681	803	1,038	1,190
Combines (000)	224	292	298	300	265	294	351	373
Trucks (000)	426	479	520	529	335	381	468	585

Note: [a]*Nedelimye fondy*, roughly corresponding to fixed capital.
Source: *Narkhoz* (1981), p. 254f, 300f.

From the above, it is easy to gain the impression that the two types of farms are converging, and some do believe that a merger of the two is a conscious policy of the Soviet leadership. Some differences do remain, however. Kolkhozy are still, at least in the formal sense, co-operatives, with elected officials, in contrast to the state-owned sovkhozy where officials are appointed. Furthermore, while sovkhozy are directly subordinated to territorial sovkhoz administrations, kolkhozy are formally autonomous, which gives them somewhat greater freedom, although they are still subject to control by local party organs. Finally, the reforms regarding pay and financing have not yet been completed, and thus some differences continue to exist. None of these differences are important to our analysis, however, and in the discussion of kolkhozy below, it is assumed that the analysis applies equally to both forms.

While the kolkhoz, then, will be taken to represent the state sector in Soviet agriculture, the private plots will accordingly represent the substantial private sector. In the midst of state ownership and control, they truly represent private production, enjoying even the right to dispose of their produce at market-determined prices. They are a thing of the past, and policy has been vacillating between open hostility and grudging acceptance of the fact that they are necessary. In spite of the fact that cultivation is medieval — spade and hoe — they contribute 27 per cent of total agricultural output, using only 3 per cent of the land.[23] We shall return to this 'second agriculture' in more detail in Chapter 4, and until then most of our attention will be focused on the state sector as represented by the kolkhoz.

Performance

As we can see from Table 1.1 above, growth in agricultural production in the past two decades has been quite impressive. However, if we consider the costs involved, it is less so, and we shall return to this at length in Chapter 3. Meanwhile, an indication of the problem can be obtained from Table 1.3, from which we can calculate the value of gross output per 1,000 roubles of fixed capital. In 1965 it was 839. By 1970 it had fallen to 705, in 1975 to 458 and in 1980 it was down to 388, or less than half of the 1965 level. Given that other factors have been more or less constant or even increasing, and that production is stagnating, the Food Programme's reliance on further increases in investment in order to increase output must seem doubtful.

While our main interest below will be with the supply side, we should digress briefly here to discuss the demand side. As we indicated above, the problem is not simply one of lagging output, but rather one of adaptation to changing consumption patterns. The protein intake of present-day Soviet citizens is quite adequate, and definitely on a par with most other industrialised nations. However, it is consumed in different ways. Whereas in the US 70 per cent of the protein intake is of animal origin, in the Soviet Union it is only about half, and it is also interesting to note that in the midst of violent protests about reduced meat supplies, Polish meat consumption *per capita* is still higher than that of the Soviet Union.[24] Rising real incomes have caused Soviet households to demand not more food but a better and more varied diet.

This shift is typical for nations experiencing rising living standards. It is usually expressed in terms of an increase in meat and meat products at the expense of grain and grain products. In the Soviet case this pattern is evident. Income elasticities of demand for meat and bread are 0.6 and -0.2 respectively, meaning that with rising real incomes there will be a substantial shift of the relative shares of meat and bread in household budgets.[25] Table 1.4 summarises this development.

Table 1.4: *Per Capita* Consumption of Selected Food Products (kg)

	1965	1970	1975	1980	Soviet Norm (recommended)
Meat and meat products	41	48	57	57	82
Milk and dairy products	251	307	316	314	405
Eggs (pieces)	124	159	216	238	292
Vegetables and melons	72	82	89	93	146
Fruit	28	35	37	34	113
Fish and fish products	13	15	17	17	18
Grain products	156	149	141	139	110
Potatoes	142	130	120	112	97
Sugar	34	38	41	42	40

Sources: Emelyanov (1982), p. 80; Mozhin and Krylatykh (1982), p. 7.

It is evident from the table that the above-mentioned shift is taking place. Livestock products are increasing and grain products decreasing. But it can also be seen that the speed of this transformation is far too slow. Compared to established Soviet nutritional norms, the diet is too heavily weighted with starch, causing obesity. From the table we can see that there are three distinct groups: first, fruit and vegetables, meeting only one-third and two-thirds of the norm respectively; secondly, livestock products with meat and milk meeting around three-quarters of their norms; and, finally, starch-rich products such as grain and potatoes that are still above the norm, in spite of continuous reductions.

Two comments should be made on this table. First, *per capita* consumption is a poor gauge of the true situation, since in the Soviet case the difference between the privileged and the underprivileged is substantial. The perception of the problem by the bulk of the population will thus be considerably worse than is indicated by the table. Secondly, while the starch-rich diet might have been healthy in times when people were largely occupied in heavy manual labour, today it is definitely no longer so. Both these factors thus act to reinforce the population's demands for a better diet.

Soviet leaders have recognised the shift in demand and pledged to cater to it, but will it be possible to deliver? Much obviously depends on the sluggish development of domestic meat production[26] since continued increases in imports of meat and feed grains are things that the Soviet Union can ill afford.[27] However, there are important obstacles to increased meat production. First, about 30 per cent of milk and meat products originate in the private plots, and the possibilities of increasing their output are limited. Production is highly labour-intensive, and mostly takes place in the peasant's spare time. Feed supply is limited, and mostly gathered by hand – again in spare time. Marketing, finally, is primitive and would need substantial investment to become more efficient. Although the plots are important today, their output can hardly be expected to expand to any great extent. At best it will be preserved at present levels.

It remains then to increase production in the socialised sector. Here it is typical that increases in production have been achieved through the expansion of herds rather than through the improvement of yields. On this point Brezhnev says: 'The desire to have larger herds is understandable. Under present conditions, however, animal husbandry must also focus on improving yields – more milk from every cow and increased average weights in animals sold to the state.'[28] Feed balance appears to be the dominant problem. Insufficient concentrates are used, and too much grain is fed in relation to roughage which reduces the absorption of nutrients and leads to very unfavourable conversion ratios from feed to meat.[29] Once again the problem does not appear to be one of insufficient input, but rather one of poor resource utilisation.

If the desired increases in meat production are to be achieved, it will be necessary to increase feed production substantially. This, however, as we have indicated above, will mean a higher demand for grain, and grain production has already been a troublesome sector in recent years. It is doubtful whether grain production will be able to take the increased strain – particularly if the ambition of a reduced dependence on imports remains. Much of the discussion below will consequently be centred on the grain problem.

Before we proceed to this discussion, there are two further topics that should be included in this background description: first, the magnitude of the adverse natural conditions facing the Soviet Union and, secondly, the mechanisms of state control over agriculture. Let us begin with nature.

Natural Conditions[30]

> We must realise that the climatic conditions facing the majority of
> our lands are very unfavourable, and that this causes substantial
> difficulties for agricultural production. In comparison we find that
> the entire territory of the US lies south of the 48th parallel, while
> this is true only for a third of Soviet agricultural land. While only 1.1
> per cent of Soviet territory lies in areas with an annual precipitation
> in excess of 700 mm, the US figure is 60 per cent. Forty per cent of
> Soviet arable land lies in areas with less than 400 mm, compared to
> 11 per cent for the US . . . Precipitation is insufficient in two-thirds
> of the Soviet grain area . . . One year in three suffers from severe or
> very severe droughts . . . Temperature ranges as well exhibit substan-
> tial differentials. While 60 per cent of Soviet arable land has an
> average temperature of 5°C or less, this holds for only slightly more
> than 10 per cent in the US case. Vegetation periods in many Soviet
> regions are thus substantially shorter than in the US.[31]

This statement by the then Soviet Minister of Agriculture, Matskevich,
sums up much of the adverse natural conditions facing the Soviet
Union. Although its area is 2.5 times that of the US, much of it is either
too cold or too hot, too dry or too wet, or just plainly too mountainous
to be of any use in an agricultural sense. Whereas half of the area in the
US is suitable for agricultural use, the figure for the USSR is only about
a quarter. Still, the cultivated area in the USSR exceeds by 45 per cent
that in the US. Faced with low yields, the Soviets have been forced to
cultivate truly marginal lands of very dubious quality, to secure a necessary supply of agricultural products. These large tracts of land, which
are prone to droughts and other harvest failures, account for much of
the high variability in Soviet agricultural performance. Heavy use of
marginal lands makes weather an even more formidable opponent.

A Vast Land

The Soviet Union is by far the largest country in the world. Covering
2,227 million hectares, it is almost two and a half times larger than the
United States. However, only 27 per cent of the land area is agricultural,
one-third of this being arable, the rest being meadows, pasture, orchards,
vineyards, or simply left idle. The reasons for these unfavourable figures
are climatic. The bulk of Soviet agricultural land is climatically comparable to that of Canada and the north central parts of the US. Leningrad,
for example, is on the same latitude as Anchorage (60°N) and San

Francisco on the same latitude as the southernmost parts of the USSR (38°N). Very little Soviet agricultural land is in any way comparable to the famous American corn belt. In comparison, Soviet land is heat deficient, moisture deficient, and − with the exception of the black earth (*chernozem*) soils − of inferior soil quality. Let us look at these factors in turn.

(a) *Heat*. An adequate heat supply is important primarily with respect to the length of the growing season. Average daily temperatures below 10°C will rule out most crops, and the shorter the season during which temperature remains above this critical limit, the more restricted will be the choice of crops. Deficient heat supply can create another problem as well. In the northernmost parts, where the ground is permanently frozen (permafrost), the short summer may well thaw out enough of the top layer in order to allow planting. Since the lower layers will remain frozen, however, there will be no run-off of surplus moisture, and the surface will be transformed into useless bogs and marshlands. Over 30 per cent of the USSR suffers from one or both of these conditions. A growing season of 90 days or less will allow only early varieties of vegetables, and the earliest varieties of oats and barley. A further 40 per cent of the land is so cold that only hardy, early maturing crops can be grown (growing season of 90-150 days). Only 5 per cent of the total land gets enough heat to allow a wide variety of crops, including citrus fruits and winter vegetables. The comparable figure for the US is 34 per cent.

(b) *Moisture*. Although half the Soviet land mass gets sufficient precipitation, over half the *arable* land lacks sufficient and reliable moisture. One reason for this is that the wet parts coincide to a very large extent with a very cold climate. Another reason is that high temperatures, low humidity and strong winds might offset the benefits of rainfall through evaporation.

(c) *Soils*. The important chernozem (black earth) soils that allow for a wide variety of uses cover only 5 per cent of the USSR. This highly fertile land stretches from the Ukraine to beyond the Urals, and it is the counterpart of the prairies of North America. Together with the slightly less fertile chestnut soils, the chernozem covers 13 per cent of the total land mass, but accounts for more than 60 per cent of the *arable* land. The remainder is made up of other soils of good to mediocre, and sometimes highly variable, quality, which are usually in need of irrigation and fertilisation. The most important of these are grey and brown forest soils. *Podzol* and other agriculturally insignificant soils account for almost 70 per cent of total land, and only a very small fraction of this can be significantly improved.

It is against this background that Soviet agricultural performance should be seen. To supply its population and industry with agricultural produce, the Soviet Union has been forced to utilise existing resources to the maximum. Consequently, in the USSR almost all arable land is sown, whereas in the US, the figure is less than three-quarters. Furthermore it has been necessary to bring under cultivation vast tracts of inferior lands. Since 1950 almost 43 million hectares have been added, which is equivalent to an area the size of California. Today the outer limit for expansion has probably been reached. Further expansion will need heavy capital investment in land reclamation and reductions in total sown area are more likely to occur. Erosion and salinisation are considerable problems, and every year 1.5-2.0 million hectares of arable land are lost through urbanisation and industrial expansion.

These climatological conditions, together with heavy reliance on marginal lands, have made Soviet agriculture highly vulnerable, with resultant wide variations in yields. *Winter-kill* occurs every year, and sometimes as much as a quarter to a third of the area sown with winter grains can be hit. In such cases the fields will have to be resown in spring, and crop rotation patterns will be distorted. It occurs all over the country, due to freak weather damaging the citrus crops in the south, and thawing and refreezing, or simply extremely low temperatures, in the north.

Drought is another traditional enemy of Soviet agriculture, and unfortunately it strikes hardest in the best grain-producing areas. In the south the probability of drought during May to July is well over 50 per cent. These areas are also commonly affected by the *sukhovey*, dry and hot, easterly or south-easterly winds, which cause rapid drops in humidity and rises in temperature. Sukhovey last from a few hours to several days, and are especially damaging to spring wheat.

Areas that are not subject to drought, suffer frequent damage due to thunder and hailstorms instead. Orchards and vineyards are especially badly hit. In the Caucasus hail occurs on an average of 9 to 12 days a year, compared to 1 to 3 days in other areas of southern European USSR.

Fighting Nature

Apart from some more spectacular attempts at combating nature, such as the reversal of Siberian rivers,[32] considerable investment has gone into reducing vulnerability through fertilisation, irrigation and drainage.

The *fertiliser programme* has been highly ambitious, especially since the early 1960s. Between 1960 and 1973, the output of mineral fertiliser was quintupled and the use of organic fertiliser — manure, compost and peat — increased substantially as well. Deliveries of mineral fertiliser to agriculture increased from 2 million tons in 1965 to 74 million in 1975 and 82 million in 1980,[33] and although there was stagnation during the latter half of the 1970s, the Food Programme intends to restore the upward trend. During the 1980s deliveries are to increase 1.7-fold.[34]

However, quality in terms of nutrient content is poor. In 1970 it was only 29 per cent compared to 40 per cent in the US. Only 5 per cent of Soviet output is made up of multinutrient fertilisers. In the US it is more than 50 per cent. Actual nutrient available per hectare in 1972 was about 30 per cent less than in the US. Nevertheless, profitability is still positive. Soviet sources estimate that each rouble spent producing, transporting and applying fertiliser will produce 2.5 to 3 roubles' worth of additional agricultural output.[35]

Irrigation and drainage are other aspects of Sovet attempts at combating adverse natural conditions. The largest share of irrigated land is found in central Asia, but the most rapid expansion is taking place in the important but drought-ridden areas of south-eastern European USSR. The total irrigated area is planned to increase from 18 million hectares in 1980 to 23-5 million in 1990.[36] Drainage, on the other hand, forms a problem. Most of the western European parts of the USSR are excessively wet, and proper drainage could mean valuable additions to output, especially in the important non-chernozem areas. Technology is backward, however, and deficient quality hampers expansion. In the Food Programme nothing is said about drainage.

We shall not return to these problems below, since they fall slightly outside our framework of institutional problems, but it is important to bear in mind the restrictions imposed by adverse natural conditions.

Agriculture and Planning

Management of Soviet agriculture is a highly complex business. The Ministry of Agriculture has direct responsibility for animal husbandry and crop production, as well as for other functional aspects of agricultural activities. The organisation of these different branches can be seen from Figure 1.1. Administration at lower levels will differ depending on the size of the region and on its major activities. The number of levels also differs depending on where you are, but the most important ones are: the all-union or *vsesoyuzni*; the republican; the region or *oblast*; and the district or *raion* levels.

Figure 1.1: State and Party Hierarchies

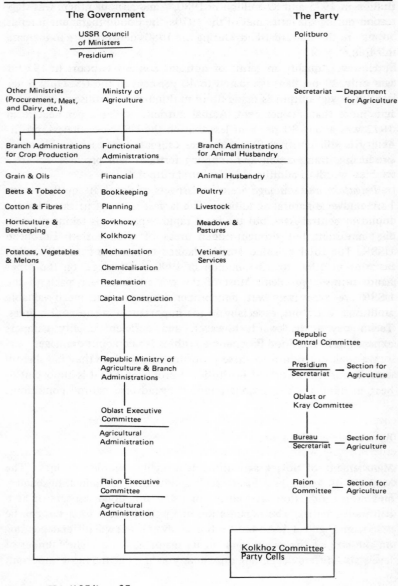

Source: CIA (1974), p. 37.

Of comparable importance to the Ministry of Agriculture is the Ministry of Procurements, which is responsible for state purchases of agricultural produce. These purchases account for the bulk of farm sales. Apart from these two ministries, there are a number of others that are directly or indirectly involved. Deliveries of equipment and machinery are co-ordinated through the State Commission for the Supply of Agricultural Machinery, *selkhoztekhnika*, and delivery of mineral fertiliser is organised through the State Commission for the Supply of Agricultural Chemicals, *selkhozkhimiya*. Individual farms cannot deal directly with the relevant enterprises or ministries. Even less direct are the links for provision of such things as transport, packaging, etc. The organisation of these functions has varied considerably over time, and especially under Khrushchev conditions were turbulent. After Khrushchev's departure, Brezhnev made a very firm commitment to stability in administration, and this commitment has been adhered to. Solutions to agricultural problems have not been sought in administrative reform, but rather in increased investment.

Alongside the state bureaucracy we find the party organisation, duplicating state functions at all levels. The leading and guiding role of the party is explicitly stated, and in case of conflict there is no doubt as to who will have the final say. Party control not only works through the formal party organisations, but also through the fact that all key positions in the state administration and in the collective farm system are held by party members. Even at the grassroots level, party cells in production brigades function to whip up enthusiasm for the daily chores. Below we shall be chiefly concerned with the district party committee, the *raikom*. The first secretary of the raikom is a key person in agricultural affairs, and he will figure prominently in our discussion.

The Planning Process

Given the highly complex administrative framework and the large number of decisions to be made by the centre, information becomes crucial to the workings of the system. Responsibility for the gathering, compilation and dissemination of information regarding all aspects of economic life lies with the central Statistical Administration, the *Tsentralnoe statisticheskoe upravlenie*, or TsSU. The TsSU has at its disposal a vast organisation of statisticians, accountants and bookkeepers at all levels, as well as a complex machinery of statistical reporting and programming.[37]

Decisions on what is desirable are taken in the party Politburo, and information on what is possible is compiled by the TsSU. It is then up to the State Planning Commission, the *Gosudarstvennaya planovaya komissiya*, or *Gosplan*, to draft a plan. The most well known plan is probably the Five-Year Plan, which is adopted at the party congresses that are currently held in the first and sixth year of every decade. The most recent, 26th, congress, which was held in 1981, adopted the 11th plan. The Five-Year Plans, which become Soviet law, are not operational. For the direct control of production, disaggregated annual and quarterly versions are used. For long-term planning there are also 15-year perspective plans, which deal with major investment decisions, transfer of resources between sectors, etc.

'Fulfilling the plan' (in the short term) is probably the most basic of all tenets of Soviet life. Income depends on it, status depends on it, and promotion (or demotion) depends on it. At the end of every month or quarter when accounts are made and plans are checked, the so-called *shturmovschina* (frontal assault) sets in. To meet the deadline, the pace is stepped up considerably (sometimes to an unreasonable extent), and as a result quality naturally suffers. After the deadline the pace slackens again. This cyclical pattern of production is highly detrimental because of its disruptive effects, but at the same time a natural consequence of the way in which party control is exercised.

Drafting a working plan is a complicated process of trial and error.[38] Gosplan drafts a starting plan that is broken down and submitted to everyone involved. These agencies, institutions and enterprises in turn draft a counter-plan, stating their production possibilities. The process continues until something approximately workable is arrived at. When this occurs all production quotas, input requirements, etc., as well as whom to deliver to and where to get inputs, become binding and for obvious reasons cannot be changed without great difficulty. Money plays a very limited role in the Soviet economy since firms do not have the right to buy and sell in the Western sense.

In agriculture the principal plan targets are state procurements. Production as such is not subject to planning, although this has not always been the case.[39] The plan also contains some other minor variables that we will return to in Chapter 4. One obvious problem connected with the process of drafting a plan is that it will pay to conceal productive capacity. If a low plan target can be obtained, it will be easy to over-fulfil the plan, and over-fulfilment means bonuses and perhaps promotion. Evaluation of given information becomes a critical undertaking.

Special Features of Agricultural Production

That biological production is something far removed from production in heavy industry is something that has been painfully brought home to generations of Soviet planners. The great versatility of land as a factor of production poses a requirement for large amounts of information to be collated in order to make correct decisions on what, where and when to grow. The optimal use of a hectare of farmland is obviously much harder to determine than the optimal use of, say, a die cast, for which there can only be one use. This problem is aggravated by the fact that what is optimal one year will probably not be so the following year. If the optimal use for a certain type of machinery in an industrial plant has been found, this can be repeated over a longer period of time without much harm in terms of reduced output or profitability. If, however, it is found optimal to sow a field with barley one year, and this is repeated over a number of years, the field will finally not reproduce seed. Industry has no equivalent to crop rotation problems.

Nicolas Georgescu-Roegen summarises these specific features of biological production under three headings.[40] First, the scale factor is entirely different. A few grains of corn or a tomato plant can be grown in a flower pot in your back yard, which is hardly true for the production of a modern tractor. The need for large scale in industry has been transplanted into agriculture to the obvious detriment of the latter. Huge unmanageable complexes have been promoted and efficient small-scale units suppressed.[41] Secondly, the time factor is entirely different as well. Industry knows no equivalent to the 'unflinching rhythm of nature'. Faulty timing in industry will in most cases only create a nuisance for consumers and other plants. In agriculture it can be disastrous. Certain operations have to be performed in given sequences and at given points in time, otherwise entire crops might be destroyed by frost, rains, drought or simply overripening. Weather of course is the major villain here. Since weather conditions will always form an unplanned – and unplannable – residual, absurd consequences such as the ploughing of fields still under snow are bound to result from centralised planning of farm operations.

The third factor is again related to scale, but in a more subtle way. In industry, an important way of exploiting economies of scale lies in methods that speed up the production process. In agriculture this is seriously impeded by the fact that biological production depends crucially on natural forces that are still largely uncontrollable, at least in positive terms. The inability to produce major reductions in gestation periods constrains the number of harvests that can be obtained from a field — sometimes down to zero — as well as the number of offspring that can be obtained from an animal.

A highly important point in our argument will be that early Soviet planning was based on fundamental misconceptions about these basic facts of life, and that this had serious consequences for future agricultural production. The approach to agriculture was largely the same as that to industry. Farms were regarded as rural factories, and planners attempted to control them in much the same way that industrial plants were controlled. Soviet agricultural history is to a large extent about different attempts at finding the best way of exercising this control, without questioning its existence. Many of today's problems derive from these attempts at control.

Marketing

The most important feature of control over agriculture today concerns the transfer of agricultural produce from producer to consumer, and we shall complete our background description by looking briefly at these flows.

Soviet farms have three different outlets for their marketable output, namely the state procurement organisation, the consumer co-operative organisation, and directly to the 'free' collective farm markets. These flows are shown in Figure 1.2. State purchasing is handled exclusively by

Figure 1.2: Flows of Agricultural Produce

From the source to the consumer

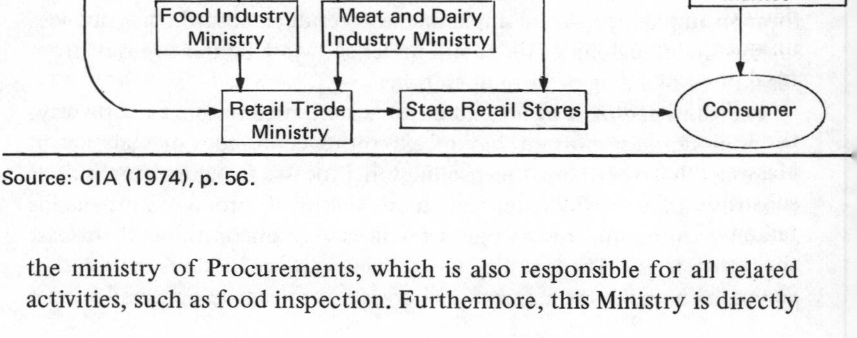

Source: CIA (1974), p. 56.

the ministry of Procurements, which is also responsible for all related activities, such as food inspection. Furthermore, this Ministry is directly responsible for the purchase, storage and proper utilisation of all state grain resources. Virtually all of the output of technical crops is purchased in this way. The other purchasing organisation is the Central Union of Consumer Cooperatives (*tsentrosoyuz*). Formally this organisation is independent of the state apparatus. In particular, livestock, potatoes, vegetables and fruit are purchased in this way. In addition, the tsentrosoyuz not only buys from the farms, but also from the private plots of the individual households. The final option is the free market, where households and farms alike have the right to market produce, with the sole restriction that they must themselves be the producer of what is sold. No private middlemen are allowed. The functioning of these markets will be dealt with extensively in Chapters 4 and 5.

Plan of the Study

Given the climatological restrictions set out above, we shall now turn to investigate what can be done to solve the serious problems presently facing Soviet agriculture.

At the centre of the analysis will be a conflict between *continuity* and *change* in development. We shall argue on the one hand that there has been throughout a marked continuity in the structure and institutions of agricultural production and decision making. On the other hand, there have been marked changes in overriding policy, particularly in the period following Stalin's death. These changes, however, have not been accompanied by the necessary institutional change, and it is precisely in this conflict that we shall seek many of our explanations.

In Chapter 2 we shall start by outlining how the tsarist legacy of emancipated serfs was taken over by the Bolsheviks, and transformed into the collective farm system that still exists. Our emphasis will be on demonstrating how an institutional structure has developed which was uniquely suited to a Stalinist policy of forceful extraction of agricultural produce from an uncooperative peasantry.

In the following chapter (Chapter 3), we will proceed to show how the leaders who succeeded Stalin radically altered the overriding policy. Massive increases in inputs to agriculture and in peasant incomes were substituted for Stalinist repression. Our emphasis here will be on the failure of the new leadership to implement corresponding changes in the institutional framework. As a result of this lack of institutional change the new policy failed. Success in the short run rapidly turned into stagnation as the bureaucracy adhered to its old practices, thus preventing the newly created incentives from having any long-run effect. In later chapters we will use this experience as a yardstick to judge the prospects for present policy, which will be shown in important respects not to differ from that of Khrushchev or Brezhnev.

Following the presentation of how the present structure of Soviet agricultural production emerged and developed into what it is today, Chapter 4 will set the stage for our analysis of its present functioning. Production in a typical collective farm will be seen as a game played by three different actors. The farm household will be a decision-making unit striving to maximise private utility. The party organisation will be its counterpart, striving to maximise deliveries of agricultural produce to the state, and in the middle we find farm management, trying to make decisions on production, given the restrictions imposed by the other two players.

The next two chapters will then be devoted to the conflicts that arise between these three players. Chapter 5 will deal with problems relating to planning, pricing and procurements, as external restrictions on farm decision making, while Chapter 6 will concentrate on problems relating to the internal utilisation of resources within the farm, such as the allocation of labour between the plots and the collective fields.

Chapter 7, finally, will first present the Soviet view of the problems, and then contrast their proposed cure with our experience of what might be possible. Our conclusion will be that the present Soviet leadership is caught in a form of no-win position, where a continuation of the present policy carries highly unpleasant political implications in terms of increased social unrest, but where a change carries equally unpleasant political implications, in terms of allowing a wider play for market forces, and a consequent relaxation of political control. The dilemma is made all the more acute by the rapidly deteriorating food situation that is bound to force the hand of Andropov within the very near future.

Appendix: Methodological Problems

The study of the Soviet system is seriously complicated by the limited availability of information. To make up for gaps and lack of information, it frequently becomes necessary to adopt unorthodox methods that to scholars of other disciplines might seem slightly — or highly — 'unscientific'. It might perhaps be worthwhile to make some comments on some of the more salient features of these specific problems.

The Role of Information

At the root of the problem lies the role of information in Soviet society. The secrecy that surrounds at times the most trivial matters gives a Western observer an impression of almost an obsession with secrecy. Any attempt, even by Soviet citizens, to get information that is slightly out of the ordinary will almost certainly be followed by the question: 'Why do you want it?' Intimidation by bureaucrats will frequently discourage people from finding information that is not 'really' secret. The borderline between what is classified and what is not is a highly fluid one, even to Soviet citizens. One consequence of this state of affairs is the fantastic spread of rumours, which today are an ingredient of Soviet life.[1]

Perhaps the most spectacular example of secrecy concerns political succession. Relations between different actors in the Soviet power elite are notoriously difficult to interpret. This difficulty has given rise to the peculiar, and to some perhaps amusing, branch of social science that is known as *kremlinology*.[2]

The basic assumption of the kremlinologist is that there is a constant power struggle in the Kremlin. Since there are no formal rules governing succession, the actors will unceasingly manoeuvre to improve their positions. In this manoeuvring process various forms of 'esoteric' communication are used to transmit changes in relative positions of power, for the benefit of subordinates. The most well known example of this is probably the line-up on the Lenin mausoleum at May Day parades in Red Square. People who over the years move closer to the centre are assumed to be on their way up, and vice versa.

Communication takes on many other forms as well, however, such as the use of capital letters in, or the changing of, official titles, presence or absence at official functions, etc. The basic contention of the kremlinologist is that these 'esoteric' signals form an essential part of the Soviet power game, and that if they can be read and understood by Soviet bureaucrats then they can also be read and understood by Western scholars. If this is the case, then it will be possible to shed some light on the political process, and thus perhaps to make important predictions on coming changes in policy or in the system as such.

We shall not venture here to pass judgement on the relative virtues of kremlinology as a science, although it should be noted that there are precious few other ways of gaining information on the political process in the Soviet Union.[3] Our purpose in bringing it up has rather been to use it as a striking example of the problems facing a scholar of Soviet studies. Absence, unreliability and distortion of officially published information seriously complicate any attempt to proceed along the methodological lines that are common in the West. Let us look at these problems in turn.

Some forms of information do not exist at all, simply because they are not collated or, if they are, only secretly. One example of this is information on the distribution of incomes. Isolated investigations of various geographical regions are made at times, but no systematic, regularly published data exist.[4] The reasons are not known. Another example concerns prices. The last major price revision was in 1967,[5] and present prices obviously cannot reflect relative scarcities of goods and services. It is assumed that Soviet planners use some form of shadow prices in the planning process, but once again, we do not know. These types of problems are clearly the most disturbing, since it is very hard to compensate for them.

Another type of problem is that where the data does exist, but is clearly misleading. The worst form of this problem is where the bias is unknown, as in the case of Soviet national accounting. Explicit expenditure on the entire KGB apparatus, for example, is nowhere to be found. However, it must be accounted for somewhere, otherwise national income statistics in terms of expenditure would be incomplete. Where then is it to be found? Is it under 'transfer payments to old-age pensioners', or 'repair and maintenance of public baths'? We do not know, and this is obviously a major problem, since the heading to which it has been added will be inflated. One possibility of course is that it has been spread out evenly across the board, in which case the relative shares of various headings will not be distorted.

A similar situation is that of military expenditure. Western estimates indicate that what is actually found in the budget far underestimates the true figures.[6] Where then can we find the rest? Will we find a nuclear submarine under 'subsidies to dairy production'? We simply do not know. Compared to the first category, however, these problems are less disturbing, since they can sometimes be corrected for in various indirect ways. Furthermore, when it comes to trends, these will not be affected, unless distortions are at random — which of course is quite possible.

A third kind of problem concerns distortions which are obvious and predictable. An excellent example of this is the reporting of yields in agriculture that was mentioned above.[7] The obvious reason for the Soviet practice of reporting *bioyields* and *bunker yields* is to inflate statistics, and if we want statistics that are comparable to those in the West or that reflect what is actually available for consumption, corrections will have to be made. Such corrections can be made and are made regularly,[8] but they can only be approximate. Waste and losses will depend heavily on local conditions at the time of harvest, and such information will necessarily be scant. Again, we do not know the true situation. Compared to the first two problems, however, these distortions are less serious.

An Indirect Approach

How then does one go about conducting research under such conditions? Obviously whatever information there is will be used, with varying degrees of care and correction. This greatly depends on the historical period involved. During the period immediately following the revolution there was an open and very lively debate. Highly qualified scholars of various disciplines regularly published materials in scientific journals.[9] From this period much valuable information can be derived. Of course, one is still confronted with the usual problems of historical statistics, although they are less subject to suppression and distortion.

Following Stalin's takeover there was a radical change. Many journals were simply discontinued[10] and publishing of various forms of official statistics abruptly stopped. This difficult situation lasted until the mid-1950s, when the thaw following Stalin's death led to a normalisation in many ways. Today the availability of information in press, journals and official statistics is probably better than many think. There are important gaps, however, which will have to be filled in some way, and this is where 'unorthodox' methods come into play.

Newspapers. The most important way of filling these gaps in officially available information is by scrutiny of daily newspapers and above all of *Pravda*, the official organ of the Communist Party. This form of research is far less suspect than it might appear. If someone were to quote the *New York Times* as a source on the economic policy of President Reagan, this may or may not be in line with the actual policy pursued. Since there is no direct line between this paper and the White House, we cannot know. The case of *Pravda,* however, is different. The editor of that paper is a highly influential person with direct links into the Politburo, which is the top decision-making body in the Soviet Union. What is published in *Pravda* will unquestionably correspond with official policy, or with what the leaders want to be known as official policy, which in essence amounts to the same thing.

For the benefit of other major newspapers that do not have daily contact with the top leaders, conferences are arranged regularly to outline current priorities in policy. The understanding is that news selection will be such that it forms an integral part of that policy. In the case of minor newspapers, editors are assumed to follow the leader, and in any case, all material that is to be published has to pass the censors, who are usually people with highly developed political instincts.

Two types of information can be gleaned from this screening of newspapers. First, there are indications of overall policy. Since the Soviet bureaucracy is not only a gigantic machine, but is also one where functions on all levels are duplicated into party and state organs, an effective mechanism of control and guidance is badly needed. This, it is believed, is the role of the *Pravda* editorial in particular, and of news reporting in general.[11] Here Soviet bureaucrats are given daily orders on what should currently be given priority. During 1982 one such area has been animal husbandry. In editorials and news reporting, the importance of this sector has been constantly repeated. If our assumptions about the role of media are correct, then Western observers can also interpret the signals, and predict changes in policy.

The second type of information concerns the running of daily matters, and is probably more important in helping to form a picture of how Soviet society really works. Let us take an example. If we look at official statistics and find that the production of mineral fertiliser has doubled, then we might infer that this would have a beneficial effect on agricultural production. If, on the other hand, we find a cartoon showing a field with mountains of fertiliser turned into concrete through exposure to the elements, then we might infer that much of the increased output of fertiliser never reaches the field, at least not in the intended way.

It is precisely this gap between what is shown in official proclamations, speeches and statistics on the one hand, and what actually happens in real life on the other, that is the root of many problems in Soviet studies. An uncritical reading of official programmes and proclamations can give a picture that is far removed from Soviet reality. Official statements are a means of influencing the bureaucracy, to bring about desired changes. However, it can be dangerous to believe that these desired changes actually take place. Sometimes they do and sometimes they do not. The important task here is to find out what the real situation looks like, and this is where a patient scrutiny of the newspapers can help.

The basic contention is that cartoons, articles, letters from readers, etc. will not be published at random, but rather as *sanctioned* and integrated parts of official policy, where policy is defined to include criticism of mistakes and inadequacies. The degree of correspondence between official policy and editorials, news reporting, cartoons, etc. is highly important. Given the way in which Soviet society works, the media acquire a role that is different from that in the West. Since Soviet citizens are never given a choice of different policies, it becomes of paramount importance for the Soviet leadership to legitimise its existence by showing that its policy is for the common good. There can be no doubt that what is printed in *Pravda is policy*. Consequently, the information that can be obtained in this way can hardly be overestimated.

Fiction. Another, principally different, kind of information is found in novels, short stories and poetry. When writing fiction the author will unintentionally but necessarily supply a lot of background information on the daily life of Soviet citizens, such as housing standards, public communications, availability of various forms of consumer goods, etc. Once again, this information can be used to fill the informational void between the 'official' and 'real' Soviet societies.

For the same reasons as outlined above, the sort of materials dealt with in fiction will also be in close correspondence with official policy. Some themes are 'out', whereas others are tolerated or even encouraged. The prime example of changes in this policy on publishing is the appearance of *A Day in the Life of Ivan Denisovich* by Alexander Solzhenitsyn.[12] This marked the beginning of an open attitude to the release of materials on the GULAG system. The 'camp theme' was soon discouraged, however, and very little was actually (officially) published.[13]

The mainstay of the policy on publishing is that of Soviet realism, and of a positive attitude to 'Soviet man'. Writers form an integral part of the Soviet system and their writings can definitely not be regarded as some form of private activity. The official doctrine is that they must shoulder their share of responsibility for furthering the system and its advance towards communism. Consequently, *criticism of the system* is out. Writers must point out the *positive features* in Soviet life, in order to encourage the citizens to further increases in their efforts to develop the system. Thus one does not turn to literature for evaluations or descriptions of the system as a whole.

What one does get is information on how the system works at the local level. Criticisms of malfunctions at the local level have never been prohibited, rather the opposite. This type of information will be a valuable complement to that which can be derived from the daily press, since it originates from a different angle. Whereas the press usually deals with malfunctions of isolated agencies, party organs, government administrations, etc., or isolated problems, such as public transportation or housing, fiction will deal with the *ensemble* of these problems from the point of view of a single or a few Soviet citizens. Hence, we get the much desired picture of the 'real' Soviet society.

Relevance for our Study

In our study we will rely on all these sources of information. Existing Western sources will be used where available,[14] on the one hand to create a background of Soviet agricultural development, and on the other as a source of factual material to substantiate our hypotheses on the emergence of Soviet agricultural *policy*. Such sources, however, are not available for more recent developments, and here we shall turn to Soviet publications.

We shall use primary statistical material[15] for typical time series data, such as livestock herds and grain output. These data are of a high reliability if only used to study trends. For other materials, such as prices, costs, returns to investment, etc., we shall use Soviet journals.[16] These data will be of more limited reliability, since the authors often do not explain their calculations or refer to their sources. Here we shall not attempt a critical evaluation of the data used, which would be a tall order, but rather limit our use to cases where there are obvious trends, and where reliability can thus be deemed to be high.

To create a picture of the 'real' Soviet society, we shall use clippings from the press.[17] These data will be even less reliable, since they apply only to a given point in time, and perhaps also only to a single farm or a single district. However, we will use them under the assumption that they have been published in order to criticise a common problem, and thus we will assume that their reliability is high. In particular, this holds for cartoons from *Krokodil*, which will be used in order to corroborate the existence of problems that we shall derive from our theoretical analysis of the system. If the problem did not exist widely, the cartoon would not be funny.

Finally, to solve the most difficult problem in our presentation — that of the day-to-day operation of party control over agriculture — we shall use fiction, and we shall use it under the same assumption as for press clippings. If the writer's account of Soviet reality did not correspond with the true situation, his works would either be stopped by the censors (if overly critical) or not read by the public (if overly glorifying). The picture that is derived from fiction will then be contrasted with accounts from the press, and thus we shall arrive at the closest possible approximation of the true situation. Any official Soviet accounts of how this process works obviously do not exist.

Notes to Appendix

1. See Zinovjev (1980) for an excellent literary account of these problems.
2. The standard works in kremlinology are: Nicolayevsky (1966), Conquest (1961), Rush (1958), Tatu (1969) and, with special reference to agriculture, Ploss (1965). The role of media in particular is analysed in Hopkins (1970). Journals in which kremlinological articles frequently appear are: *Problems of Communism, Survey and Osteuropa.*
3. For a further discussion of the merits of kremlinology, see Nove (1964a).
4. Various fragments that do appear can of course be used to form an indirect picture. See for example Nove (1982b) and McCauley (1982).
5. The final report was published in hundreds of volumes, which gives an indication of the magnitude of the task. See further Schroeder (1969).
6. One way of double checking is to add up all industrial output that is accounted for by the civilian sector. What remains will give a very rough estimate of what is used by the military sector.
7. See also further Chapter 2.
8. OECD (1979), pp. 56ff.
9. There are numerous sources to this debate, Lewin (1974a) perhaps being the best place to start.
10. For example *Ekonomicheskoe Obozrenie (Economic Review), Statisticheskoe Obozrenie (Statistical Review)* and *Biulleten Koniunkturnogo Instituta (Bulletin of the Business Cycle Institute).*
11. An excellent analysis of this function is found in Tarschys (1978).
12. Solzhenitsyn (1962).
13. Much of course was published as *samizdat.*
14. The most important works here are Nove (1969) and Volin (1970) for a broad sweep, Carr's many volumes for the period up until 1929, and Lewin (1968) for the collectivisation process. Apart from these works, Western sources normally deal with a limited time period or with a narrow problem. This is where it is hoped that the present study will fill an important gap in the literature on Soviet agriculture. Authors who have a similar approach as ours to the emergence of Soviet agricultural policy are Lewin (1974b), Roberts (1970), Szamuely (1974) and Taniuchi (1981). Their accounts, however, are confined to the period prior to 1930.
15. In particular from the statistical yearbook *Narodnoe Khozyaistvo*, which will be quoted below as *Narkhoz*, followed by the year of issue.
16. The most important are *Voprosy Ekonomiki, Ekonomika Selskogo Khozyaistva, Planovoe Khozyaistvo* and *Sotsiologicheskie Issledovaniya*. In footnotes these will be quoted by the author's name, followed by the year of issue.
17. Here the more important ones are the daily *Pravda*, the weeklies *Ekonomicheskaya Gazeta* and *Literaturnaya Gazeta*, and the satirical magazine *Krokodil*, which appears approximately every ten days. In footnotes these will be rendered as above, followed by the date or number of issue.

Notes

1. See USDA (1981), p. 29, and also CIA (1979) and Desai (1981).
2. On the nature and effectiveness of this embargo, see Scherer (1981), pp. 180ff.
3. The target for 1976-80 was 220 million tons and that for 1981-5 is 239 million. Harvests in 1979 and 1980 were 179 and 189 million tons respectively, and Western estimates for 1981 and 1982 are 149 and 176 million tons respectively. See *Narkhoz* (1981), p. 202, *Pravda*, 18 November 1981 and *Radio Liberty Research Bulletin*, no. 475/82, 1 December 1982.
4. Information on the availability of food is largely obtained from foreign officials living in or visiting the Soviet Union. See *Radio Liberty Research Bulletin*, no. 321/82, 11 August 1982, for a collection of such letters that have been published elsewhere in the West.
5. It is an indication of the gravity of matters that the plenum was held in the middle of a plan period, when very few major changes could be made. Full documentation on the plenum can be found in *Prodovolstvennaya* (1982).
6. Brezhnev's speech can also be found in *Pravda*, 25 May 1982.
7. The share of agriculture in total Soviet investment is presently one-third and rising. That of Hungary, for example, is 15 per cent and falling. See Buzdalov and Bukh (1982), p. 97.
8. Returns to investment in agriculture fell by 14 per cent in 1966-70, by 26 per cent in 1971-5 and by 27 per cent in 1976-9. See Kleimyshev (1982), p. 71.
9. FAO, *Production Yearbook* (Rome, 1980). The comparison will vary substantially over time, particularly due to uneven Soviet performance, but it is still rather striking.
10. See OECD (1979), pp. 56ff.
11. The poor condition of roads aggravates this problem, causing losses to agriculture in the vicinity of 5-7 billion roubles annually. Five per cent of the grain crop and 10-15 per cent of all hay is lost as vehicles are forced to cross growing fields. See *Izvestia*, 10 October 1981.
12. At the November 1981 plenum, Brezhnev complained about the fact that nearly all grain purchased by the state is first taken to often distant elevators, only to have a large part of it shipped back at a later date. See *Pravda*, 9 December 1981. *Izvestia*, 16 June 1981, has similar complaints.
13. See *Kommunist*, no. 11 (1982), p. 7.
14. Industrial growth in 1982 was 2.8 per cent, which should be compared to the target of 4.7 per cent, and to the past impressive double-digit rates. See further an article by Gosplan head Baybakov in *Pravda*, 24 November 1982.
15. Over the past 18 years, around 15 million people have left the farms. For further details on this migration, see Perevedentsev (1975) and Zaslavskaya and Korel (1981).
16. Irregular supply of power can have dire consequences. Imagine, for example, a power cut in a fully mechanised large-scale dairy farm.
17. We shall return to the debate on this issue in Chapter 2.
18. *Narkhoz* (1980), p. 7.
19. Ibid., pp. 312, 387.
20. Our ambition here is simply to give a very rough picture. For a fuller understanding, it would be necessary to make a number of corrections, such as for the double counting of people working both on the plots and on the communal fields. See further de Pauw (1968) and Grossman (1968).
21. Some of the largest farms have an area that is well over 100,000 hectares, the parallel of which is hard to find in the West. In 1979, 66 per cent of the

kolkhozy had more than 300 households and 36 per cent had more than 500. Seventy-six per cent had more than 1,000 head of livestock and 13 per cent had more than 3,000 head. In the sovkhoz case figures are even greater. Twenty-one per cent had more than 3,000 head of livestock and 5 per cent had more than 5,000 head. Only 0.3 per cent of kolkhozy had no livestock. *Narkhoz* (1980), p. 287.

22. See further Nove (1977), pp. 120ff.

23. See Nove (1982b) and Shmelev (1981), p. 69. See also Hill (1975) on definitions of 'private plots'.

24. See also OECD (1979), pp. 19ff.

25. Data presented in Movshovich (1977), p. 457, and quoted in OECD (1979), p. 8. The total food elasticity is 0.8, and over the period 1970-80 expenditure on food has risen by only 59 per cent, while non-food has risen by 93 per cent, thus reducing the share of food in household budgets from 56 to 51 per cent. See Lokshin (1981), p. 82. Interpretation of these elasticities is difficult in the Soviet case, since most markets for consumer goods are subject to supply constraints, thus causing a larger expenditure on food than might otherwise have been the case. See further Karcz (1966), appendix, for a discussion of these problems.

26. Meat production was 11.6 million tons in 1966-70 (annual average), 14 million in 1971-5 and 14.9 million in 1976-80. *Narkhoz* (1981), p. 201f.

27. Meat imports have increased substantially, from 0.1 million tons (annual average) in 1966-70, to 0.3 million in 1971-5 and 0.5 million in 1976-80. *Vneshnaya Torgovlya SSSR*, selected years. See also USDA (1981), pp. 15ff.

28. *Pravda*, 25 May 1982.

29. *Kommunist*, no. 11 (1982), p. 6, claims that a poor feed balance increases feed requirements by 25-30 per cent in meat production, and by 40-50 per cent in milk production, given the same output.

30. Unless otherwise indicated, all climatological data given below are taken from CIA (1974).

31. *Ogonek*, no. 4 (1973), p. 4.

32. The rivers concerned are mainly the Pechora and the Ob, both of which flow into the Arctic. Water is to be diverted southwards, in the first case to the Volga and in the second to the area around the sea of Aral. See CIA (1974) for details, and Gustafson (1981) for a discussion of the prospects and importance of these projects.

33. *Narkhoz* (1981), p. 237.

34. *Pravda*, 25 May 1982.

35. OECD (1979), p. 31f.

36. *Narkhoz* (1981), p. 239, and *Pravda*, 25 May 1982.

37. See Susiluoto (1982), pp. 161ff, for an account of the emergence of the 'cybernetics' school, and for the ensuing debate. After a long silence it seems that it might again be on the rise. See *Ekonomicheskaya Gazeta*, no. 22 (1980).

38. See Ames (1965) for an account of this process.

39. Until 1955, not only procurements but all forms of production were planned.

40. Georgescu-Roegen (1960), p. 5.

41. This extreme belief in the benefits of large scale is far from a thing of the past. See *Radio Liberty Research Bulletin*, no. 253/80 (1980), for recent examples of 'gigantomania'.

2 EMERGENCE OF THE COLLECTIVE FARM

In this chapter we shall present the first phase in the evolution of modern Soviet agriculture — that of the transition from serfdom to collective farming. We shall show how the Bolsheviks, after the revolution of 1917, inherited an agricultural sector that bore the mark of an emancipated but largely dissatisfied peasantry, and how this inheritance was transformed step by step into the collective farm system that still remains largely intact.

Our presentation will rely heavily on a contrast between *continuity* and *change* in development. Change is not difficult to find, but it shall be our endeavour here to identify two important strands of continuity in this period of chaotic upheaval. One strand relates to the basic institutions of agriculture, such as the organisation of production and relations with the state, while the other strand concerns the basic attitude of the Bolsheviks to the peasantry. By holding up the zig-zag pattern of actual development against these two strands of continuity, which continue today, we hope to explain how Soviet agriculture was shaped into what it is today and what this historical experience means for today's policy makers.[1]

We shall start with a brief exposition of the emancipation of the Russian peasantry from serfdom and of the developments that led up to the Bolshevik Revolution. Then we will look in more detail at the consecutive steps of a development that culminated in Stalin's total domination and in the establishment of the foundations of collective agriculture. The following chapter will then study what Stalin's successors did in attempts to change this system.

Russian Peasants

The origins of Russian serfdom are shrouded in uncertainty, and we shall not venture to penetrate that veil here.[2] What is important for our purposes is the large extent of serfdom and the fierce opposition from the landed classes to its abolition.

In the 1858 census, the agricultural population was divided into four categories. There were 20 million private serfs. Another million were serfs in various forms of mining and factory work, with mixed ownership, while a further 2 million were serfs owned by the imperial family. To these should be added a further 18 million 'state peasants', who were formally free. In reality, however, the tsar could make gifts of their persons, thus converting their freedom into serfdom.[3]

The most relevant group for our purposes are the private or manorial serfs. These were subjected to the harshest conditions. Apart from direct household serfs, lacking land, there were two forms of subjection. The most common form was day labour, or *barschina*, which accounted in 1861 for three-quarters of all private serfs.[4] These serfs had their 'own' land, and apart from their labour services on the manor led their own life within the village community. The other form of subjection, *obrok*, was common in areas where agricultural yields were low. Instead of labour, the serfs were asked for quit-rents, which sometimes forced them to seek gainful employment elsewhere, for example in a nearby city. This arrangement was beneficial for both parties, yielding higher income for the landlord and more freedom for the serf. For our purposes, it was important in that it provided a possibility for accumulation, and thus created the conditions for economic differentiation.

Emancipation

It was these 20 million private serfs who were mainly affected by the emancipation legislation of 1861, which abolished 'forever' serfdom from 'all of Russia'.[5] Three main principles can be distinguished in this legislation. First, the liberated peasants were to be landed, i.e. they were to be allotted holdings that would enable them not only to gain a livelihood, but also to pay taxes and to produce the surplus necessary to pay for the land allotted to them. Second, the landlords were to be paid a fair price for land given over to the peasants. This price was to be paid at once by the state, which would then collect it from the peasants in long-term instalments. Third, *no* payment was to be made for liberating the serfs as persons.

Predictably, the legislation provoked much resentment from the landed classes, and after intense lobbying the law was amended in several ways, all of which aimed at diminishing peasant holdings. As a result 75 per cent of the households received holdings that were less than two-thirds of the established maximum norm.[6] Furthermore, the landlords reserved for themselves the best part of the land and, most importantly, an element of compensation for the loss of serf labour was included in the payments, in clear breach of the law.[7] It should also be noted that whereas landlords could force the peasants to redeem their land, the reverse was not true. Thus, when redemption was finally made compulsory in 1881, 20 per cent of the households had still not redeemed their land.[8] The peasants started off their new-found freedom poorly and it was to get worse.

It became readily apparent that tax and redemption payments constituted a heavy burden on the peasantry. In spite of measures such as corporal punishment to extract payments, arrears immediately started mounting up. The fact that taxes were collected immediately after harvest, thus forcing peasants to sell when prices were depressed, further added to the problems of minuscule holdings and high payments. In 1883 taxes were lowered and arrears cancelled. However, the pressure continued to be high, and peasant land was still taxed at several times the rate of estate land. Thus, apart from being formally free from serfdom, the emancipation bill had little impact on peasant welfare.[9]

Not even the formal right to your own person was of much value, however. When serfdom was abolished, titles to the land were transferred, not to the individual peasants, but to the village community — the *mir* — as common property.[10] We shall not in this context carry out any detailed examination of the mir as a social organisation.[11] Its role in the emancipation legislation, however, is of crucial importance to our argument on three separate counts. First, the mir exhibited communal land tenure. Secondly, all labour was performed for the private gain of the individual household. Finally, communal matters were decided by the village gathering, at which presided the village elder, or *starosta*, who also represented the mir to the outside.

During serfdom, the mir proved an efficient social organisation where the landlord only had to deal with the elder, who then acted as his representative to the serfs. Following emancipation it came to serve much the same purpose. The newly freed serfs were responsible for the payment of taxes and redemptions for their land, but instead of making them individually responsible together with individual property rights, via the mir they were made collectively responsible, with communal property rights.[12]

The joint responsibility made it necessary to prevent able-bodied persons from leaving, and for this purpose the mir was empowered to prevent its members from travelling more than a short distance away from the village without a passport.[13] Passports would only be issued with the consent of the village elder.[14] These responsibilities, especially in poor farming areas, often made additional holdings a liability rather than an asset, and there are stories of entire villages flatly refusing to accept allotments of land.[15] Furthermore, it is easily visualised what this collective responsibility meant for individual incentives to buy various implements — implements that could later be sold to pay for your neighbour's tax arrears.[16]

We shall see below how Stalin would later reverse history by 'rediscovering' the mir as a basis for the kolkhoz. Here, the features of joint responsibility and of the role of the village elder and the village gathering would be helpful, whereas the feature of production for private gain would be a major obstacle.

The last part of the nineteenth century witnessed a rapid deterioration of the situation in agriculture. Small holdings on inferior land, combined with high liabilities for taxes and redemption payments, created a tremendous squeeze on the peasantry, culminating in the disastrous famines in 1891, 1897 and 1901. The situation was also further aggravated by a rapid growth in an urban population that had to be fed. Between 1871 and 1901, the number of people living in the cities grew from 7 million to 17 million.[17]

From the government's side little was done. Its overall attitude is probably best reflected in a statement by the Minister of Finance, I. Vyshnegradskii: 'We will starve, but we will export' ('Ne doedim, no vyvezem').[18] Transfer of resources from agriculture was of course necessary to feed the nascent industrialisation. Moreover there was little else to export but agricultural produce. The consequences for the peasantry, however, were dire, and at the turn of the century the situation changed. The largely peaceful and submissive peasantry of the nineteenth century was becoming violent. The year 1901 witnessed widespread unrest, and the abortive revolution of 1905 was largely a peasant revolt. The demand for more land continued to be a central issue.

The most important feature in this process is the peasant's perception of property rights. Even before emancipation, land was regarded as a right given by God. This was expressed in the plea of the serfs to their squire: 'We are yours, but the land is ours.'[19] The tendency for the peasantry to see 'more land' as a panacea for all their troubles is a well known phenomenon in all developing countries and in Russia it was particularly strong. Land hunger was to overshadow all other problems, and it soon became obvious that the emancipation of 1861 had done nothing to solve the problems in agriculture, but had merely postponed them. Consequently, land reform became a burning political issue, and several political parties and groups were riding on the wave of discontent.

The Stolypin Reform

The course of events after 1905 was to be heavily influenced by the new Prime Minister, P.A. Stolypin. His policy[20] came to be known as the 'wager on the strong'.[21] The mainstay of the new policy was that the mir, with its communal land tenure and strip farming, was the main obstacle to development, and should thus be broken up by the introduction of reform measures.

The reform contained two important parts.[22] The first part was a recognition of the difficult financial situation confronting the peasantry, and aimed at easing financial conditions, by writing off all remaining redemption payments. This was done in 1907. The second part, however, was the most important one, in that it attacked the very foundation of rural organisation — the mir. The new legislation decreed that any member of the mir could demand that 'his' holdings be transferred to him personally, and that all his scattered strips be consolidated into one plot. This land would then become hereditary possession.

In cases where no repartition had taken place, so that the peasants were tilling the same land as prior to the emancipation, the mir was simply declared dissolved, and the land became private property. In other cases, the mir could voluntarily abandon communal tenure by a two-thirds majority vote. A reflection of the highly individualistic nature of the reform is that while land had been previously allotted to the household, it was now made personal property of the head of the household. One restriction stipulated by the legislation is worthy of mention. Land that became private property could not be mortgaged to private individuals or institutions, nor could it be sold to anybody except peasants. There was a clear determination to prevent the remaining big estates from regaining economically the power they had lost in the emancipation of the serfs.

The impact of the reform was substantial. Between 1907 and 1915 around 2 million households secured conversion of their land by petition, another half million due to the fact that their village had never been repartitioned, and finally a further 140,000 due to a vote by the mir to dissolve.[23] Thus, by 1915, over 2.5 million households out of a total of about 15 million had secured private hereditary holdings. However, the bulk of conversions took place prior to 1910, and several writers[24] have advanced the hypothesis that there were two well defined groups that were interested in conversion, and that once these had left, the large group of middle peasants was left relatively unaffected by the reform. The first group would have been those who wanted to migrate, either to seek employment in urban areas or to take up farming elsewhere, notably in Siberia. The second group would then have been those who had managed to hold on to more than their due share of land. If this hypothesis holds, it means that the long-run effects of the Stolypin reform would have been limited, even had it not been interrupted by the revolution in 1917.

However, the short-run effects on production were dramatic. The index of crop production for the period 1909-13 rose by 36.9 per cent, compared to 1896-1900, and Russia became a leading exporter of grain.[25]

In summary, then, as the revolution was drawing near, the agricultural scene was dominated by two very marked trends: the growing land hunger of a dissatisfied and increasingly violent peasantry and an increasing economic differentiation amongst the peasantry, fuelled by the Stolypin programme. Obviously, this was a highly flammable mixture, and in February 1917[26] it exploded. Although the February Revolution was hardly a peasant uprising, the peasant element in it cannot be discounted. In Lewin's words, it was a 'proletarian revolution, flanked by a peasant war'.[27] Yet, in the eyes of the peasantry, the revolution failed to deliver. The large estates remained and peasant holdings were unchanged. Once again they had been frustrated, but for the last time.

Peasant discontent was skilfully exploited by Lenin and the Bolsheviks. As early as May, Lenin wrote in *Pravda* that the entire 'agrarian question' was all about whether 'the peasants here and now should take over the land, without paying compensation, or if they should wait for the constituent assembly' (which was to be convened in November).[28] This policy proved a great success in the short run. Support for the Bolsheviks amongst the predominantly rural population increased dramatically, and by October they were ready to take over. The Great October Revolution was a smooth and virtually bloodless affair.

Revolution and War Communism

One of the very first things done by the Bolshevik government upon seizing power was the issuing of the famous decree 'Concerning Land' ('Dekret o zemle').[29] The basic tenet of this decree was the abolition of private property rights in land. Other paragraphs, such as the setting up of organs for the redistribution of land, rapidly became a dead letter. Largely out of control of the authorities, the peasants started a land reform of their own, displaying considerable violence. The 'Stolypin peasants' were deprived of their gains, and the large estates were broken up. The Soviet government was reduced to *ex post* legalisation of peasant actions. Thus the peasants finally got their land reform, and this was the price that the Bolsheviks had to pay for their previous support. The first step in the evolution of Soviet agricultural policy consisted of pure accommodation.

However, events also got out of control in areas other than agriculture. Immediately following the October Revolution, the Soviet state was besieged not only by foreign aggressors but also by the White Armies, led by tsarist officers attempting to crush the revolution. Peace with Germany, signed in April 1918,[30] was soon followed by the war with Poland in May-October 1920. A final military peace was not established until the beginning of 1921, when the last remnants of the White Armies were crushed in the Crimea.

Quite predictably these events brought chaos to the country. Industrial production was falling drastically, rapid inflation destroyed the monetary system, and all communications were more or less paralysed. The little food that existed was either kept on the farms or traded on the black market, since there was nothing to offer the peasants in exchange for their products. Famine spread rapidly, and sometimes led to outright starvation in the Red Army and in the cities. In the beginning of 1918, for example, bread rations in Petrograd were down to 50g per day, even for workers.[31] The very fact that the large estates disappeared probably contributed to the problems, since these had been the main suppliers of commercial grain. The Bolsheviks soon had to tackle the problems with force.

The following step in the emergence of a policy is probably the most important of them all, and it incorporates all the measures that came to be known as 'War Communism'.

The *first stage* was the important decree on 'Food Dictatorship'[32] which established a state monopoly on all trade in agricultural produce, in order to secure food for the cities and the army. The importance of this decree can hardly be overrated. It was to influence agricultural policy for decades to come. The aim was directed at 'speculation', i.e. possession of surplus grain, and a refusal to deliver to the state. It laid the foundation of Soviet agricultural policy. The problem was not how to get the peasants to produce more grain, but rather how to extract from them what they already had.

Shortly afterwards, in response to a delegation of Petrograd workers, Lenin sent a telegram urging workers to save the revolution by enrolling in the 'food detachments' (*prodovolstvennye otryady*) that were organised by the Commissariat of Production (*Narkomprod*). In effect, this meant that armed bands, backed by the new law, were sent out into the countryside to forage. A week later a further decree gave the Narkomprod a monopoly on the distribution of all objects of 'prime necessity'.[33] This was the *second stage* of War Communism.

At this time the clouds of civil war were gathering. Shortly after Lenin's telegram came the first outbreaks of violence. The revolution had not yet had its first birthday. The situation rapidly deteriorated. Famine was spreading, and the black market flourished in spite of death penalties for 'speculation'. Inflation was so rapid that money lost all meaning.[34] Trains and local services were free of charge, and wages were paid in kind, if at all. In 1920 there was even an experiment with a 'money-free' budget. The shortage of food was so serious that it forced a mass exodus from the cities, and in three years the urban proletariat was reduced by more than half.[35] With relatives in the villages there was at least a chance of finding food. The proletariat being the power base of the Bolsheviks, something had to be done, and out of this situation grew the *third stage* of War Communism.

At the local level 'Committees of Poor' (*kombedy*) were set up, consisting of poor peasants who were loyal to the state.[36] Their purpose was simply to facilitate the work of the 'food commandoes' who were sent out by the Narkomprod. They would split the peasant front against the government by directing resentment against better-off neighbours, and they would provide the food detachments with valuable local information, i.e. many peasants acted as informers.

This policy came to be known as 'Food Extraction', or *prodrazverstka,*[37] and the principle was to confiscate[38] everything above a stated minimum required for seed and on-farm consumption. Sometimes literally everything was confiscated. Naturally the peasants did not submit peacefully to these confiscations. As the villages were bristling with demobilised soldiers, who had frequently kept their weapons, encounters sometimes resulted in pitched battles.

In terms of requisitions, the system was quite successful. More than twice as much grain was procured in 1920/21 as in 1918/19.[39] Starvation, if not hunger, was avoided. The cities and the army were saved.

In terms of overall output or peasant welfare, however, it was nothing short of a disaster. Deprived of all incentives to produce, peasants reduced or concealed their sowing, and went to great lengths to hide whatever grain they did produce.[40] It is an interesting point to note that reductions in sowing were greatest in areas that benefited from Soviet rule throughout, i.e. that were spared the devastations of the Civil War.[41] The consequences for production were disastrous. In 1920 the grain harvest was down to 54 per cent of the 1909-13 average, and in 1921 it fell even further to 43 per cent.[42]

There are important lessons to be learnt from these first few years of Soviet rule, since history would repeat itself a decade later. First of all, the basic problem was that of a total breakdown in relations between state and peasantry. The terms of trade deteriorated to such an extent that the peasantry chose to withdraw into subsistence, leaving the cities to starve. Secondly, the reaction of the leadership to the crisis was to use compulsion and force. Initially this policy was no doubt made necessary by the circumstances. In the words of Merle Fainsod, 'the policy of War Communism was the rule of the besieged fortress'.[43]

Subsequent events, however, are open to controversy. The basic features of the prodrazverstka agree very well with the Marxist principles of non-market allocation and distribution, and some writers go so far as to suggest that War Communism was from the start a wholly planned policy.[44] Others play down the importance of ideological factors and stress the disruptions and chaotic conditions that forced *ad hoc* decisions and actions.[45]

What the original intention was is not important for our purposes, and we shall not pursue that point further here. What is important, however, is the *actual form* that the policy took. Since many of the same elements were to return later, we shall highlight them here.

In our interpretation,[46] the three most important features of the policy of War Communism were the decree on 'food dictatorship', the organisation of food commandoes, and the setting up of the kombedy. All these were elements of the policy of prodrazverstka — first a law on state procurement of grain, then a system to collect it, and finally a local organisation to help out and prevent peasant obstruction.

The common denominator is that of the basic attitude towards agriculture. For the first three years of Soviet power, food supply had been regarded as a collection and distribution problem. It was necessary to force the peasants to *deliver*. No thought was given to production. Now, faced with drastic reductions in output, it began to be realised that it was a production problem as well. Typically, however, the solution to this problem was found along lines similar to the previous policy. It was necessary to force the peasants to expand production. For this purpose it was decided to set up 'sowing committees' to induce expansion of sown areas.[47]

This was the last, stillborn, product of War Communism. Three months later the situation was desperate. The sailors at Kronstadt, the pride of the revolution who had fired the opening rounds from the cruiser *Aurora*, openly revolted against the Bolsheviks. The wind changed abruptly. The New Economic Policy was introduced.

Interlude

The first discussion of a change in course took place in the Politburo on 8 February 1921, where Lenin presented a draft for a new policy. This came as a total surprise even to leading Bolsheviks, since any change in policy had been consistently and categorically denied in spite of growing difficulties. Two weeks later the ground was prepared by suggestive articles in *Pravda*, and a detailed draft was submitted to the Central Committee. The first public indication of the reform came on the last day of February, at a meeting with the Moscow City Soviet. Here Lenin said that it was reasonable that the peasants should know in advance what was expected from them, and that maybe a tax in kind (*prodnalog*) should be substituted for the hated prodrazverstka.[48]

A New Economic Policy

At the 10th party congress in March the suggestions were realised, barely a month after their first mention. The speed of decision making is indicative of the magnitude of the problem. The resultant decree abolished requisitions and introduced a progressive tax in kind.[49] The tax was deliberately set very low, at only a little more than half the delivery quota for grain in 1920/1. Trade and exchange were relied upon to bring the total up to the required minimum.[50] Furthermore, the decree stated that any surplus after the tax was paid could be sold on the free market. As a consequence of this, middlemen gradually began to operate again. There is no indication that the Bolsheviks had either foreseen this development,[51] or that they tried to prevent it. Interference from local party officials died hard, but all attempts to interfere with the operation of middlemen were rapidly swept away by the momentum of the reform.

This New Economic Policy (NEP) came too late for the sowing in 1921, however, and things were to get worse. The year 1920 had brought drought and a very poor harvest, and by the summer *Pravda* carried an article stating that 25 million people were stricken by famine.[52] When 1921 came with a second year of drought, the disaster was a fact. At the end of the year it was stated that out of 3.8 million hectares of sown land in the European areas, the harvest was a clear failure on 1.4 million hectares. Instead of an estimated 3.9 million tons, the tax in kind yielded only 2.4 million.[53]

But 1922 proved to be the real turning point. In this year a new Land Code was enacted.[54] The starting point for this legislation was the legalisation of existing land holdings, which had largely been brought about by the peasants themselves, outside Soviet control. Once again, the legislator was very careful not to allow the reappearance of estates with absentee landlords, and the law stated that the tiller also had to be the occupier (*trudovoe polzovanie*). Another matter of considerable importance was that it adopted a neutral stance on the issue of land tenure. Private tenure was just as acceptable as various forms of collective and communal holdings. Needless to say, formal ownership of the land still rested with the state and accordingly plots could not be sold or mortgaged. Furthermore, land was again allotted to the household (not to the head of the household as in the Stolypin programme), and holdings were made into perpetuities.

The result of the freedom that was granted the peasants in the new legislation was a powerful stimulus for private production as well as trade. In 1922/3 around 75 per cent of all retail trade was in private hands,[55] and Table 2.1 shows the response in terms of increases in sown area. The rapid expansion of the sown area was matched by an equally rapid expansion in agricultural production, which led to a new crisis. Partly due to the rapid expansion of supply in agriculture, which tended to depress prices, and partly due to inefficiencies and supply constraints in industry, which tended to raise these prices, a gulf opened up between agricultural and industrial prices. The 'scissors crisis' started, with the scissors being the respective price indices. Peasants again reacted by threatening to withdraw into subsistence, but this time the leadership acted swiftly to prevent renewed disaster by partly closing the 'scissors'.[56]

Table 2.1: Total Sown Area (million hectares)

1913	1921	1922	1923	1924	1925	1926	1927	1928	1929
117	90	78	92	98	104	110	112	113	118

Source: Volin (1970), p. 176

The year 1925 witnessed the height of NEP. Private traders faced virtually no competition from the official distribution system. Trade margins in the consumer co-operative network[57] were sometimes so high as to be prohibitive.[58] In Moscow the private traders – the so-called NEP-men – controlled 14 per cent of wholesale and 83 per cent of retail trade. At the same time the number of private farms grew rapidly, from 17-18 million in 1918, to 23 million in 1924 and 25 million in 1925. In 1927 private farms accounted for 98.3 per cent of own area, with state farms having 1.1 per cent and various forms of collective farms only 0.6.[59]

Early 1925 saw the last wave of liberalisations for decades to come.[60] The general policy was reflected in the decisions at the 14th party congress in December,[61] the most important changes being relaxations in the restrictions on leasing land and hiring labour. Minor changes included a reduced agricultural tax and a general crackdown on local administrative abuse.

Thus in 1925 agriculture was booming. Compared to 1922, the sown area was up from 78 million hectares to 104 million, and the grain harvest was up from 50 to 72 million tons.[62] In spite of this, however, sales were dropping and the cities could only be supplied at the cost of a fall in exports.

The *magnitude* of the fall in peasant marketing, on the other hand, is controversial. At the time Stalin presented data to support the belief that it was substantial,[63] and that the peasants were using the increased output to improve their own standard of living, at the expense of the urban population. Later research has challenged these data as being too high, and it is important to note that at the time Stalin used them to motivate a tougher stance against the peasants. This new crisis in food supply sparked off serious dissent in the Politburo. The left wing, notably Trotsky, Kamenev and Zinoviev, emphasised the risk of the kulaks strengthening their position, with a resultant spread of capitalist conditions in rural areas. The right wing, notably Bukharin and Rykov, downplayed this threat and claimed that strong peasants were good for the state. In the middle ground Stalin was operating.[64]

At the 15th party congress in 1927, yet another Land Code was enacted, which this time deliberately discriminated against the kulaks.[65] Collectives were given preference, taxes were raised and progression sharpened, restrictions on the lease of land and hire of labour tightened, and finally the control over the mir by poor peasants was strengthened by depriving the kulaks of suffrage. With the grain situation again growing progressively worse, the government once more resorted to violence, which was only vaguely condemned by the Bukharin wing. Although it officially lived on until 1932, in 1928 NEP was for all practical purposes dead. The peasants were quick to respond, and in 1928/9 procurements of wheat and rye were down by 20 per cent compared to the previous year.[66]

For a while official statements on policy were vague, due to the conflict in the Politburo, but by the fall of 1929 the Bukharin wing had been defeated. The interlude was over and the stage set for one of the most dramatic acts in Soviet history. Before we turn to this, however, let us look briefly at the impact of the first decade of Bolshevik policy on the institutions of Soviet agriculture.

Institutional Change

As we have seen above, by the time of the October Revolution, the traditional form of land tenure and production mode, known as the mir, was in a state of dissolution. As a result of the Stolypin reform, almost half of the households in European Russia had left the mir.[67] After the revolution, however, there was a steady flow of peasants back to the traditional ways of life, and by the time NEP was introduced, the mir was again the dominant form of tenure, and various forms of collective farms were still insignificant.[68] Yet little more than a decade later the mir would be dead and there would only be collective farms. How was this transformation accomplished?

It is a fact that today's system of state and collective farms in many respects did emerge out of the mir, but not according to any obvious plan. Parallel with the introduction of 'Food Dictatorship' we can also discern an element of structural policy in agriculture. Starting in the autumn of 1918 it was decided to launch sovkhozy, state farms to be the equivalent of rural factories, and the importance — economically as well as politically — attached to these new farms can be seen in the formulation of the law:

> Soviet farms are being organized (a) to obtain the greatest possible increase in supplies, by raising the productivity of agriculture, (b) to create conditions for a complete shift to communist agriculture, and (c) for the purpose of creating and developing centers of the best farming techniques.[69]

Priority was also given to sovkhozy in the allocation of land. By a decree the most valuable of the remaining estates were transferred to the Commissariat of Agriculture and converted into state farms. After exhausting the initial supply of estates, however, growth rapidly stagnated, as can be seen from Table 2.2. While over three thousand farms were established in 1918 alone, less than a hundred were added in 1921. Total sovkhoz area then started to decline, and fell from 3.4 million hectares in 1921 to 2.3 million in 1926. Following a spurt of investment in 1926-8, sown area again picked up to the 1921 level, but improvements in farming techniques were insignificant, and yields were only slightly above the national averages, in spite of the allocation of first-class land and equipment. In the light of expectations, therefore, the experiment must be deemed a failure, and party leaders do not seem to have been impressed.[70]

Table 2.2: Numbers of Sovkhozy

1918	1919	1920	1921
3,101	3,547	4,292	4,391

Source: Volin (1970), p. 156.

Parallel with the attempts to develop a state farm system, attention was given to various forms of co-operative farming, and here there were three different forms.[71] The *kommuna* (commune) was the most 'communistic'. Everything was held in common possession, and frequently people slept in dormitories and had their meals in diners. All productive activities were performed jointly. The *artel*, which was to develop into today's kolkhoz, was less demanding. Here households would have their own houses, kitchen plots, and maybe even some animals and implements. The *toz*, or *tovarichestvo po obschestvennoi obrabotki zemli* (co-operative for the common cultivation of land) finally, was the least demanding. In the toz co-operation sometimes did not extend beyond joint ploughing.

The first of these to develop was the kommuna, with the pioneers being demobilised soldiers who, upon returning to their villages, found things in such a state of disorder that they decided to join together in communes. During the spring and summer of 1918, heavy support was given from the government, financially as well as in preferential allocation of land and livestock from expropriated estates. A separate 'Division of Communes' was organised within the Commissariat of Agriculture, and a model charter for communes was drawn up. No provision was made for individual incentives, and all surpluses over and above needs were to be delivered to the state. Initially the communes increased rapidly in numbers, only to be outpaced by the rival artely. The rapid stagnation in the growth of the communes was in part due to an intense dislike amongst the majority of the peasants, and in part to a change in government attitudes.

The initial directives on preferential treatment soon changed, as it became obvious that the communes needed heavy subsidies and that they frequently were made up of poor peasants who joined the communes expecting to be fed, but who had little to contribute.[72] At the end of 1918, the Commune Division became the Collective Farm Division, and all collectives were treated equally. In *Izvestia* the communes were denounced as a road to socialism, and in *Pravda* Bukharin said that communes were only acceptable as a step towards the sovkhoz.[73] By early 1919 the party had rejected communes as a goal, and during the NEP period virtually nothing was heard about them. Lenin himself attacked the communes forcefully in 1920 and 1921, saying that 'artificial false communes are the most dangerous of all', and that it was 'harmful, even fatal for communism to try to put in effect prematurely purely and narrowly communistic ideals'.[74]

The toz, finally, never really was an option. Party leaders considered it too bourgeois and too close to private farming. It did have some appeal amongst the peasants, though, since it made it possible to get subsidies without really engaging in co-operation, and especially at the height of NEP it grew rapidly.

It is difficult to form a picture of the numbers and performance of these various forms of collective farms, since the data are of poor quality. Definitions are unclear, and the dividing line between the toz and the artel appears to have been especially thin. It also appears to have been a frequent occurrence that peasants set up 'false' collectives in order to receive preferential treatment. Moshe Lewin quotes numerous sources indicating that in certain areas as many as 50-60 per cent of newly formed collectives were liquidated by the authorities as false.[75] One indication of this unclear situation is the differing opinions between three involved authorities (the Collective Farm Association (Kolkhoztsentr) and the Commissariats of Agriculture (Narkomzem) and Finance (Narkomfin) respectively) as to the actual numbers of artely that were formed. The only firm picture that emerges out of this development is that the contribution of these new forms of rural organisations was insignificant throughout the NEP period. The mir was still very strong, and by 1921 — which was the end of War Communism and determined policy — only 625,000 out of a rural population of 100 million people had joined collectives. Their share of total sown area was less than 1 per cent.[76]

A major reason for the slow growth of collectives was the vagueness of official policy. The 1917 decree on land established that communal tenure should be the 'normal' form, though there was freedom of choice provided that the occupant also was the tiller (trudovoe polzovanie).[77] A new law in 1919 disposed with the previous vague formulations. The principle of state ownership of land was firmly established, and it was also stated that the 'individualistic' style of farming was dying out, to be replaced by state and collective farms. Priority was to be given in the order: sovkhozy, communes, other forms of co-operatives, and lastly small-scale peasant farming.[78] This priority ranking soon vanished, however, and the 1922 land code again provided for a free choice of tenure.

Table 2.3: Numbers of Artely According to Various Sources

	Kolkhoztsentr	Narkomzem	Narkomfin
1924	12,005	9,718	8,641
1925	15,974	12,609	9,277
1926	11,851	12,099	8,023

Source: Lewin (1968), p. 108.

It was not until 1927 that party preference was clearly established. The Land Code of this year was clearly in favour of the artel, which was to become the kolkhoz of today. This was the great winner. At the beginning of NEP there were 16,000 artely, accounting for about 1 per cent of all households.[79] During NEP there was a slight decline, to 14,832 in June 1927.[80] The original kolkhozy also were tiny affairs, averaging 12.5 households and about 40 hectares of cropped land in 1928.[81] With the change in agricultural policy, however, expansion picked up dramatically, and by June 1928 their numbers had increased to 33,258.[82] By this time the kolkhoz could hardly be called voluntary. This was the prelude to the great collectivisation drive.

Continuity or Change

Before we continue to the events that followed NEP, let us recapitulate this important period and try to discern underlying trends.

The collapse of agriculture in 1921 brought War Communism to an end. The first step of the New Economic Policy was the introduction of the tax in kind, and after that things began to happen at an ever increasing pace. This speed of events is important in understanding policy making. In the words of Moshe Lewin, 'this first move triggered the rest and led to a remarkable *volte-face*, which astonished the world as well as the Bolsheviks'.[83] He further summarises Lenin's position as

The antimarket practices and theories of War Communism still strongly influenced these initial moves. First, Lenin thought that the peasant, unhappy about the requisitions, would settle for an organized and predictable direct barter (*tovaroobmen*) between state industries and peasants without trade, markets and intermediaries.[84]

Lenin's statements at the time also show bewilderment and insecurity about the future. At the 10th party congress, when NEP was adopted, Lenin was worried about how the policy should be explained: 'we must muster . . . all our theoretical forces, all our practical experience, in order to see how it can be done'.[85] He also presents a programme that is very vague: 'Because if we are to be absolutely definite, we must know exactly what we are going to do over the year ahead. Who knows that? No one.'[86] Bukharin's stand is equally confused:

> We thought that we could, at a blow and swiftly, abolish market relations. Yet it turns out that we shall reach socialism through market relations . . . In other words, War Communism was seen by us not as military, i.e. as needed at a given stage of civil war, but as a universal, general so to say 'normal' form of economic policy of a victorious proletariat. The illusions of War Communism burst at the very hour when the proletarian army stormed the Perekop.[87]

One is thus given a strong impression that once War Communism was abandoned it was not replaced by any other policy. The New Economic Policy was rather the absence of a policy. In this sense 1921 represents a clear break. The distinct and explicit policy of prodrazverstka was replaced by a state of gradual yielding to peasant opposition. Afterwards this series of retreats came to be known as the 'New Economic Policy', but there are no indications that it was either planned or consistent. Nowhere is this better illustrated than in the policy on land tenure.

Two conclusions can be drawn from a study of agricultural policy during the NEP period. First, actual measures taken exhibit a distinctly haphazard pattern, lending support to the hypothesis that total disarray followed the abolition of War Communism. NEP was the absence rather than the presence of a policy, characterised by abrupt changes such as those relating to the legislation on land tenure.

Our second point is more subtle. If we accept as a fact that the prodrazverstka was a deliberate set of measures forming a distinct policy, then we can advance the hypothesis that NEP is an example of a period where practical policy measures became disconnected from overall, desired policy. Prodrazverstka continued to be the *desired* policy, but faced with peasant resistance, practical policy was forced into a retreat. As none of the leading Bolsheviks wanted the retreat, there was no alternative policy − hence the disarray. Much of the political struggle then came to be centred around the issue of how to reconcile ambitions with reality, the left wing wanting to continue with force and the right wing wanting to lower ambitions. The distinction is important to make, since at the end of the interlude actual policy would be brought back up to the level of original ambitions.

Stalin Takes the Helm

The consequences of leaving the economy rudderless at a time like this were, predictably, disastrous. NEP was not a stable reform that could run safely under its own steam, and its price policy proved particularly unfortunate.[88] Not only were prices low,[89] but there was also a distortion in that prices for livestock and technical crops had been increased, but not those for grains. If they sold grain at all, peasants would sell it to the private traders who had still not been eliminated. A grain procurement crisis developed. Lewin also argues that neglect of the emerging collective farms and of training in agricultural matters served to aggravate the situation.[90]

The first signs of danger came in early 1928, when it was obvious that grain procurements would fall far below the necessary minimum. The failure was most acute in Siberia, the Volga and the Urals, where the harvest had been good.[91] Clearly, the peasants had accumulated stocks and reserves of cash during the good years, and were now holding out for higher prices.

A Ural-Siberian Method

Stalin took a tough stance. In January threats were issued to local party officials: 'Fulfil the plan or else . . .' By February the situation was becoming desperate, and the so-called 'Ural-Siberian' method was born.[92] Together with detachments of police and procurement officials, Stalin personally went to Siberia, and procured large quantities of grain, using the Penal Code's paragraph 107 against 'speculation'.[93] Parallel with Stalin, other members of his faction, notably Zhdanov and Andreev, went to the southern provinces on similar missions. In Moscow the whole operation was co-ordinated by Mikoyan, the Commissar of Trade.

In the short run the method proved a success. During the first half of 1928, 28 per cent more grain was procured than during the previous record year. Moreover, this was from a crop that was 7 per cent smaller.[94] The degree of abuse and excesses was such, however, that the remaining opposition in the Politburo objected violently, and at a Central Committee plenum in April a resolution was accepted condemning the method and stating that it was never to be repeated again.

The 'Ural-Siberian' method was presented as part of the class struggle. Grain was to be taken from kulak speculators, and part of it was to be rechannelled to poor peasants. In practice there were many similarities with the prodrazverstka of the War Communism period. Payment for procurements[95] was made in government bonds which were of no interest to the peasants. A large amount of force and violence was involved. Free markets were closed, road blocks set up, and heavy penalties were enacted for refusals to deliver. The repeated attempt to split the peasant front by singling out the rich peasants, the kulaks, as the target, failed partly because of a deep mistrust of the government and partly because the bulk of the grain was in the hands of the middle peasants who consequently had to be attacked as well.

Three particular consequences are brought out by these events. First, the kulak was brought back to the front page after not having been mentioned in the press for several weeks. In a long letter to party officials[96] a campaign was proclaimed against the kulak, and from this date they did not vanish from the press until they had been removed altogether.[97] Secondly, it meant the definite break of faith between the party and the peasantry, a faith which has still not been fully restored. Although Stalin repeatedly stated that the campaign was directed against the kulak and that the middle peasant should not be affected, this cannot have been very credible against the background of events. Third, this was the first time that Stalin acted on his own, without first consulting the Politburo — an ominous sign.

For our purpose, the events in 1927/8 become of crucial importance. Stalin's actions were nothing but a full dress rehearsal. While still fighting Bukharin in the Politburo, he was drilling his troops and preparing for an inevitable showdown with the peasantry.[98]

As a result of the campaign, peasants again cut back on sowings. A special sowing campaign (which has been repeated annually ever since) had to be organised to follow up procurements. By December food rationing was introduced in the cities, and the black market was booming. From that time on there was a continuous decline in procurements, and it became increasingly clear that something drastic had to be done. The outcome was the second application of the 'Ural-Siberian' method, but this time on a national scale.[99]

In 1929 Stalin gained the upper hand in the party, and all political opposition to the campaign was firmly put down. There was even a minor purge of 'difficult' officials — again an ominous sign. Peasant resistance was fierce, entailing concealment and destruction of crops, armed resistance, arson and attacks on newly formed collective farms. From the party 'plenipotentiaries' (*upolnomochennyi*), agents with very wide powers, were sent out to organise the campaign at the local level. Again the campaign was a success in quantitative terms. During July-October, twice as much grain was procured as during the same period in 1928.[100]

To back up the procurement campaign another new feature was introduced, the *kontraktatsiya*, or contract system. Contracts had been introduced in 1927 to induce peasants to grow technical crops, the point being that prior to sowings a contract was signed specifying, amongst other things, prices and deliveries, and awarding some advance payments.[101] Since the government immediately went back on its obligations, however, the extension of kontraktatsiya to cover grains can only be seen as a component of the Ural-Siberian method. Only 7 per cent of the 1928 harvest was obtained through contracts. For 1929 they covered a fifth of the area sown with grain.[102] In the autumn of 1929, signing up was made compulsory.[103] Stalin praised the system as a method of replacing trade at free prices. No attempt was made to estimate the losses suffered by the peasantry.[104]

With regard to long-run decisions the situation was characterised by extreme disorder. Work had started on the first Five-Year Plan, but little attention was given to agricultural problems. Thirty research institutes were studying problems related to industry, but none dealt with agriculture. It is also significant that the Commissariat of Agriculture, *Narkomzem*, and the central body of collective farms, *Kolkhoztsentr*, were not formed until the end of 1928.[105]

The re-emergence of the prodrazverstka under the Ural-Siberian method represents the third step in the development of agricultural policy. On the one hand, an important reason for the failure of the prodrazverstka during War Communism had been peasant resistance, and Stalin had learned that lesson well. This time the necessary force would be applied. On the other hand, it had also become gradually more evident that if free exchange with the peasantry was to lead to the production of the necessary food surpluses, the upper strata of the peasantry must be allowed to expand, quite simply because they were the most efficient producers. In 1927, Kondratief summarised the situation very pointedly: 'If you want a higher rate of accumulation then the stronger elements of the village must be allowed to exploit the weaker'.[106]

The leadership was thus caught on the horns of a dilemma. If relations with the peasantry were to be based on *voluntariness*, this would lead to the spread of capitalism and in particular to the private domination of trade in agricultural produce. The only way to avoid this development was by a return to the forceful policies of War Communism, and this is where we find the continuity that bridges over NEP. When Stalin resumed the prodrazverstka, he thus took over its basic principles but improved its format. Instead of the simple decree on 'Food Dictatorship', the system of contracts, kontraktatsiya, was introduced, giving a legal framework for harsher measures against peasants who failed to meet their contractual obligations.

While the basic principle of administrative extraction of grain was thus maintained, the Ural-Siberian method and the kontraktatsiya provided it with a more efficient framework to replace the haphazard confiscations of the prodrazverstka. We shall now proceed to see how the fourth and fifth steps served to replace the kombedy, the 'Committees of Poor', with a more efficient local organisation to facilitate extraction.[107]

Full Collectivisation

Against the background outlined above, it is not strange that the collectivisation drive seemed to emerge out of chaos. This is another important point in our argument. Until Stalin finally came out in favour of the artel, various departments supported their own favourites for further *experimentation*. There was no talk of *wholesale* collectivisation. It is also important that both the left and the right wings in the party emphasised Lenin's old warnings against the use of force in relation to the peasantry.[108] We shall thus argue that mass collectivisation was an *ad hoc* measure that was in no way derived from a *premeditated party strategy*. In the words of Arthur Wright, it was a 'sudden, desperate lunge to extricate the leadership from a deep economic and political crisis, a crisis which was largely of its own making'.[109]

The first signal of a change came in October 1929: 'all forces gathered for the procurement campaign must be thrown into the collectivisation campaign'.[110] Then in November Stalin published his famous article 'The Great Turn',[111] which is generally considered as the go-ahead signal for the collectivisation campaign. Trotsky was forced into exile, the Bukharin group was ousted, and as a finishing touch came the celebrations of Stalin's 50th birthday, where he was hailed as the greatest Marxist-Leninist and best strategist ever. The personality cult, or *kult lichnosti*, was born.

Once the campaign was started, the pace of events gathered increasing momentum. In April 1929 Gosplan was planning for 5 million households in collectives, cultivating 21·2 million hectares by 1932-3. In June Kolkhoztsentr was aiming for 7-8 million households on 8 million hectares by the end of 1930, and to have the total needs of the nation covered by collective farms by 1933. During the autumn months Gosplan gradually revised the estimates from 13 million hectares (September) to 30 million (December).[112] Initially the campaign was run on wholly local initiative, and the attitude of the leaders towards the behaviour of local officials is reflected in a statement by Kaminskij in January 1930: 'If you are arrested and found guilty of excesses, remember that you have been arrested for revolutionary deeds.'[113] Local officials were told to achieve full collectivisation (*sploshnaya kollektivisatsiya*) in two days or hand in their party membership cards.[114] The attitude was to get things over with before the spring sowing.

A growing debate on the fate of the kulak was abruptly ended when Stalin declared the liquidation of the kulaks as a class.[115] On the fate of individuals he said: 'Dekulakisation is now an essential element in forming and developing kolkhozy. Therefore to keep discussing dekulakisation is ridiculous and not serious. When the head is off you do not weep about the hair.[116] It was not until January 1930 that a decree was published outlining a plan for the campaign.[117] The decree set up deadlines for the completion of collectivisation in different areas. The most important areas were to be completed by the autumn of 1930. It also stated that the artel was the only acceptable form of organisation, and called for a Model Charter to be drawn up. In February a further decree revoked the rights to rent land and hire labour.

With dekulakisation (*razkulachivanie*) acting as a catalyst, showing middle peasants the alternative to joining the newly formed kolkhoz (artel), the campaign became a landslide. Between July 1929 and March 1930, the number of households in collectives increased from 4 to 56 per cent.[118] During these first months of 1930, the official version, and that of the press, was that the peasants were willingly and *en masse* flocking to the kolkhoz. The truth of course was different. Whereas peasant resistance during the previous years had been largely passive (concealing grain), the situation now changed into outright civil war.[119] The official terror was met by peasant terror. Official representatives were murdered and mutilated. Attacks were made on newly formed kolkhozy, and arson was frequent. The most important consequence, however, was a wave of wholesale slaughter of livestock. Under the threat of having their animals 'collectivised', the peasants preferred to eat them.[120] The consequences of this depletion of livestock herds were to be felt long after.

To manage the operation locally,[121] committees of three, *troikas*, were set up. These included the first secretary of the district party committee (raikom), the chairman of the local Soviet Executive Committee (*raiispolkom*), and the local head of the Secret Police, the OGPU. These troikas made up lists of kulaks and kulak property, and in so doing frequently accepted 'recommendations' on additions to the lists from poor peasants and agricultural workers.[122] The operation rapidly degenerated into pure looting and opportunities for personal revenge.[123]

Eventually the abuse and excesses took on such dimensions that Stalin himself had to intervene.[124] The situation was now similar to that in 1921 when Lenin ordered a change to the New Economic Policy. Stalin's reaction was different. In a famous article in *Pravda*[125] entitled 'Dizzy with Success: Problems of the Kolkhoz Movement', he placed the full blame on local officials. They had become 'Dizzy with Success', and thus committed mistakes and abuse. The reaction from local officials to this 'Dolchstoss' is reflected in a letter to Stalin from a prominent party secretary named Khataevich, who argued that many of the excesses condemned by Stalin had been carried out on direct orders from the Narkomzem and the Kolkhoztsentr.[126] Khataevich would not survive the Great Purge.

Following Stalin's intervention there was a flow of other articles in the press, giving examples of local abuse and terror,[127] and consequently the operation lost momentum. By the summer the number of households in collectives was down to 23 per cent, and many dekulakisation cases were reversed.[128] However, the retreat was only temporary. In June the mir was formally dissolved and replaced by the kolkhoz. By the autumn the campaign picked up speed again, and by summer 1931 the 50 per cent mark was reached anew.[129] The operation was now pursued with all available means. Peasants outside the kolkhozy, who were nevertheless not kulaks, were given poor soil, high delivery quotas and high taxes. They were also subjected to various forms of intimidation, ranging from administrative pressure to outright violence.[130]

The renewed war with the peasantry again brought famine upon the country. On this occasion no foreign aid was applied for. On the contrary grain exports continued, and in 1930-1 even increased.[131] In 1932, the situation had deteriorated so far that grain delivery quotas had to be reduced from 29.5 million tons to 18.1 million.[132] In order to strengthen incentives, peasants were allowed to sell surplus grain on the free market. To starving peasants this can have done little else but add insult to injury. Middlemen were still prohibited, however, and penalties of 5-10 years' prison camp were established for 'speculation'.[133] This was a major difference in comparison with NEP, and it greatly reduced the value of the liberalisation. The severity of the situation is illustrated by the mandatory death penalty for theft of kolkhoz property, including crops in the field.[134]

Collectivisation represented the fourth step in the development of Soviet agricultural policy. Given the principle of administrative extraction of produce and the system of forceful collections developed under the 'Ural-Siberian method', kolkhozy offered a perfect local organisation. By choosing the mir as a model for the new collectives, two important advantages were gained. One was that, as in the mir after emancipation, the peasants could be made jointly responsible for delivery obligations, and the other was that the number of farms was drastically reduced, which facilitated control. The latter point is of major importance.

The Final Touch

The final step in this process is composed of two different events. At the first count, early 1933 saw the start of reporting 'biological yields'. This system meant that special officials made estimates of the 'biologically possible' yield as the crop was still standing in the field. As we recall from Chapter 1, common practice in the West is to report 'barn yields', i.e. what is actually harvested and brought under cover. The difference consists of theft, wastage and other losses, and could frequently amount to as much as 20-30 per cent.[135] The obvious aim was to facilitate procurements. Since contracts were signed on the basis of bioyields, all harvest failures would be borne by the peasantry.

A corollary of this practice was that only underreporting of yields was considered a crime, which is reflected in the many decrees against lowering quotas, but none to the reverse.[136] Parallel with the introduction of bioyields, the best economics and statistics journals were closed down, with the result that statistics in the proper sense were abolished for over two decades.[137] The system of bioyields was not abandoned until after Stalin's death in 1953, and it was not until 1959 that it was revealed that the actual barn crop of grains on average had been 23 per cent lower than published for the period 1933-7.[138]

The other important event — and indeed the finishing touch to the development of Soviet agricultural policy — was the utilisation of the Machine Tractor Stations (MTSs). At an early stage it was clear that mechanisation of agriculture would have to be an essential ingredient in policy, not only to win over the peasantry,[139] but also to make possible the huge transfer of resources out of agriculture that would be necessary to fuel the industrialisation drive. To achieve this, machinery rental points, seed cleaning stations and land reclamation stations were set up, all of which were beyond the means of individual farmers to set up and operate.

Towards the end of the 1920s, these various organisations were consolidated into the MTS network, which in 1930 was given exclusive responsibility for rural mechanisation.[140] Initially the MTSs were given priority in machinery allocation, but soon they were given a monopoly on all mechanised farm operations. In 1934 the kolkhozy were stripped of all agricultural machinery.[141] Payment for the services rendered by the MTSs was made in kind, and this became an important channel for government grain procurements. The grip of the MTSs over the kolkozy was consequently very strong.

In January 1933 Stalin decided to use this leverage.[142] Special political departments (*politotdely*) were set up at all MTS stations, with the vice-director of the station as acting head, and with the local head of the secret police as second in command. The philosophy behind these politotdely was to bring party control to bear directly on production.[143] Political control was to be substituted for other inputs. No thought was given to agronomic detail. People sent out to the farms as plenipotentiaries came from all sorts of backgrounds, and previous knowledge of agricultural matters was far from essential. Their function was not to give advice, but simply to make sure that party directives were followed. Exhortation and extraction were more important than production. Peasant reaction was again fierce, and after two years of disruptions, the politotdely were abolished.

With this fifth and final step our picture is complete. Russian serf agriculture had been transformed into Soviet collective farming, and gradually a policy had emerged that clearly defined the roles of state and peasantry. Peasants were reduced to residual claimants of their own produce, and the step into a full wartime economy was not a large one. All that was needed under the German onslaught was a reinstitution of the MTS politotdely to get the necessary leverage. Let us summarise the steps in this development.

Conclusion

In this chapter, we have shown the step-by-step emergence of Soviet agricultural policy, and the establishment of an institutional framework suited to this policy. In highly simplified terms this development took place in three distinct phases. The *first phase* was the War Communism period, where the basic principles were laid down. The prodrazverstka established the principle of administrative extraction of agricultural produce, and made an attempt at finding a suitable format for this policy. Peasant resistance, however, was too strong and the attempt failed.

The *second phase* was the NEP period, when the Bolshevik leadership learnt the lesson of making concessions to the peasantry, and when the future of Soviet agriculture was still very much an open question. The *final phase* was Stalin's reintroduction of the prodrazverstka in the shape of the 'Ural-Siberian method', during which the break with the peasantry became definite. The principle of administrative extraction was maintained. Contracts were introduced to facilitate planning and execution of this extraction. Kolkhozy were set up to make the peasantry a residual claimant. Biological yields were introduced and scientific journals closed, in order to cover up what was happening, and as a final touch, the MTS political departments, the politotdely, were established to bring party control to bear directly on production.

The most important conclusion to be drawn concerns the very close correspondence between policy and institutions. The basic principle of Soviet agricultural policy, as it emerged during the first years of Soviet rule, was the reduction of the peasantry to the status of residual claimants, i.e. to force them to absorb natural fluctuations in production. On three important counts the institutional structure was helpful in this respect. *First*, the machinery for administrative extraction of produce at fixed prices was established, thus giving the state complete control over the terms of trade with the peasantry. *Secondly*, the machinery of party control over the farms was established, which offered the state a means of preventing the peasants from withdrawing into subsistence. *Thirdly*, and most importantly, the structure of the new collective farms was chosen in order to fit into this system of control.

In many respects the kolkhoz exhibits great similarities with the old mir, but there are highly important differences. Livestock and equipment in the mir were private property, whereas in the kolkhoz they were communal property, and while all work in the mir was for private gain, in the kolkhoz the link between effort and reward was removed.[144] Both these modifications were essential in order to remove the basis for peasant claims to a share in output.

In the following chapter, we shall demonstrate on the one hand how basic policy was changed in favour of the peasantry, and on the other how institutions remained unchanged. The procurement system, with fixed prices and delivery quotas, still remains. The system of party control down to minute detail is also still intact, and the structure of the kolkhoz is largely unchanged. In Chapter 4 we will present this conflict between policy and institutions as it stands today, and in subsequent chapters we will use it to analyse the present crisis in Soviet agriculture. Before we proceed, however, let us listen to Moshe Lewin's verdict, in 1974, over the period we have just studied:

> Soviet agriculture has not yet managed to effect a real technological revolution similar to the one which took place some time ago in other developed countries. Agriculture is still rather primitive and a great problem and there is no doubt that the consequences of the first quarter of a century of kolkhoz history still weigh heavily and are far from having been definitely overcome.[145]

Notes

1. It should be pointed out from the start that we are not attempting to show an actual plan or strategy of development. On the contrary, our endeavour is to show that as a result of a basic attitude on how to deal with the peasantry, a series of *ad hoc* measures came to be contiguous steps in the emergence of Stalinist agriculture. There is a substantial difference between this view and one that sees an explicitly devised strategy. See for example Wickman (1981).

2. See above all Smith (1968) and Volin (1970), Ch. 1. See also Maynard (1962a, 1962b) and Robinson (1961) on conditions for the peasantry during the nineteenth century.

3. Volin (1970), p. 21.

4. Ibid., p. 17.

5. See Gsovski (1949), vol. I, pp. 667ff for the contents of this law.

6. The importance for future developments of this reduction in peasant land holdings is reflected in a contemporary Russian source: 'Now, however, the peasants have to lease the very same plots at excessive rentals. What fertile ground for the idea that the landlords illegally own peasant land.' Quoted by Volin (1970), p. 76.

7. Several sources testify to this, notably Count Witte at an agricultural conference 25 years later: 'The redemption payment in most areas considerably exceeded the income [rent] of the land, and thus the landlord was receiving what amounted to a concealed compensation for being deprived of his rights over the person of the peasant.' Quoted by Volin (1970), p. 51.

8. Ibid., p. 50.

9. An alternative interpretation is that the failure to meet tax and redemption payments indicates a *refusal* to pay rather than an *inability*, and that the peasants actually were rather well off. See for example Simms (1977).

10. The only exception to this was a small plot of land around the house, which was held in hereditary possession. These plots would later develop into today's private plots in the kolkhozy.

11. Male (1971) and Taniuchi (1968) give excellent accounts of the crucial final stage of the mir in the 1920s.

12. One obvious reason for this was the desire to avoid creating a landless proletariat, which would no doubt have resulted from a system of individual property rights. See further Emmons (1968) on the whys and wherefores of emancipation.

13. Without this passport, it is still not possible to travel inside the Soviet Union. It must be carried at all times, and in it are recorded such information as marital status, age and current address. It was not until 1975 that it was decided that such passports should be generally issued to the peasantry.

14. Maynard (1962a), p. 36.

15. Ibid., p. 40f.

16. It is important to note that implements and animals were held in private possession, since precisely these property rights would be a major stumbling block in the collectivisation campaign that was to come.

17. European Russia. The total population was approximately 100 million. Volin (1970), p. 63.

18. Ibid.

19. Maynard (1962a), p. 36.

20. The reform that was carried out in these years is credited to Stolypin by convention, although most of the work had been done by others before his arrival in St Petersburg. Witte, Krivoshein and Gurko were especially involved.

21. 'The Government has placed its wager, not on the needy and drunken, but on the sturdy and strong.' Quoted by Robinson (1961), p. 194.

22. See Gsovski (1949), vol. I, pp. 682ff.

23. Volin (1970), p. 104f.

24. See for example Volin (1970), p. 105.

25. Volin (1970), p. 110.

26. We shall consistently be using dates according to the Julian calendar that was in use in Russia at the time. Our Gregorian calendar is 13 days ahead and the revolutions in 1917 would thus have occurred in March and November.

27. Lewin (1968), p. 132.

28. Carr (1952), p. 31.

29. It was actually worked out by Lenin during the night following the storming of the Winter Palace, and it immediately triggered an intense political struggle. It was not until February of the following year that it was actually made law, 'On the Socialisation of Land'. See Carr (1952), pp. 39ff.

30. The very severe peace of Brest-Litovsk.

31. Nove (1969), p. 55.

32. Carr (1952), pp. 51ff.

33. Ibid., p. 53.

34. Between November 1917 and mid-1921, the quantity of paper money in circulation increased by more than 100 times, and prices by even more. Volin (1970), p. 144.

35. In 1917 it was 2.6 million. By 1920 it was down to 1.2 million. Nove (1969), p. 66f.

36. See Carr (1952), p. 53f.

37. Volin (1970), pp. 147ff., gives a detailed account of this system. Detachments were to be a minimum of 75 workers with two to three machine guns, and it rapidly developed into a veritable army, numbering between 20,000 and 45,000 people at various points in time.

38. True, the officially fixed prices were paid to the peasants, but with the purchasing power of money being virtually nil, the difference is purely academic.

39. Grain procurements in the first four years after the revolution were as follows (000 tons):

1917/18	778
1918/19	1,767
1919/20	3,481
1920/1	4,636

See Carr (1952), p. 151.

40. Dobb (1966), p. 117, states that in 1920, between 14 and 20 per cent of the sown area, and as much as 33 per cent of the harvest, was concealed from the authorities.

41. In European Russia and in Belorussia the sown areas were reduced to 75 and 78 per cent respectively, whereas figures for the Ukraine and Siberia were 96 and 98 per cent. Volin (1970), p. 149.

42. Nove (1969), p. 86.

43. Fainsod (1963), p. 93.

44. This new interpretation was pioneered by Roberts (1970) and by Szamuely (1974).

45. This traditional view has been championed above all by Dobb (1966).

46. See also Lewin (1974b) for a similar interpretation of early Soviet agricultural policy as being built on *extraction*.

47. Carr (1952), p. 172.

48. Nove (1969), p. 83.

49. Carr (1952), pp. 280ff. See also *Izvestia*, 23 March 1921.

50. The delivery quota for grains in 1920/1 had been 6.9 million tons, and the tax was set to yield 3.9 million. The required minimum was 6.5 million tons. See Carr (1952), p. 283f.

51. See further Lewin (1974a), Ch. 4.

52. *Pravda*, 26 June 1922. See further Fisher (1927) for a description of the horrors of this famine.

53. Carr (1952), p. 284. It is an indication of the seriousness of the problem that aid was finally accepted from the Hoover Program (American Relief Association – ARA), which at its peak fed 10 million people daily. See further Volin (1970), pp. 174ff.

54. 'Fundamental Law on the Exploitation of Land by Workers'. Carr (1952), p. 289.

55. Nove (1969), p. 88.

56. Ibid., pp. 93ff, has an account of the causes and development of this crisis, as well as of the government measures taken to alleviate it.

57. Retail outlets operated by the Consumer Co-operation, tsentrosoyuz.

58. Nove (1969), p. 103.

59. Ibid., p. 106.

60. In the vanguard of this movement was Bukharin, who in an article in *Pravda* (24 April 1925) coined the expression *obogaschaites* ('Get Rich'). His basic tenet was that strong peasants were good for the state, and thus should be

encouraged. He also went so far as to suggest that maybe even better-off peasants — the kulaks — could eventually be assimilated into society. Since precisely these people had been singled out as the main enemy, however, other leading Bolsheviks were outraged, and Bukharin was forced into a public *démarche*. See further Nove (1969), p. 123. An excellent biography over Bukharin is found in Cohen (1980).

61. See Volin (1970), pp. 177ff.

62. Nove (1969), p. 110.

63. In 1928 Stalin presented data showing that grain sales in 1927 were down to half of the 1913 level, or down to 13 per cent of total production. The table was compiled by the well known statistician Nemchinov, and it long went undisputed. Recently, however, a debate has arisen over its reliability, and Karcz, for example, argues that 'the calculation, as published by Stalin and reproduced by Nemchinov, is completely misleading and provides an exceedingly distorted picture of the relation between 1913 and 1926/27 grain marketings'. Karcz (1967b), p. 402. See also Davis (1970), Kahan (1963) and Karcz (1979a). The disputed table is reproduced in Karcz (1967b), p. 402.

64. There are several excellent accounts of this decisive power struggle. See for example Carr (1958), Ch. 4, Lewin (1974a), Chs. 6 and 12, and in particular Cohen (1980) and Deutscher (1949) on the respective roles played by Bukharin and Stalin.

65. Volin (1970), p. 195. This was also the congress where Trotsky and his followers were expelled.

66. Volin (1970), p. 168.

67. Robinson (1961) has a lengthy discussion of these flows out of the mir. He puts the 1917 figures at 7.3 out of 17 million households as holders of private hereditary tenure. These figures have subsequently been questioned as being too high. See Male (1971), p. 19.

68. Ibid., p. 27, quotes figures that for most areas are around 90-5 percent for the mir, and on p. 19f he also discusses the causes for this flow back to the mir.

69. Jasny (1949), p. 236.

70. Volin (1970), p. 107.

71. See Lewin (1968), Ch. 5.

72. Lewin (1968), p. 108.

73. Izvestia, 6 December 1918, and *Pravda*, a few days later.

74. Wesson (1962), p. 343. See also further Wesson (1963).

75. Lewin (1968), p. 112f.

76. See further Volin (1970), p. 154.

77. Volin (1970), pp. 128ff.

78. Ibid., p. 153.

79. Jasny (1949), p. 298.

80. Ibid., p. 299.

81. Ibid., p. 50.

82. Ibid., p. 304.

83. Lewin (1974a), p. 84.

84. Ibid., p. 84.

85. Quoted by Roberts (1970), p. 252.

86. Ibid., p. 252.

87. Quoted by Nove (1974), p. 188.

88. At the 15th party congress in 1928, Molotov referred to it as a series of 'colossal stupidities', and Kaminsky deplored its 'enormous influence on the instability in marketings'. Quoted by Lewin (1965), p. 165.

89. In 1925, limit prices were introduced for procurements, and at this time the official price was only half of the average price paid by private traders. Davis (1980a), p. 56.

90. Lewin (1974a), p. 214. See further Narkiewicz (1966), who elaborates on the point of an inadequate output of trained specialists. This argument, of course, supports our thesis that there was *no premeditated strategy or plan* for the development of Soviet agriculture.

91. Here procurements were down by 63 per cent compared to the previous year. Nove (1969), p. 151.

92. See Lewin (1974b) and Taniuchi (1981) for a background to the events.

93. This Code was introduced in 1926 and paragraph 107 made it an offence to raise prices by agreement between traders, or by withholding produce from the market. Penalties were imprisonment of up to three years and possible confiscation of property. The paragraph was not originally directed against the kulak, but was rather an integral part of the new law. It was not used until Stalin 'discovered' it. See Beerman (1967), p. 127f.

94. Volin (1970), p. 210.

95. It is significant that the term *zagotovki*, which means 'procurement', was later changed to *zakupki*, which means 'purchases'.

96. *Pravda*, 15 February 1928.

97. See Lewin (1968), Ch. 17.

98. Arthur Wright summarises the situation as: 'Can the interests of the ruling political group and the dominant economic group be reconciled to their mutual satisfaction?' Wright (1979), p. 7.

99. Davis (1980a), pp. 21ff.

100. Ibid., pp. 104ff.

101. Lewin (1968), pp. 268ff, argues that if this system had been seriously implemented, it might have had very positive long-run effects. It was used very successfully in Poland after the abolition of collective farms in 1957. See also Lewin (1974b), p. 284.

102. Davis (1980a), p. 19.

103. Lewin (1974b), p. 285.

104. Davis (1980a), p. 62.

105. Lewin (1968), p. 274.

106. Quoted by Nove (1964a), p. 27.

107. It is important to note again that we are not trying to present the evolution of a policy as proceeding according to some form of strategy. As Lewis has it: 'NEP went under before any alternative forms or structures had taken shape, even in the minds of the leadership.' Lewin (1965), p. 162. The continuity we are trying to indicate is that of a basic attitude that produced a systematic type of reaction to a series of crises.

108. Wright (1979), p. 7.

109. Ibid., p. 6.

110. *Pravda*, 31 October 1929.

111. Ibid., 7 November 1929. See also Davis (1980a), p. 155f, for details.

112. Lewin (1968), p. 438.

113. Nove (1969), p. 165.

114. Ibid., p. 165.

115. *Pravda*, 29 December 1929.

116. Quoted by Davis (1980a), p. 198.

117. This decree was prepared by a Politburo commission, chaired by Yakovlev, the Commissar of Agriculture. The commission was appointed on 5 December and given two weeks to prepare its draft. This was then presented to a specially convened conference, and submitted to the Politburo on 22 December. After a redraft the final version was approved on 5 January. Davis (1980a), pp. 185ff. Again, the speed of events supports our thesis that there was no plan, but only a series of *ad hoc* decisions.

118. Volin (1970), p. 222.

119. Narkiewicz (1966), p. 30, argues that it was not so much the collectivisation as such, but rather the procurement campaign that sparked the revolt.

120. Sholokhov's superb novel *Virgin Soil Upturned* tells of nights when there was meat on the table in every hut, and when the peasants were staggering, drunk from overeating. Sholokhov (1934), p. 152.

121. An invaluable source on the actual practices of carrying out collectivisation on the local level are the so-called Smolensk Archives. These were classified documents on the campaign in the Smolensk area which were captured by the Germans in 1941, and subsequently fell into US hands in 1945. They have been compiled, translated and published in Fainsod (1958).

122. Volin (1970), p. 217f. See also Davis (1980a), p. 188f.

123. Although this was explicitly prohibited, 'ideological kulaks' would also be deported. These were persons who had made influential enemies, or quite simply poor peasants who had resisted collectivisation. Fainsod (1958), p. 245.

124. Endless stories can be told about this period. Davis (1980a), p. 222, has an account of how one village was collectivised: The organiser poses the question: 'Who is against Soviet Power?' and when nobody answers the village is declared unanimously in favour of collectivisation. See further Davis (1980a), Ch. 5; Lewin (1968), Ch. 17; and Volin (1970), Ch. 10. Over 100,000 troops were specially trained to 'help', which gives a flavour of the operation.

125. *Pravda*, 2 March 1930. See further Volin (1970), pp. 228ff.

126. Nove (1969), pp. 170ff.

127. Stalin's private attitude is reflected in an exchange of letters with the writer Mikhail Sholokhov. In reply to complaints about local abuse, Stalin answers that although there was no bloodshed, the peasant reaction of cutting down production was indeed an act of war; 'War by starvation my dear comrade Sholokhov'. Reprinted in *Pravda*, 10 March 1963. See Volin (1970), p. 213.

128. Ibid., p. 229.

129. Ibid., p. 230.

130. Lewin (1968), pp. 430ff, gives an account of these practices.

131. Volin (1970), p. 232.

132. Nove (1969), p. 178.

133. Volin (1970), p. 242.

134. The famine that resulted is described in Dalrymple (1964, 1965).

135. Volin (1970), p. 254.

136. Ibid., p. 254.

137. *Ekonomicheskoe Obozrenie (Economic Review)*, *Statisticheskoe Obozrenie (Statistical Review)* and *Biulleten Konyunkturnogo Instituta (Bulletin of the Business Cycle Institute)* were all closed in 1930.

138. *Selskoe Khozyaistvo* (1971), p. 196.

139. Lenin's statement: 'If we could only provide the peasants with 100,000 tractors, they would turn communists' would become famous. See Miller (1970), p. 1.

140. Miller (1970) is the *magnum opus* on the MTS and its role in Soviet development.

141. Jasny (1949), p. 279.

142. See Miller (1966).

143. We shall return to this 'production principle' in Chapter 4.

144. We shall return to this in detail below, the most important point for the moment being that remuneration for labour is reduced to a share in the potential surplus of the farm at the end of the year – if any.

145. Lewin (1974a), p. 318.

3 POLICY REVERSAL

In the previous chapter we showed the gradual emergence of an apparatus that was wholly suited to a policy built on repression and forceful extraction of agricultural produce. We shall now continue to follow the development of this policy, along two lines. On the one hand, we shall argue that in all important respects the agricultural bureaucracy and the planning framework have remained intact, whereas on the other, there have been important changes in overriding policy towards the peasantry. Force and repression have been replaced by material incentives.

Following Stalin's death in 1953, Khrushchev attempted to introduce certain changes in agricultural policy, and a second attempt at change was made in Brezhnev's programme, which was started in 1965. The common denominator of both these programmes was a massive increase in the amount of resources allocated to agriculture, combined with a failure to change the basic institutions of agricultural production.

This chapter attempts to demonstrate that without such a change, any change in policy regarding the flow of funds will be of only limited assistance. We shall start with an examination of the Stalinist legacy for the new leaders. Then we will look at Khrushchev's and Brezhnev's programmes, respectively. Finally, we will argue that the situation facing the Soviet leadership under Andropov is in important respects similar to that which faced Khrushchev and Brezhnev, and that without institutional change, the present crisis will continue to deteriorate.

A Stalinist Legacy

The acid test of the workability of Stalin's model as a vehicle of extraction came with the German attack in 1941. The initial rapid German advances resulted in the loss of the best agricultural lands and the best manpower. Forty-seven per cent of the pre-war crop area and 45 per cent of livestock were overrun. Included in the losses were the best agricultural lands, which had an even more drastic effect on output. In comparison only 10 per cent of the crop land was overrun in World War 1.[1] At the beginning of 1945, the number of able-bodied males remaining on kolkhozy was down to a third of that four years previously, the rest having been called up by the army or war industry.[2]

The expansion eastwards also meant falling yields due to the utilisation of poorer soils, and the food situation in general was severely
strained by the influx of refugees into the uninvaded zone, boosting
the population there from 105 to 130 million.[3]

The shift to wartime measures which would have been necessary in
most countries to cope with the crisis only meant a firmer application
of existing policy in the USSR. The MTS political department, the
politotdel, was reintroduced and remained in operation until after the
victory at Stalingrad. Delivery quotas were changed from being based
on sown area to being based on arable land. Yields were measured in
biological terms, and prices were very low. Sometimes outright force
was used to extract the nesessary grain.

The saving grace, as it had been before, and would be again, was the
private plot. During the war, individual gardening both by kolkhozniks
and by urban dwellers was encouraged. Areas of unused land around
the cities were allotted to various institutions and enterprises. In 1944
these included 1.4 million hectares, or almost twice as much as in 1941.
Total output was close to 10 million tons of potatoes, vegetables and
other crops.[4]

An indication of the excellence of the system as a vehicle of maximum food extraction is the fact that the Germans initially preserved it.
In the German high command there was a dispute over policy. Those
who wanted to secure a supply of provisions for the army were in
favour of the kolkhoz, whereas those who wanted above all to secure
the co-operation of the Ukrainian nationalists were against it. By the
summer of 1943 the balance tilted. The Germans desperately needed
support, and promises of individual property rights were given to the
peasants. However, by then it was too late. People who had greeted
the Germans as liberators had learned their lesson well.[5] The failure
on the part of the Germans to change the system greatly facilitated
the return of Soviet rule.

The agricultural scene at the end of the war was depressing. Total
grain production was less than 50 per cent of that in 1940. Twenty-five
per cent of all tractors, 19 per cent of all combines and 78 per cent of
all trucks had been lost. In addition, the number of horses, which in
1940 had been only 58 per cent of that in 1928, was halved again by
1945.[6] Yet the policy for recovery was one of crackdown rather than
one of stimulation. By a decree of 1946, a return to the old strict rules
of the last pre-war years was proclaimed. Amongst other things, 5.9
million hectares of land were returned to the kolkhoz from the greatly
expanded private sector. Stalin's basic policy towards the peasantry

had not changed.

In the longer term, the programme for recovery included two features that would have important consequences. The first was the campaign for amalgamations, which was to transform the original tiny kolkhoz into today's large-scale enterprises. In 1949-50 alone, the number of kolkhozy was reduced from 250,000 to 124,000.[7] Apart from administrative reasons, the campaign was based on an almost unlimited belief in the benefits of large-scale production. An outstanding example of the latter is the kolkhoz 'Gigant', which was formed from 84 single kolkhozy, spreading over three districts and encompassing 135,000 hectares of land.[8] This trend has continued up to the present.

Even more serious was the emphasis on the introduction of new techniques of cultivation. The man behind this scheme was V. R. Williams, an American-born biologist who came to Russia as a railway builder, but soon became a soil scientist, and ended up as a professor at the famous Timiriazev Agricultural Institute in Moscow. The core of the new approach was the introduction of grasses into crop rotation, so-called *travopolnyi sevooborot*, to improve the quality of the soil. As such there was nothing wrong with this programme. The problem lay in its implementation.

The great populariser of William's teachings was Trofim D. Lysenko, who is probably better known as the man who destroyed Soviet genetics for some time to come.[9] Lysenko rapidly found Stalin's ear, and hence was able to impose his ideas on the rest of the profession. The consequences of this were twofold. On the one hand, virtually all research along other lines than those sanctioned by Lysenko was stopped, and on the other hand the methods favoured by him were introduced everywhere, whether locally feasible or not. Increases in grasslands became a political issue, the acid test of the loyalty of local party secretaries. During 1940 to 1953, grasses increased by 50 per cent, or from 10 to 15 per cent of total sown area.[10] The long-run costs would prove to be substantial.

The flagship of Stalin's contribution to agriculture was the great 'Stalin Plan for the Transformation of Nature', which laid emphasis on afforestation and planting of tree shelter belts to conserve moisture and prevent soil erosion.[11] On 5 March 1953 Stalin died, however, before his plan got off the ground. His legacy was an agricultural sector that was in shambles.

A New Strategy

After the death of Stalin a troika was formed, consisting of Beria, Malenkov and Molotov, all three of whom were part of the state apparatus. This was representative of the new form of 'collective leadership' that was to replace the Stalin cult. In the background, Khrushchev had risen through the party hierarchy to the post of First Secretary of the Central Committee. What made Khrushchev different from the other top leaders was his peasant origin. In the struggle for power, which was in full swing at the time of Stalin's death, he exploited this difference, building his power base on agricultural matters.

The new leaders found themselves confronted with substantial problems. Livestock holdings in 1953 were still below 1928 levels, as were major crop yields for the period 1949-53. Farm income had fallen by 30 per cent in the period 1928-52, and peasants had in many instances survived thanks only to their private plots.[12] Soviet agriculture had thus, in the quarter of a century following collectivisation, still not progressed beyond the level it had reached in 1928.

Stalin's successors did not have the necessary power, nor probably the desire, to continue the old policy. Drastic changes were made, and in the ensuing struggle for power, Khrushchev gradually came out on top. The new strategy bore his firm imprint. Broadly speaking, this new policy had three different components. Administrative reform was to bring party control to bear directly on production, a massive expansion of sown area was to bring about a rapid increase in production, and improved economic incentives were to make agricultural production an economically sound undertaking. Let us proceed to look at each of these components in turn.

In Search of an Administrative Solution

The dominant feature for which Khrushchev will probably be remembered was his 'organisational itch'. He was constantly engaged in a search for an administrative solution to the problems facing him. This was partly to solve economic problems, and partly to improve his own political position. These manoeuvres or their motives will not be investigated here, but instead an attempt will be made to outline the significance of the measures actually taken for the further development of Soviet agriculture. Three different steps can be discerned, all aimed at strengthening party control over agriculture.

The *first* step was the above-mentioned amalgamation campaign. Given the large number of farms and the low degree of party membership in rural areas, very few kolkhozy had a Primary Party Organisation (PPO), which was the smallest organisational unit in the party.[13] Consequently, party control had to be exercised from without, which was not very satisfactory. In this light, amalgamations seemed like an excellent idea. If the smaller farms could be merged, the number of farms that had sufficient numbers of Communists to form a PPO would increase, and so would overall party control. Although this was not the only reason for the campaign, it must have been an important one. The process was started in the last years of Stalin's rule,[14] and it yielded quick results, reducing the number of farms by half in the first year alone, and by a further half by 1958.[15] Thus, part of the problem was solved. The number of units to control had been reduced.

With the reduction in numbers, most kolkhozy now had a PPO,[16] and with this strengthening of party control at grassroots level, the logical *next step* was to turn to the management level. In the 1930s Stalin had sent around 20,000 people to the farms to increase his grip over agriculture, and Khrushchev decided to repeat this campaign.[17] On this occasion, over 100,000 volunteered, with a final number of 32,000 being sent, most of whom ended up as farm chairmen.[18]

With these two campaigns, the party's grip over the kolkhoz had been significantly strengthened, both from below — via the PPO — and from above — via the increasing number of chairmen who were also party members. The time had come, in a *final step*, to turn to the raikom, the district party committee which was the body of external control over the kolkhozy. The struggle to find the right format for rural party organisation would last throughout the remainder of Khrushchev's rule.

At the time of Stalin's death, Khrushchev had built up a power base that was solid enough for an all-out attack on the system of agricultural administration.[19] The main thrust was aimed at the 'depersonalisation' of party leadership in the village. Raikom officials had become too bogged down in paperwork to be able to assert their influence. There was a need to bring party control closer to production, and a decision was taken to decentralise the raikom.[20] As a result, its agricultural department was abolished and power transferred to the MTS. Each station was assigned a resident secretary who was in charge of an Instructor Group (IG). The raikom first secretary was to remain in the raion centre to co-ordinate the activities of the zonal secretaries.

This represents a highly important further step in the evolution of Soviet agricultural policy. What Khrushchev had done was in essence to *restore the politotdel,* the political department that Stalin had attached to the MTS stations. As we recall from Chapter 2, the purpose of these departments was to bring party control to bear directly on production, and the purposes with the IGs were no different. Exhortation and political control were still more important than production, though one difference was that this time organisation was more refined and internal control over the farms was stronger. It is precisely these points that make it a further step in the evolution of policy. Stalin's politotdel had largely been confined to controlling the kolkhoz from the *outside*. Khrushchev's Instructor Groups could work from the *inside*, via the PPO and the chairman.

To protect his new creation, Khrushchev launched a simultaneous attack on the state agricultural administration. Shortly after Stalin's death, he subjected the Ministry of Agriculture to a major reorganisation.[21] The All-Union Ministry was transformed into a co-ordinating body, and all operational control devolved to republican ministries. The local branch of the Ministry was completely abolished and all its important functions transferred to the MTS. Thus, in the mid-1950s Khrushchev had not only managed to strengthen his own power base by tightening his grip over agriculture, but he had also managed to reduce that of his enemies by downgrading the state agricultural bureaucracy.[22]

However, his new creation did not fare well. It was based on much the same principles as the politotdel and it ran into much the same trouble. Attempts at detailed party control over minute agricultural matters caused mounting disruption in production. Furthermore, the recruitment task for the IGs proved overwhelming, and on top of being understaffed they immediately ran into jurisdictional conflicts with the raikom. The system came under heavy attack in 1955, and was only saved by Khrushchev's personal intervention, arguing that it needed more time, and that the principle of 'closeness to production' was important. But in 1957 it vanished quietly, and thus ended the attempt to use the MTSs for political control.[23] The following year would see the end of the MTSs altogether.[24]

The last years of the 1950s were characterised by various attempts at filling the gap left by the MTSs, as well as by a continued political struggle, but for our purposes nothing of consequence[25] happened until 1961, when Khrushchev struck again. The Ministry of Agriculture was demoted to a research institute and most of its personnel transferred out of Moscow. As a result the power base of the Minister of Agriculture, Matskevich, was finally destroyed.

At the same time, two new organs were created. The first was the *soyuzselkhoztekhnika* (Farm Machinery Association), which through its local organs took over all the remainders of the MTS system. The other was a 'State Inspectorate of Procurements', which was created to bring together all the procurement agencies, assuming responsibility not only for procurements but also for supervision of the kolkhozy. With regard to these two new organs, the first one became well established, and is still in operation, whereas the second was just another in a series of attempts at controlling kolkhoz production. Parallel with these institutional changes there was an extensive purge of local as well as higher officials.[26]

The changes in 1961 brought an end to the attempts at decentralising control, and in the following year the process was reversed. A completely new and fairly complex agricultural bureaucracy was set up.[27] The most important part of it was the local level where so called Territorial Production Administrations (TPA) were organised. Each TPA consisted of a group of Inspectors-Organisers, each of whom were responsible for a small number of farms. There were 960 TPAs in 3,421 rural raions.[28] Most interestingly, a party committee was attached to each TPA, and thus the reform once again tried covertly to reintroduce the politotdel mode of party control.[29]

The TPA immediately came into conflict with regular party organs at raion and oblast level.[30] As the situation became untenable, Khrushchev intervened with a speech, trying to force the raikom into submission.[31] When this did not help it was simply abolished. Thus, Khrushchev had again created a whole new centre of gravity in agricultural administration, and in so doing succeeded in destroying not only the state machinery but also the old party structure. The new structure predictably ran into the same old problems, since it was built on the same principles as previous attempts with the politotdel. By the summer of 1964, there were rumours that yet another major reshuffle was in the offing, to be announced at the ordinary November plenum. However, before this could happen, Khrushchev was overthrown in October 1964.

Two very important conclusions can be drawn from this first part of Khrushchev's programme. First, in terms of basic attitudes regarding the role of the party in agriculture, there is a *distinct continuity* from the Stalin period. All the attempts at reorganisation are in various ways modelled on the politotdel principle of direct party control over production. In spite of negative experiences, it keeps returning in new external guises. We shall see below how this important continuity from the Stalin period extends into and over the Brezhnev period as well.

The second conclusion is a corollary to the first. In spite of several attempts, Khrushchev did not succeed in finding a *format* that would allow the politotdel principle to work without negative effects on production. What did result, though, was continuous disruption that finally led to his own overthrow. We shall see below that Brezhnev made a point of ensuring administrative stability, along the lines that existed before Khrushchev's arrival on the scene. Hence this first part of the programme was neither characterised by anything new, nor by anything lasting. When we turn to the second part of the programme, however, we shall find the reverse to be true. This brought a lasting and massive expansion of the total cultivated area.

Expansion

In the last years of Stalin's rule, agricultural policy began a period of intensification, with the Stalin plan and the Williams system at the front of the effort. Under the impact of a renewed food crisis, however, this strategy underwent a drastic change. A growing urban population placed increasing pressure on food production, with an especially rapid rise in the demand for meat. Parallel with this, there was a growing need for exports of agricultural produce. The shortfall in production was substantial, and something had to be done. Yet there was a considerable difference of opinion over which course was to be chosen. This marked the beginning of a war between Malenkov and Khrushchev, between state and party, between light and heavy industry, and between intensification and expansion in agriculture. The struggle was to end with Malenkov's resignation in 1955.

A few days after Stalin's death, Malenkov stated his views on agriculture in an article in *Kommunist*, the theoretical organ of the Central Committee.[32] The stance was hard-line Stalinist. The Stalin plan was to be continued and 'free' kolkhoz marketings suppressed. At a meeting with the Supreme Soviet in August he presented his programme, which also included an increased emphasis on light industry and on the output of consumer goods. The urban population was to be courted at the continued expense of the peasantry. Khrushchev reacted quickly, calling a Central Committee plenum on agriculture, where he outlined his own programme.[33] His attack on the Williams system and his condemnation of the Stalin plan are of major interest. Khrushchev argued that a policy of intensification would fail because there was insufficient capital for the necessary investments in infrastructure and land improvement. There was only one way out, to go east, to plough up virgin soil, thus achieving the necessary increase in output. There was nothing essentially new in Khrushchev's programme. Colonisation of the east had been going on since the end of the nineteenth century, and on a couple of occasions there had been determined campaigns.[34] What was new was the immense scale. Following the September 1953 plenum[35] a rapid process of escalation was set in motion. The first published figure came in December, calling for half a million hectares to be cultivated.[36] In January Khrushchev wanted 13 million hectares. By August it had been revised upwards by more than 100 per cent.[37]

Scattered opposition was launched by the 'anti-party group', notably the Stalin men Molotov and Kaganovich, but also by Kazakh party officials, claiming that the necessary infrastructure, such as roads, warehouses and grain elevators, should be built before undertaking such a massive project.[38] All opposition was steamrollered, however, and actual performance far outstripped even the most ambitious goals.[39] At the end of 1954, 18 million hectares had been ploughed up, and by the following year the total had reached 30 million. A crop failure in 1955 slowed down progress,[40] and in the following two years only 9 million hectares were added. A bumper crop in 1956 was followed by another poor crop, and the programme virtually ground to a halt. It was not until 1960, following two good crop years, that another 2 million hectares were added, bringing the total up to a record 41 million hectares.[41] By now, the limit for the agricultural area in the Soviet Union had been reached. Any further attempts at expansion were frustrated by the dropping out of marginal lands.[42]

To illustrate the immensity of this achievement, the area brought under cultivation was equal in size to the entire cultivated area of Canada, or to that of France, the UK, West Germany, Belgium and Scandinavia taken together.[43] Between 1950 and 1960, total sown area increased from 146 million to 203 million hectares,[44] the bulk of which was virgin land. As far as expansion goes, the project must therefore be deemed quite a success. In terms of output as well, the programme was important. The dominant crop in the new lands was grain, over half being spring wheat, and the contribution to total grain production was substantial.[45] From Table 3.1 we can see that the contribution of the new lands was between one-third and one-half of total Soviet grain production. On average, total grain production increased from 81 million tons in the years 1949-53 to 131 million in the years 1960-4, which can hardly be termed a marginal addition to output.[46] In particular, 1958 brought the largest crop ever in the Soviet Union to that date.[47]

Yields in the new lands were uneven, however, and consistently lower than in other parts of the country. In Table 3.2 we can find a comparison between two traditional farming areas — the Ukraine and the North Caucasus — and three of the most important new lands. Only West Siberia achieved the target set by Khrushchev at 10 centners per hectare. In some years the Tselinnyi Krai produced barely enough to replace seed, and studies of the costs of producing grain on the Virgin Lands show this area to be considerably less profitable than other areas.[48] Grain from Kazakhstan, for example, was about 20 per cent dearer than the national average from 1954 to 1960.[49]

Table 3.1: Grain Harvests (million tons)

	1953	1954	1955	1956	1957	1958	1959	1960
USSR total	82	86	104	125	103	134	120	125
of which Virgin Land	27	38	28	64	38	59	59	59

Source: McCauley (1976), p. 88.

Table 3.2: Grain Yields, 1954-61 Average (centners/hectare)

North Caucasus	13.5
Ukraine	14.7
West Siberia	10.4
Urals	9.1
Tselinnyi Krai[a]	7.9

Note:[a] This consists of the five northern regions of Kazakhstan, an area equal in size to France, Denmark and the Benelux together, with 22.4 million hectares of arable land.

Source: Volin (1970), p. 487.

What then was the reason for the poor performance in the new areas? Weather naturally was one adverse factor. Most of the new areas were steppes, with low annual precipitation, and no funds were available for investment in irrigation. Indeed the whole rationale for going east was a lack of funds, so these problems should have been anticipated.[50] Considering the large areas brought under cultivation, drought was likely to affect some parts every year,[51] and in addition severe winters made the growing season very short.[52] Furthermore, the sukhovey, the very dry winds coming from the desert and semi-desert areas of Central Asia, aggravated the situation. These winds not only reduce humidity and increase temperature during summer, but also blow the snow from the fields in winter, thus exposing crops to winter-kill and removing a possible source of moisture.[53] Apart from adverse weather, however, the programme also encountered other difficulties, which illustrate important limitations in the system.

As we have seen above, the dominant crop in the new lands was spring wheat. All attempts at introducing winter crops were rejected, and over time an extremely vulnerable monoculture developed. After a few years, yields predictably began to fall rapidly.[54] A major reason was a massive weed infestation.[55] Between 1954-7 and 1958-61, the amount of grain containing more than 5 per cent weeds rose from 6.1 per cent to 50.5 per cent. Losses in grain due to weed infestation were estimated at 4.2 million tons out of the 1964 Kazakh crop.[56] These losses can only be ascribed to monoculture and a reduction in clean fallow. The reason as to why it happened lies at the very heart of the system.

In order to start such a vast project, Khrushchev had to exert considerable personal pressure from Moscow — it became a 'campaign'. The very fact, however, that the operation was largely led and controlled from Moscow put a serious limitation on the number of variables that could be considered. On the one hand, it was technically impossible to collect a lot of detailed information at the centre, and, on the other, it was equally impossible to check the performance of local officials if they were given several variables to act upon. The campaign needed a simple slogan, and it got it: 'Sow spring wheat in the new areas.'

In addition to this technical problem there was the political dimension. Given the political struggle over what course to take, it was necessary to plan and implement the programme at the highest possible speed. Naturally, this resulted in many imbalances. The lack of time for selection led to the predominance of spring wheat. Haste in implementation also led to bottlenecks in the infrastructure, and Khrushchev complained that each year 'literally millions of poods of grain rot and spoil' due to inadequate storage facilities.[57] Finally, haste also contributed to the notorious shortage of machinery and personnel. Large groups of inexperienced *Komsomol* (communist youth organisation) were attracted by 'patriotic calls', which further aggravated the machinery problem, since many of these recruits had neither the experience nor the interest necessary for proper care and maintenance.

Two conclusions should be drawn from the Virgin Lands programme. First, whatever the problems and difficulties of the campaign, it should be remembered that it did alleviate the acute food crisis by substantially increasing output, and thus succeeded in buying time for a more carefully devised policy. Secondly, it provided the perhaps most spectacular example of the difficulties involved in exercising direct control from the centre. This 'campaign mode' of control, and the role of local officials in the process, will be dealt with extensively in Chapters 4 and 5 below. Whilst being most spectacular, the Virgin Lands programme was not the only example of this problem, and we shall look briefly at two other similar campaigns.

One important result of the increase in the output of grain was the release of high-quality land in the west for growing feed crops. An increase in feed production was necessary to satisfy the growing demand for meat. The crop chosen was corn, which is an excellent feed grain.[58] Corn had previously been a minor crop compared to other feed grains such as oats and barley, largely due to the fact that the Soviet Union is located far to the north of the famed 'corn belt' in the US. In addition to the short growing season, most areas are too dry for successful, unirrigated corn growing.

In 1955, however, Khrushchev proposed to expand the corn area from 4.2 million hectares in 1954, to close to 30 million in 1960.[59] The fact that in many areas there would not be time for the corn to mature was overcome by recommending harvest at milk-wax stage, using it for silage. The ears could be fed to hogs and horses, and the stalks to cows and sheep. Research on hybrid corn had been started early but was interfered with by Lysenko, and in the early 1950s there were no varieties suitable for Soviet conditions. In addition, the use of mineral fertilisers was not even mentioned.[60] Hence, the corn programme had similar features to the Virgin Lands programme. As a result, it encountered similar problems. It took off rapidly, expanding by over 13 million hectares in the first year alone. A peak was reached in 1962 with 36 million hectares, out of which only 6.8 million were for dry grain, the rest being for silage.[61] It is easy to envisage how the switch from other crops to corn became a test of political reliability for local officials, and the fact that coercion and force were used is borne out in a statement made by Khrushchev himself at the February 1964 plenum: 'Some officials sometimes force kolkhozy to plant corn which they cannot profitably grow.'[62]

The rapid expansion of the corn programme meant that something else had to give besides grain. Two targets were singled out, grasses and fallow. The use of perennial grasses in crop rotation was part of the famous *travopole*, or Williams crop rotation system. This system had been controversial throughout its existence, but especially so during Khrushchev's reign. Already in 1954, Khrushchev had attacked it. At this time, he criticised those who saw it as a panacea for all problems, and he explicitly stated that there could be no system that was equally applicable everywhere.[63] Soon this was all forgotten, however, and travopole was the main enemy — everywhere. Grasses died hard, though. Under the first onslaught there was a reduction from 16.8 to 14 million hectares. In 1961 it had increased to 19.2 and a renewed campaign was necessary to bring it back down to 14 million.[64] To illustrate the political importance of adhering to the campaign, there are accounts of local officials ordering kolkhozy to plough up fields of growing clover in order to be able to report reductions in grasslands.[65] As a reflection of the resistance to the anti-grass campaign, a kolkhoz chairman remembers how clover plantings were hidden from well travelled roads, for 'who would want to be known as a malicious travopolschik (one who adheres to the travopole system)?'[66]

The other target for Khrushchev's attack was summer fallow. Although he had been fighting fallow throughout the 1950s in order to release land for corn, success had been modest, reducing fallow from 29 million hectares in 1953 to 24 million in 1958. At the beginning of the 1960s the campaign was intensified, however, and fallow was reduced to 6 million hectares by 1963.[67] Once again, the campaign was a success in quantitative terms. The qualitative consequences of both these campaigns, on the other hand, were quite serious. There was a good case for reducing summer fallow in the humid north and central regions. Here fallow was not needed to preserve moisture. It was a left-over from the three-field system. Fallow was not 'clean'. It would be rapidly overgrown and used for pasture. Consequently, a reduction in fallow would increase production in both the short and the long run. Implementation in the dry zone, however, only served to make the lack of moisture an even more acute problem.[68] In the case of grasses, the situation was the opposite. There was a very good case for reduction in the dry zone, where yields were low. In the humid zone it was highly detrimental. Not only were yields high, but the introduction of grasses also served the purpose of breaking up the old three-field system and of increasing fertilisation. Reduction in grasses was a step back.[69]

The campaigns for corn and against grasses and fallow thus reinforce the conclusions drawn from the Virgin Lands programme. Any attempt by the centre to effect a major change will have to take the form of a 'campaign', in order to make sure that things happen at the local level. Such programmes will on the one hand necessarily be built on seriously limited information on local conditions, and on the other provide a strong incentive for local officials to score political points via the campaign, even if it is a disaster in the specific area. The consequences of Khrushchev's campaigns could have been predicted, and we shall see that the Brezhnev period did not feature any such activities. Let us now turn to the third part of Khrushchev's programme.

Incentives

The most important part of the new strategy that was implemented after Stalin's death was the marked emphasis on economic incentives to increase production. The first sign of a change came with the presentation, in August 1953, of the annual budget.[70] The agricultural tax was lowered, made simpler in character, and all arrears were cancelled.[71] As usual in policy reversals, this was only the first in a long series of changes.

The next step came with the presentation of the new agricultural programme at the September plenum, where Khrushchev was made First Secretary. The conflict between 'superindustrialisation' and improvements in rural living standards was recognised, the use of 'bioyields' condemned, and a promise issued that the publication of statistical data would be resumed. During the post-war years, not a single statistical yearbook had been published, and only a trickle of other information had appeared. The Khrushchev period witnessed the resumption of regular publications, and although much remained wanting, there was a clear desire to produce more reliable data. In 1961 a law was passed making it a serious offence to falsify reports and accounts.

Following the September plenum, drastic changes were made. The procurement system left by Stalin was characterised by high delivery quotas and low procurement prices. It was also characterised by a large degree of arbitrariness. Placed under heavy pressure to fulfil their plans, local officials continually revised upwards the quotas of any kolkhoz for which this appeared feasible.[72] The new policy brought higher prices, lower quotas, more stability and a revival of the bonus price for above-quota deliveries that had existed before the war. The price rises continued for four years, and were quite substantial, as can be seen from Table 3.3. The organisation of procurements was highly complicated. First there was the compulsory delivery quota, *obyazatelnye postavki*, for which the lowest prices were paid. Then there was the above-quota delivery, for which substantially higher prices were paid, sometimes by a factor of two or three. Thirdly, there was the system of contract procurements, kontraktatsiya, which had originally been introduced for technical crops, but then as we saw in Chapter 2 had been extended to grains by Stalin as a part of the Ural-Siberian method. Finally, there were separate procurements from the household plot. Up until 1958 there had also been payments in kind for the services of the MTS. After 1958 these were reduced to a mere trickle.

Table 3.3: Index of State Procurement Prices (1952 = 100)

	1952	1953	1954	1955	1956
All crops	100	132	171	169	207
Grains	100	236	739	553	634
Livestock	100	385	579	585	665

Source: Volin (1970), p. 384.

Initially the procurement system was kept in this form, but following the second stage of the reform it too came under attack. In 1957 the private plots were exempted from deliveries, on the grounds that the growth of the 'socialised' sector had made procurements from them uneconomical. In the following year, the whole procurement system was reorganised.[73] There was now to be only one form of delivery, with one single price for each commodity, in each region. Moreover, payments to the remaining MTS was to be in cash, not in kind. Symptomatic of the change in policy was a change in terminology. The old term *zagotovki* was abolished in favour of *zakupki* (*purchases* instead of *procurements* were to be the new basis of relations to the peasantry). Certainty was introduced into the system by fixing prices and quotas for a number of years ahead. This was partly intended to curb the display of arbitrariness on behalf of local officials. There was a loophole, however, in the form of an annual revision to raise quotas and lower prices in the case of a large harvest. There was no provision for the reverse in case of a small harvest.

It should also be mentioned that compulsion remained with respect to state purchases. This had been Stalin's 'First Commandment of Collective Farming', and so it would remain. Quotas could be lowered but never abolished. It should also be mentioned that the practice of fixing quotas per unit of land instead of sown area remained as well. A further important change concerned transport costs. The previous responsibility for the full transport cost to delivery points was limited to the first 25 km. Considering the lack of hard surface roads and shortage of rail track, this was a major point.

Finally, procurement prices were to be based on average production costs in state and collective farms over the past four to five years. This actualised the problem of costs as such. Studies of farm costs had been carried out in the 1920s[74] but after the purge of leading economists and statisticians in the early 1930s they were discontinued. During the Stalin period the concept of cost was largely ignored, and when it was brought up again in the mid-1950s, two questions immediately arose: what items should be included in cost, and to what degree should cost govern pricing?

Several problems were connected with these questions. Costs must inevitably be based on labour cost, since land rent and interest on capital are not recognised as costs in Marxist economic theory. Labour, however, was a residual claimant via the complicated work-day system,[75] with payments made partly in cash and partly in kind. Hence, there were no good statistics on labour costs, and a proxy had to be sought. Two schools emerged on this problem.[76] One argued that payments actually made to the kolkhozniks should be used, whereas the other argued that state farm wages should be used. Both systems have obvious drawbacks. If you use the former, there is no common denominator, and farms can be made to look profitable simply by reducing payments to labour. If on the other hand you use the latter, you will use a measure that might have little to do with reality in the individual kolkhoz. The matter was resolved in 1966 when the kolkhozy started paying a minimum based on sovkhoz wages.[77]

Initially, the response to the created incentives was very favourable, but soon the upward trend ground to a halt. During the period 1950-65 agricultural production in the Soviet Union increased by 70 per cent, but more than *half* of this increase fell within the period 1956-60, and on an annual basis growth was highest in the first two years of the programme.[78] Average factor productivity grew by 25 per cent in the years 1950-65, but all this growth occurred in the period before 1959. The remainder of the growth in output was due to an increase in inputs by a third.[79] The Virgin Lands programme is obviously important here.

Towards the end of the 1950s all hopes of decreased food prices through improved agricultural efficiency were frustrated.[80] The early years of the 1960s saw a new round of price increases, plus a commitment by the government to absorb all transport costs for procurements to delivery points.[81] This time the increase in procurement prices was matched by an increase in retail prices, and the anxiety with which this measure was taken is indicated by the fact that it was announced in a joint appeal to the people by the Central Committee and the Council of Ministers.[82] The price increases were substantial — 35 per cent for livestock and poultry for example — and the anxiety was well founded.

Food riots are rumoured to have resulted in some cities.[83]

These, then, were the ingredients in Khrushchev's programme for agricultural revival. Let us summarise their relative importance.

Khrushchev's Contribution

The *first* part of the programme marked the continuity with the past in preserving the basic principle of political control over production, and at the same time it preserved the format of the apparatus that exercised this control. All attempts at changing it resulted only in chaos. In this respect, Brezhnev would preserve the *status quo*. The *second* part of the programme removed another area of options for future policy. By expanding cultivated area to the point where no more land was available without heavy investment,[84] only intensification remained as a path to higher production. At the same time, the various campaigns also brought out the limited ability for the centre to influence development. Brezhnev would show that he had learned this lesson as well. The *third* part of the programme represented something essentially new, and is therefore of major interest for our purposes. Instead of repression, it was decided to rely upon material incentives to elicit production. At the same time, however, we have seen that there was no institutional change to accompany the change in policy. Farms were given higher prices but still lacked the freedom to adjust production. Peasants were given higher incomes but there was no link between pay and effort, etc. This contradiction seriously limited the returns to the substantial resources that were poured into agriculture.

While Khrushchev's leadership was thus highly dynamic, not to say flamboyant, it failed to solve the basic problems of agriculture. It did bring about a radical change in attitude on how the peasants should be made to work — carrot instead of stick — but it failed to bring about a concomitant change in the apparatus that controlled agriculture. As a result of this failure, the problem of low productivity in agriculture persisted. Although this was obviously not the only cause, it must surely have contributed considerably to the change of leadership in 1964. Let us now proceed to examine the impact of the Khrushchev legacy on the Brezhnev programme.

Perpetuation

The agricultural scene confronting Brezhnev was perhaps not as depressing as that which had faced Khrushchev, but on the other hand policy options were fewer and something still had to be done. No quick gains could be made by bringing new land under cultivation. No quick solution could be found in administrative reorganisations, and no easy way existed of exercising direct control from Moscow. There was no other way but that of restoring order and raising yields via investment and improved profitability.

On the first count action was swift. Only six months after Khrushchev's resignation, the agricultural bureaucracy was restored to its status at the beginning of his rule. The Ministry of Agriculture was resurrected even to the point of reinstating the former Minister, Matskevich. All the way down through the administration, the old order was restored. To consolidate further, firm promises were issued that there would be no more campaigns, and these promises have been kept. The most important promise concerned the private plots. Well aware of the fact that these plots were serious competitors for the time and effort of the peasants, Khrushchev had initiated an attack in 1958 aimed at reducing plot sizes and private livestock holdings.[85] Clearly, this had caused much resentment, and the lifting of these restrictions was a popular measure with the peasantry. In 1964 the plots still provided almost half of household income, cash and in kind.[86]

Apart from restoring order, Brezhnev's programme featured improved incentives, increased investment, emphasis on livestock production and a programme to develop the non-black earth area. Let us look closer at these in turn.

Incentives

The first part of the programme continued Khrushchev's effort at strengthening incentives to produce by providing more money, and great concessions were made via the budget. Procurement prices were raised again, in some cases by considerable amounts,[87] and the 50 per cent bonus for above-quota deliveries was reintroduced.[88] Furthermore, tax rates were altered to reduce total tax revenue from the kolkhozy from 1 billion to half a billion roubles per annum.[89] Finally, 2 billion roubles of debt were written off, and additional credits amounting to 7 billion were granted for 1965, compared to 4.5 billion in 1964.[90]

For the kolkhozniks there were two important provisions, apart from the lifting of restrictions on their plots. First, at last they were able to qualify for pensions, and at the same age as for workers, i.e. 55 for women and 60 for men. The second provision was of even greater importance. In July 1966, guaranteed minimum pay was introduced, to replace the old system of residual claim[91] where the kolkhozniks were paid only after all other liabilities had been met. At times there had been no pay at all, which explains the importance of the private plot. In order to make this change possible, the state bank was ordered to forward credits to farms in financial trouble. This was also an important step in bringing kolkhozy and sovkhozy closer together, since the minimum pay was based on sovkhoz wages.[92]

This part of the programme thus continued Khrushchev's policy of infusing more funds into agriculture. It failed, however, in linking this flow to improvements in productivity. The financial position of the kolkhozy was improved via higher prices and lower taxes, but there was no change in the structure that determined agricultural production. The income of the kolkhozniks was improved, but there was no attempt at linking this to increased productivity. (We shall argue below that it is not so much the low *level* of kolkhoz pay as the *system* of remuneration that constitutes the problem.)

Most importantly, the programme failed to bring prices in line with costs. From Table 3.4 we can see that the price increases left a pattern where some products were loss-makers while others were highly profitable. Given that the farms are told to a great extent what to produce, there will be a large element of good or bad luck involved.

Table 3.4: Procurement Prices as Percentage of Costs, 1966

Grain	170	Milk	98
Potatoes	227	Beef	110
Sunflowers	498	Pork	119
Cotton	132	Eggs	95

Source: Nove (1970), p. 395.

So far there is thus nothing new in Brezhnev's programme. It is merely a continuation of that of Khrushchev — more funds and no structural change.

Investment

The second, and dominant, part of the programme started an ever increasing spiral of agricultural investment, which is still rising. Deliveries of machinery, equipment and fertiliser were to double during 1966-70, compared to the previous five-year period.[93] Table 3.5 summarises these flows. Although the share of agriculture in total investment rose sharply, deliveries to agriculture failed to materialise at the planned rate, largely due to industrial supply constraints. Declining farm output and consumer discontent in 1969 led to a renewed emphasis on agriculture which in turn led to an increased flow of resources. Plan fulfilment in the years 1971-5 was more satisfactory.

After 1975, however, there was renewed stagnation and the 1976-80 plan targets were not met. Nevertheless, the 1981-5 plan targets were revised upwards (with the exception of tractors), and the new agricultural programme for the 1980s envisages further, substantial increases in the supply of inputs to agriculture. In the years 1971-5 agriculture and the branches supporting it received 34 per cent of the total investment in the economy. Agriculture proper received around 20 per cent.[94] It has since risen continuously and the latter figure alone is now more than one-third. The problems connected with this increasing flow of resources will be dealt with in detail in Chapter 6.

Table 3.5: Agricultural Investment by Purpose (thousands, annual averages)

	1966-70		1971-5		1976-80	
	(Plan)	(Actual)	(Plan)	(Actual)	(Plan)	(Actual)
Tractors	358	293	340	333	380	361
Combines	110	94	109	90	108	108
Trucks	220	143	220	220	270	268
Fertiliser (million tons)	41	37	61	61	93	78

Source: Carey and Havelka (1979), p. 59f.; *Narkhoz* (1981), pp. 218, 237.

While the first two parts of Brezhnev's programme thus represented a continuation of Khrushchev's policy of increasing the flow of resources into agriculture, the latter two parts did represent something new. One programme was aimed at increasing livestock production, in order to supply the consumers with more meat, and another was started in order to compensate for the long-standing neglect of the important non-black earth (*nonchernozem*) area around Moscow. Let us look briefly at these two programmes.

The Livestock Programme[95]

As we outlined in Chapter 1, the Soviet food problem is one of dietary composition, rather than one of being unable to feed the population. The diet is heavily weighted with starch, and there is a growing consumer demand for, above all, more meat. The regime has pledged to cater to these demands, something that has proven very costly.

Not only are capital requirements for investment in the livestock complex very high, but there is also an increasing strain on grain production. Increased demand for feed usually translates into increased demand for grain, since production of forage-type feed increases very slowly, and in addition such feed is bulky and inconvenient to use in large-scale production units. Today, concentrates (grains) account for one-third of the total feed balance. This is the background against which the constant emphasis on the grain problem should be viewed.

The initial advances of the programme were achieved fairly easily, largely due to neglect of the livestock sector under Khrushchev's last years. The removal of restrictions, raised prices and increased investment led to rapid expansion, and the targets for 1966-70 were met. After these positive results, even more ambitious targets were set, and the expansion of livestock herds outstripped the expansion of the feed base, which continued to be unreliable. The government's commitment to the programme remained intact, however, and instead of distress slaughterings, large quantities of grain were imported to make up for shortfalls. After the moderate harvest failure in 1972 this strategy worked, but following the drought in 1975 imports were insufficient and herds were depleted. In particular the hog population, which can be most rapidly rebuilt, declined by 20 per cent.

Table 3.6: Livestock Inventories (million head, end of year)

	1966-70	1971-5	1974	1975	1976	1977	1978	1979	1980
Cattle	96.9	106.6	109.1	111.0	110.3	112.7	114.4	115.1	115.1
Pigs	56.3	67.6	72.3	57.9	63.1	70.5	74.7	73.9	73.4

Source: Carey and Havelka (1979), p. 67; *Narkhoz* (1981), p. 245.

The Russian Nonchernozem Zone[96]

One consequence of the incorporation of the Virgin Lands was the creation of an agricultural sector that is extremely sensitive to the capriciousness of weather conditions. The resultant heavy fluctuations in harvests constitute a major problem, and to combat this Brezhnev launched a programme to develop the Russian Nonchernozem Zone (RNCZ).

The benefit of this zone is that it has a guaranteed supply of precipitation, and is consequently protected from the year-to-year fluctuations that plague the traditional southern farming areas. The drawback is that it is riddled with unproductive tracts of land, such as swamps, streams, sandy and stony stretches, etc., that present a very different picture from the vast steppes of Kazakhstan, for example. The aim of the programme is to alleviate these restrictions, and thus to create a zone of guaranteed and stable output, which is badly needed for the expansion of the livestock programme.

In 1976-90 the RNCZ is scheduled to receive 35 billion roubles in fixed capital investment, which is more than anywhere else in the farm belt. Today it absorbs about one-quarter of agricultural investment, and only contributes one-sixth of output. It accounts for 12.7 per cent of the total land mass of the Soviet Union but for only 8.5 per cent of the cultivated area.

Investment is to be geared into all facets of rural development, such as land melioration, mechanisation, increased construction, both for productive uses and to improve standards of living, and finally a broader application of agrochemicals as well as scientific methods in order to improve efficiency. For example, 9-10 million hectares are to be drained, and 2-2.5 million hectares irrigated, which represents a six-fold increase over levels at the start of the programme. As a result, it is hoped that expansion will be more rapid than in other areas. During the 1980s RNCZ grain production, for example, is to increase by two-fifths, whereas other areas are to increase by only one-fifth.

Ambitions are high, and much of future development will depend on the success of this undertaking. Yet it is off to a slow start. Investment is lagging and targets have not been fulfilled. The number of unfinished projects is accumulating. The reasons are largely a repetition of what has been said above. Structural constraints hamper implementation, and we shall return to these at length below.

Performance

Agricultural production performance after 1965 has shown many of the same features as it did during Khrushchev's time. Initial rapid advances turned into stagnation in spite of substantial increases in resource inputs. From Table 3.7 it can be seen that grain production did increase. However, it only met plan targets on two occasions after 1970. The past four years have been clear failures, and figures for the past two years have not even been disclosed.[97] Moreover, it should be noted that the bulk of these increases has been due to increased inputs. Over the period 1966-75, only one-third of increased output was due to improved efficiency. In addition, all of the improvements in efficiency came during the period 1966-70. All previous increases in output had been due purely to increases in inputs. These relations can be seen from Table 3.8, which shows that in the period 1966-70 more than two-fifths of the increased output was due to increases in inputs, and that in the following period inputs grew more than output. This trend has continued after 1975 and today poses a very serious problem. The solution obviously does not lie in more inputs. However, this is precisely what was suggested at the July 1978 and May 1982 plena on agriculture. Let us summarise the historical evidence presented in the past two chapters.

Table 3.7: Planned and Actual Output of Grain (million tons)

	1966-70	1971-5	1976-80	1981	1982
Plan	167.0	195.0	220.0	(238-43)	
Actual	167.6	181.6	205.0	n.a.	n.a.

Source: Carey and Havelka (1979), p. 64; *Narkhoz* (1981), p. 201f.

Table 3.8: Average Annual Growth Rates (per cent)

	1966-70	1971-5
Output	3.1	1.6
Total inputs	1.3	2.0
Factor productivity	1.8	− 0.4

Source: Carey and Havelka (1979), p. 64.

Conclusion

In Chapter 2 we showed three distinct trends: the transformation of the old mir into today's kolkhoz; the emergence of an agricultural policy built on administrative extraction of produce; and the development of an apparatus to support this policy, featuring centrally fixed prices and quotas as well as an elaborate organisation for local party control over production. Our basic contention has been that, on the one hand, policy and institutions were well suited to each other and that, on the other, this system, while conducive to *extraction*, was highly detrimental to *production*. Peasants were increasingly alienated, and the old threat of withdrawal into subsistence partly materialised in the form of a preference for the private plot over communal production.

In the present chapter we have shown how the new leaders following Stalin attempted to cure these problems by changing from an overall policy built on extraction to one built on incentives and investment. In one important respect, this attempt has failed. The basic structure remained unchanged.

Khrushchev's programme consisted of three different parts. The first part was an attempt to find an administrative solution, which merely served to underline the continued existence of the principle of detailed political control over production. The second part was a vast expansion that brought under cultivation all arable land in the Soviet Union, but meant little else. The third part, finally, was the important break. A programme of expansion of agricultural inputs was started, but led only to a short-lived boost in production. None of the important features of the Stalinist apparatus were changed.

Brezhnev's programme has meant a continuation of the policy of increasing inputs. Investment and procurement prices have been increased greatly, but once again only a short-lived increase in production has been attained. Brezhnev did not attempt to change the basic principles of administrative and political control over production.

The remainder of this presentation will be devoted to an investigation of the prospects for the leadership under Andropov. Present policy, as it was outlined at the May 1982 plenum, is merely a continuation of the programmes of Khrushchev and Brezhnev. The prospects for success on this occasion, however, are even slimmer than before. In 1953 farm income was extremely low, and increased procurement prices provided an incentive to increase production. In 1965 agriculture was starved of investment, and increases yielded high returns. Today, however, the relation between peasant incomes and the availability of consumer goods is such that the marginal utility of money is very low. Increased procurement prices can thus be expected to have strong income effects, leading to a reduction of the arduous work on the plots. Furthermore, the return to investment is now so low that little should be expected from this quarter. We shall now proceed to see what can and might be done with this legacy.

Notes

1. Volin (1970), p. 274.
2. Ibid., p. 276.
3. Ibid., p. 280.
4. Ibid., p. 289.
5. For a detailed account of these conflicting goals of the German High Command, see Brandt, Schiller and Ahlgrimm (1953) and Dallin (1957).
6. Volin (1970), p. 307.
7. Hough (1971), p. 109.
8. Davis (1980a), p. 124. This kolkhoz was established already in 1928, which shows that the process of gigantomania had started early.
9. See Joravsky (1970) for an account of the influence of Lysenko, who would not be dismissed until after Khrushchev's resignation.
10. Volin (1970), p. 315.
11. Details of this plan can be found in *Pravda*, 5 January 1949, p. 1, and

Bolshevik, no. 20 (1949), p. 3. See also Volin (1970), pp. 313ff.

12. Karcz (1971), p. 122. Obviously the war with Germany is one important explanation for this, but most important is that the losses incurred during the collectivisation process were almost on par with those inflicted by the Germans.

13. In 1949, only 36,000 out of a total of 240,000 kolkhozy had PPOs. Swearer (1963), p. 19.

14. See *Pravda*, 7 March 1950. It should be noted that Khrushchev had already started his struggle for the top in 1949, when he was made First Secretary of the Moscow *obkom*.

15. In 1949 there were 250,000, in 1950 it was down to 124,000 and in 1958 to 68,000. Hough (1971), p. 109.

16. In 1954, 76,000 out of 87,000 kolkhozy had PPOs, and in 1956 only a little more than 7,000 lacked them. Swearer (1963), p. 19.

17. Most of the people sent by Stalin had left and been replaced by local people. See further Hough (1971), p. 103.

18. Ibid., pp. 108ff. Like the amalgamation campaign, this process was started during Stalin's final years, but it did not gather momentum until 1953, when Khrushchev was made First Secretary of the Central Committee.

19. This was delivered at the September 1953 plenum of the Central Committee.

20. Miller (1970), p. 291f.

21. Miller (1971), p. 81.

22. An excellent account of this power struggle is given in Ploss (1965).

23. It should be noted that the agricultural department (*otdel*) at the raikom was not reintroduced.

24. Miller (1970), p. 312, especially Table 13.1. Various factors contributed to the demise of the MTSs, but that of closest interest for our discussion was the amalgamations. The farms were now large enough to have their own machinery as well as a functioning PPO. Thus, both economic and political reasons for the existence of the MTSs had been eroded. Some of their functions, such as repairs, were taken over by a network of Repair-Technical Stations (RTS). This system would have only a short life. See further Durgin (1960).

25. See further Swearer (1963), pp. 25ff.

26. Fainsod (1963), p. 226.

27. See Fainsod (1963), p. 226, Miller (1971), pp. 94ff, and Swearer (1963), pp. 28ff.

28. Miller (1970), p. 95.

29. An organisational chart of this is given in Fainsod (1963), p. 567 (RSFSR only).

30. Complaints about this can be found in *Sovetskaya Rossiya*, 25 May 1962, and in *Pravda*, 19 June 1962.

31. Reprinted in *Pravda*, 30 June 1962.

32. *Kommunist*, no. 4 (1953), pp. 53ff.

33. At this plenum he was made First Secretary.

34. In 1928-32 a number of large-scale state farms were established on virgin lands to alleviate the grain crisis, and in the early 1940s the German attack forced expansion eastwards. In the first case 12.8 million ha were added, and in the second 16.3 million. See Durgin (1962).

35. Mills (1970) discusses this prelude.

36. Ibid., p. 60.

37. Ibid., p. 62.

38. Ibid., pp. 61ff.

39. See McCauley (1976), pp. 80ff.

40. Durgin (1962), pp. 259ff. This crop failure was evidently a major political

setback for Khrushchev, especially following the success in 1954. His basic philosophy towards the Virgin Lands programme, however, is reflected in a speech at the 20th party congress in 1956. Responding to criticism, he said that if during a five-year period there were two good harvests, one average and virtually nothing the other two years, the project would still have shown a big profit. *Pravda*, 15 February 1956.

41. Of this 75 per cent was in Siberia and Kazakhstan. McCauley (1976), pp. 81ff.

42. Actually, at the 22nd party congress in 1961, Khrushchev called for a further 8 million hectares to be cultivated, putting the total close to 50 million hectares. In a speech to the Central Committee in December 1963, however, he admitted that the limit had been reached, and that further expansion would necessitate heavy investment for reclamation purposes. Ibid., pp. 81ff.

43. There are some difficulties with statistics here: 41.8 million hectares were actually ploughed up, but arable land only increased from 188.6 to 200 million hectares during 1953-60, which means that there was considerable dropping out of non-virgin lands, as well as of areas found unfit for cultivation in the new lands. Increase in the sown area in the Virgin Lands comes to 36 million hectares. Ibid., p. 82.

44. *Selskoe Khozyaistvo* (1971), p. 16.

45. As a result of the programme, the area under spring wheat increased from about 30 million hectares in 1953 to about 50 million in 1962-3. Volin (1970), p. 485.

46. McCauley (1976), p. 86.

47. The bumper crop in 1964 must have been a bitter irony to Khrushchev, whose resignation was probably at least speeded up by the crop failure in 1963.

48. McCauley (1976), p. 147.

49. Ibid., p. 151. See also Durgin (1962), pp. 269ff, Bush (1975), p. 3, and Volin (1970), pp. 493ff.

50. Indeed, in retirement Khrushchev claimed that Soviet economists had estimated that yields of only 5 centners/hectare would be needed to make the programme profitable. See Talbott (1974), p. 124.

51. During the bumper crop of 1956, for example, when the Urals and West Siberia doubled their results from the previous year, the Volga region failed to repeat its results.

52. Low temperatures also restrict the choice of crops. Winter wheat, for example, is easily destroyed, and the resultant concentration on spring wheat made the cropping pattern very vulnerable.

53. See further the account on climatological problems in Chapter 1.

54. Grain yields in the Tselinnyi Krai (quintals/hectare) were:

1958	1959	1960	1961	1962	1963
9.0	9.2	8.5	6.4	5.9	3.1

Source: Zoerb (1965), p. 34.

55. The record goes to one farm in the Kochetav *oblast*, where 3,700 shoots of wild oats were counted on one square metre of cropland. The roots went down 20 centimetres. McCauley (1976), p. 181.

56. Ibid., p. 182.

57. *Pravda*, 24 June 1960. We shall see in Chapter 6 below that this problem still remains.

58. Khrushchev was much impressed by the cornfields of the American Mid-West, and even dubbed corn the 'Queen of the Fields'. See further Jasny (1968).

59. *Pravda*, 3 February 1955. See also Volin (1970), p. 497.

60. Ibid., p. 498.
61. Ibid., p. 498.
62. Ibid., p. 502.
63. McCauley (1976), p. 124.
64. Volin (1970), p. 505.
65. Nove (1969), p. 363.
66. *Selskaya Zhizn*, 9 December 1964.
67. See further Volin (1970), p. 505.
68. See further McCauley (1976), pp. 504ff.
69. The old system consisted of a spring crop (usually oats), summer fallow, and then a winter crop (usually rye).
70. In *Pravda*, 6 August 1953.
71. By 1957 the total burden of agricultural taxes was down by 53 per cent, while the tax on the non-agricultural population was down by 27 per cent only. See Karcz (1966), p. 400.
72. Khrushchev's own characterisation of this situation is very striking: 'No sooner does a kolkhoz rise above the level of its neighbor, than the procuring agents proceed to trim it, just like a gardener trims bushes in the garden with his shears.' Quoted by Volin (1970), p. 379.
73. *Pravda*, 20 June 1958. See also Volin (1970), p. 382.
74. See Volin (1970), p. 386, note 19, for reference to such studies.
75. We shall return to this system in detail in Chapter 4.
76. See Volin (1970), p. 385.
77. The 1962 and 1964 Statistical Yearbooks published both versions.
78. Annual growth rates (3-year moving averages) are shown in the table below, which illustrates how the programme rapidly ground to a halt.

1951-64	1951-3	1954-5	1956-9	1960-4
3.7	2.4	8.7	4.8	1.7

Source: Diamond (1966), p. 346.
79. Ibid., p. 343.
80. Khrushchev repeatedly returned to this long-term goal. See for example *Pravda*, 29 December 1959.
81. Volin (1970), p. 395.
82. Ibid., p. 396.
83. Nove (1977), p. 187.
84. By the beginning of the 1960s, Khrushchev himself had realised that the limit for expansion had been reached. Yields had to be increased, and his final campaign was to increase the production of mineral fertiliser from 16 million tons in 1963 to 100 million tons by 1970. McCauley (1976), p. 130. Incidentally this was precisely the output that had been suggested by Malenkov in 1953. We should also point out at this time that one important consequence of incorporating the new lands was to increase drastically the weather sensitivity of Soviet agriculture.
85. See Karcz (1966), pp. 413ff, for an account of this attack.
86. Nove (1970), p. 399.
87. Bush (1975), p. 456.
88. It had been abolished by Khrushchev in 1958.
89. Bush (1975), p. 456.
90. Ibid., p. 466.
91. The so-called *trudoden* system. See further Chapter 4.
92. In 1963 the difference was 67.1 roubles per month for sovkhozy, and 28.5 for kolkhozy. Bush (1975), p. 461. At the same time the sovkhozy also underwent crucial change. Ever since 1919 these had operated at an overall loss (with

the exception of 1956), and the need for budget subsidies had been substantial. From 1965 they were placed on full *khozraschet* (accounting), which meant that they would be paid the same procurement prices as kolkhozy and in return have to finance all their costs out of revenue. The most important consequence of this concerned investment. Whereas investment pre-1965 had been financed via the government budget, it was now to be financed internally, and thus the farm autonomy over investment increased. The only remaining principal differences between kolkhozy and sovkhozy then concerned collective versus state ownership, and elected versus appointed management.

93. For details, see *Pravda*, 6 April 1965. The new programme was announced at the March 1965 plenum of the Central Committee.

94. Carey and Havelka (1979), p. 61.

95. Data given below are taken from Carey and Havelka (1979), pp. 65ff, and Schoonover (1979), pp. 103ff.

96. Data given below are taken from Carey and Havelka (1979), pp. 71ff. See also Sinyuva (1980).

97. See the estimates by *Radio Libery Research Bulletin*, quoted in Chapter 1, note 3.

4   THE COLLECTIVE FARM

In this chapter we are going to set the stage for our analysis of the present situation in Soviet agriculture. As a starting point, we shall take the conflict between overall policy and basic institutional structure as it has been outlined in previous chapters. To analyse this conflict, we shall construct a framework that will be devised as a game between three different actors. The *household* will represent the individual members of the kolkhoz. The Communist *Party* will represent government policy on agriculture, and kolkhoz *management* will represent the decision-making body of the farm.

These three actors will be presented individually, the rules for their behaviour will be defined and their respective strategies discussed. Two different types of conflict will be seen to arise: first, between management and the party, in terms of external restrictions imposed on kolkhoz behaviour, and secondly, between management and the household over the allocation of labour between the private plots and the socialised sector. The nature of these conflicts is one of divergent incentives. All actors will be assumed to act rationally, but given distorted incentives, the end product of their actions will be far from optimal. *Chapter 5* will investigate the first conflict, dealing with prices, procurements and marketing, and *Chapter 6* will deal with elements of both conflicts, restrictions on the use of capital and land imposed by party on management, and restrictions on the allocation of labour imposed by management on the household. *Chapter 7*, finally, will attempt to find feasible solutions to the indicated problems, and speculate about the future course of development in Soviet agriculture. Before we proceed to present our actors, let us first provide the general framework of the kolkhoz as a production unit.

The Kolkhoz

When Stalin embarked on his campaign for mass collectivisation in 1929, three different forms of collective farms were in existence which had developed on a more or less voluntary basis during the 1920s. These were the toz, the artel and the kommuna.[1] As we saw in Chapter 2, by the end of the 1920s, party preference was clearly established in favour of the artel, and by the end of the 1930s, this was for all practical purposes established as 'the' kolkhoz. Henceforth it will be referred to as such.

In 1935 a 'Model Charter' was drawn up for the kolkhoz, and this statute, which will be referred to as the *Kolkhoz Charter* below, is regarded as the basic law of Soviet agriculture.[2] A revised version was approved by a kolkhoz congress in 1969, but the basic principles remained unchanged.[3]

In the period from 1930 up to the present there were three major events of relevance for our argument. The first of these was the process of amalgamations, whereby the original tiny kolkhozy, with maybe a handful of member households, were transformed into large-scale enterprises. Today the average kolkhoz has 500-600 able-bodied members, 6,200 hectares of agricultural lands, 3,200 of which are sown, and it keeps several thousand head of livestock.[4] It also exhibits a surprising lack of specialisation. Early in its development it was established that all kolkhozy should have minimum holdings of the major types of livestock,[5] and this, together with compulsory delivery quotas for all major crops, has prevented a process of specialisation.

A second major event was the abolition of the MTSs, the Machine Tractor Stations, in 1958. For many farms this meant that after being prohibited from owning any machinery at all (and after having seen their previous machinery being taken over by the MTSs), many farms were now compelled to purchase from the MTSs more machinery than they could either afford or profitably use. For these farms the reform entailed serious indebtedness and overstocking of machinery.[6] Furthermore, it would mean that after having been dependent on the MTSs for mechanised operations, they would now become dependent on other state organisations (the future selkhoztekhnika) for delivery and maintenance of their own machinery.

The third event was the impact of Trofim Lysenko, which was not just limited to the travopole programme mentioned above. Research on crop rotation and hybrid varieties suffered as well, and these costs are still being paid.[7]

Internal Organisation

The functioning and internal organisation of the collective farm are laid down by the Kolkhoz Charter.[8] The charter of every single farm is based on this, and although considerations are made for local conditions, the Charter is in all important respects the law. The highest decision-making body in the kolkhoz is the General Meeting. It adopts and amends the farm's charter. It elects the Management Board and the chairman, as well as the Auditing Commission. It decides questions on the admission and expulsion of members, and finally it adopts regulations for intra-farm settling of accounts and pay, and ratifies plans for kolkhoz activities. All of these conditions are in accordance with the Charter.[9]

In practice, however, real power is vested in the Management Board. Whilst the General Meeting probably was a real decision-making unit in the original small kolkhozy, there are two trends that have contributed to changing this situation. The first is the amalgamations. With drastically increased farm sizes, the operation of direct democracy clearly became unwieldy, and provisions were instead made for representative democracy.[10]

This changing reality is reflected in different formulations in the 1935 and 1969 charters. The Management Board is still in charge of running matters: 'The collective farm's affairs are administered by the General Meeting of Collective Farm Members, and in the period between meetings they are administered by the Collective Farm Board.' A more detailed formulation on the role of the Board indicates a strengthening of its position: 'The Collective Farm Board is an executive and administrative body that is responisible to the General Meeting of Collective Farm Members, and it exercises direction over all the organisational, production, financial, cultural, service and educational activities of the collective farm.'[11] Furthermore the Board is now elected for three years and is required to convene at least monthly.

Another important difference between the two charters is that there is now provision for General Meetings and Management Boards within the sub-units of the kolkhoz. This is probably partly explained by the fact that many of these sub-units have actually been farms of their own before being merged. The devolution of power that has occurred mostly concerns the daily implementation of plans, however. All important decisions are still taken at the centre, and the Management Board has thus become a highly important body, which controls a large-scale enterprise. Today's Board usually consists of nine persons, including the chairman and the leading specialists. It convenes at least once a week and sometimes for several hours. Much of the actual power vested in this body circles around the chairman. The strength of his position derives partly from the charter which says that 'The chairman exercises day-to-day direction over the collective farm's activity, ensures the fulfilment of the decisions of the General Meeting and the Board and represents the collective farm in relations with state agencies and other institutions and organisations.'[12]

Most importantly, however, his strength derives from the increased party control over the kolkhoz. This represents our second trend. In Chapters 2 and 3 we showed how party control was improved by strengthening the Primary Party Organisations and above all by increasing the number of Chairmen who were also party members. As early as 1954 the position of kolkhoz Chairman was placed on the *nomenklatura*[13] (appointment list), which means that no appointments can be made without party approval. In practice it means that the party will select a candidate and submit him for approval. There are isolated cases of party candidates being rejected, but they are few.[14] Today the chairman is invariably a party member. Together with the raikom first secretary, he selects the Management Board and other important officials and specialists.

The picture that transpires is one of successively strengthened external control over the kolkhoz, starting with centralisation of power to the Management Board and the chairman, and ending with the integration of the latter into the party hierarchy. A modern collective farm should thus be seen more as an integral part of the overall Soviet apparatus than as an independently run collective organisation. This of course creates a very awkward position of double loyalties for the chairman, who is personally responsible to both members and party. We shall return to this at length below.

A further administrative body in the kolkhoz is the Auditing Commission, which carries out periodic check-ups of the financial position of the kolkhoz and its sub-units. This body should be the equivalent of a Western accountant, but it has never played a role of any consequence, and we shall not have more to say about it here.[15]

Revenue

The kolkhoz earns revenue in three basically different ways: first, and foremost, via sales directly to the state; secondly, via sales to the consumer co-operative, the tsentrosoyuz; and, thirdly, via sales directly on the free kolkhoz markets.[16] Of these, the state deliveries, or zakupki, receive top priority.

For this purpose, the Ministry of Agriculture and the Ministry of Procurements enter into the planning process to fix targets for quantities, prices, standards, etc., and once a final plan has been drawn up, the result will be a contract that is signed between the kolkhoz and the procurement agency.[17] This contract, or *dogovor*, is based on a 'Model Contract' that is drawn up by the Ministry of Procurements, and it usually runs for 1-5 years. It stipulates, on behalf of the kolkhoz, quantities, qualities, times and places of delivery, and other relevant conditions regarding the transaction, and on behalf of the state, an obligation to accept delivery, times and methods of payment, possible advances, prices and, if relevant, forms of assistance to be rendered.

The Russian word 'dogovor' literally means 'agreement', but the contract is probably better viewed as an order to the kolkhoz than as a negotiated business agreement.[18] The kolkhoz chairman will try to get the plan changed in his favour, but whether or not he will be successful is unpredictable. Sometimes he will succeed, sometimes he will fail. Once the contract is fixed, however, it is evident that there are precious few degrees of freedom left for the kolkhoz. Since procurements cover the bulk of its output, there will be little capacity available for the chairman to use at his own discretion. He is told what and how much to produce. He is told when and where to deliver the produce, and he is told how much to charge for it. If the kolkhoz meets the plan, represented by the dogovor, any remaining surplus can either be sold or distributed amongst the members. One way of selling is to the state, in the form of above-quota sales, for which a premium will be paid.[19] Another way of disposing of a potential surplus is by handing it over to the consumer co-operative for sale on a commission basis through its retail outlets. Conditions, such as prices, times and places of delivery, etc., will be agreed for each transaction, and although the co-operative has considerable monopoly power, there is an element of real negotiation here, since these sales are not compulsory. The final method of sale that can be adopted by the kolkhoz is to sell by its own effort on the kolkhoz markets in towns and cities. Although these markets have certainly had a stormy history, they are at present unregulated and prices are formed via the interaction of supply and demand.

Labour Organisation

Given the contract, the kolkhoz is faced with the problem of allocating its given resources between various uses. The details of how this problem is solved will be dealt with in the subsequent paragraphs of this chapter, and here we will merely present the administrative background, dealing first with labour and subsequently discussing the case of capital.[20]

As in most other parts of the Soviet economy, the approach to production carries a heavy military flavour. Work is carried out by detachments of kolkhozniks, called *ferma* in the case of livestock production, and *brigades* in the case of crop production. A ferma is a fixed production unit that specialises in meat, dairy and poultry products. It will have permanently assigned specialists and fixed facilities, which normally include barns, cattle pens, feed lots and machinery. It can be assigned to a field brigade or be administered directly by the Management Board.

The field brigade presents a more complicated picture. Organisation has changed considerably over time, both with increased mechanisation and with the growing size of farms. The abolition of the MTSs in 1958 constitutes a particular watershed.[21] Today the most frequent form is the Complex Brigade, which is generally the result of amalgamations. A small kolkhoz that is merged with a larger one will simply be incorporated as a brigade of its own.[22] This fact also partly explains the devolution of power over running matters to the brigade level.

With the growth of the brigade in size and tractive power, the role of the brigadier has become greatly enhanced. He has taken over much of the authority of the chairman of the previous small kolkhoz (which indeed he might have been), such as day-to-day supervision and the distribution of work tasks. He also keeps a workbook for each kolkhoznik, in which he records the work performed. We shall not dwell further on the brigade level, but rather proceed to the level below it.

The most interesting, and most hotly debated, feature of kolkhoz labour organisation is that of the *zveno*, or link, which is the smallest unit in the kolkhoz. The zveno as a small work team of 3-8 people has existed from the start of collective farming, but has undergone considerable change over time.[23] Initially, such groups were responsible for all forms of activities on a given piece of land, and would be remunerated in accordance with results. This was in sharp contrast with the brigade, which was shifted around the whole kolkhoz, and where pay was by piece rate.[24] The correlation between effort and reward was thus quite different between the brigade and the zveno, and this highly important difference is still at the root of the controversy over the organisation of work in the kolkhoz.

Until 1950 the zveno was the predominant mode of organisation. It was officially adopted at the party congress in 1939, and on several occasions it was advocated as being superior to the brigade. It was considered important that the kolkhozniks should be made materially interested in their own productivity.[25] Kolkhozy were recommended to strengthen existing links, and to form new ones within brigades that did not have them. In 1948, however, Khrushchev used this as an issue to pick a fight with Andreev, who was then agricultural spokesman on the Politburo. The outcome was that Andreev was removed from the Politburo and the zveno from the kolkhoz. Soon virtually no links remained at all.[26]

For a long time nothing was heard about the zveno, until in 1963 it was praised in an article in *Ekonomicheskaya Gazeta.*[27] This was followed by a speech by Khrushchev, where he said: 'The higher the harvest, the higher the pay for each quintal of produce received. This method raises the responsibility of each person for production. There is no need to send a supervisor to watch the work of a tractor driver.'[28] Further important support appeared soon after in *Komsomolskaya Pravda.*[29] In an article entitled 'Master of the Land, Who are You?', the author (V. Zhulin) brought out two important points. He argued that binding contracts must be established between the zveno and the kolkhoz, and he defended the zveno against accusations of petty bourgeois tendencies, arguing that small groups of friends who depended on each other were the only true school of communism. This argument has since been used repeatedly.[30]

In the autumn of 1965, a conference on the zveno, held in Kuban, discussed two of the most important problems of the zveno. The first concerned income differentials. Substantial differences in earnings will emerge since members of the zveno will be paid according to their (presumably) higher productivity, and not all work on a kolkhoz can be performed by such groups. This will naturally cause friction and resentment.[31] The other important problem is that of employment. In a situation where the rural supply of unskilled labour is abundant, large numbers of people will be made redundant, since the aim of the zveno is to raise the productivity of unskilled labour. Hence the picture that emerges is that the popularity of the zveno is inversely related to agricultural performance, or as G. Radov puts it: 'Every time there is a tight spot in our agriculture, people turn for help to the zveno.'[32] Today it seems that most people involved in agricultural affairs agree that the zveno is superior in terms of productivity.[33] Nevertheless, it has only been used so far in experimental form.

One factor that retards its development might be an ideological argument. There is certainly widespread opinion in some party circles that the zveno is too close an approximation of private farming to be comfortable. In this light, the debate turns into an exchange between 'pragmatics' supporting the zveno on productivity grounds, and 'ideologists' (or *apparatchiki*) opposing it on ideological grounds. The outcome of this debate is obviously difficult to predict.

The status of the zveno is probably one of the most interesting issues in Soviet agriculture at the beginning of the 1980s. In the revised Kolkhoz Charter of 1969 it is not mentioned, which Pospielovsky takes as a basis for a pessimistic view on the future of zveno production: 'In other words, for the moment at least, the history of the zveno remains a subject of interest to historians rather than the basis of any current predominant farm policies in the USSR. Its status remains the same as in the past 10 years, only, after the approval of the Statute, much less hope remains.'[34]

During the 1970s little was heard about it, but in recent years there has been an increasing flow of articles regarding the zveno and in the 'Food Programme' it is explicitly stated that it should be widely introduced. We shall return to this issue at length below, but let us first conclude our presentation of the kolkhoz with a brief discussion of the role of investment.

Capital Investment

Investment in kolkhozy comes from two sources: loans from the state bank, the *Gosbank*, and internal allocations to the 'indivisible fund', the nedelimyi fond. During Khrushchev's period state loans to kolkhozy expanded almost fivefold, and their share in gross investment increased from a quarter to a third of the total. Such massive lending naturally led to defaults, and at the important March 1965 plenum, 1,450 million roubles in debt were written off, together with 180 million in remaining debt from the takeover of MTS machinery.[35] The policy of extensive lending was not discontinued, however, and between 1965 and 1980 loans increased from 1.4 to 4.7 billion roubles, thus bringing the share of loans in total investment closer to one-half. Kolkhoz profitability has clearly not kept pace with investment.

Table 4.1: Kolkhoz Investment and Debt (billion current roubles)

	1965	1970	1975	1980
Investment	4.4	6.6	9.2	10.3
New loans	1.4	2.2	3.3	4.7
Short-term debt	0.3	2.4	10.1	25.7
Long-term debt	3.9	10.3	17.8	34.0

Source: *Narkhoz* (1981), pp. 341, 528, 531.

Two important trends can be discerned from Table 4.1. First, during the period 1965-75 investment expanded substantially, but after 1975 it stagnated. This fits well into our earlier picture of Brezhnev's programme. Secondly, we can see the important role of credit. Initially, investment expanded faster than new credit, but soon this trend was reversed. The substantial increases in new lending, coupled with the even more substantial increases in outstanding debt, show that the farms were to an increasing extent relying on outside capital. Between 1970 and 1980 the ratio of debt to own capital rose from 21 to 55 per cent.[36] Furthermore, we should also note the rapid expansion in short-term debt, which shows that not only long-term investment but also current expenditure are increasingly financed via credit.

These latter trends also fit well into our earlier picture of Brezhnev's programme. In spite of more than 25 years of continuous increases in procurement prices, kolkhoz profitability is still too low, and it is symptomatic of the leadership's attitude that the May 1982 plenum continues the old policy of writing off old debt and issuing new credit on an even larger scale, new loans on which many kolkhozy will no doubt default.

We will not dwell here on the technical details of making investment decisions on the farm, nor on the problems of financing investment.[37] Instead we shall be concerned with external control over such decisions. The latter may follow two important channels.

The first of these is the direct setting of guidelines for allocations to the indivisible fund. Over time this has shown a zig-zag path of increases and decreases.[38] There is a very good reason for this uneven pattern. By reducing allocations to the indivisible fund, allocations to the wage fund can be increased, in order to create short-run incentives for collective work. On the other hand, increased allocations to the indivisible fund will of course strengthen the kolkhoz in the long run. The dilemma is obvious. There even seems to have arisen a practice of combating income differentials between farms by forcing the successful ones to increase their allocations to the indivisible fund, thus reducing wage payments in the short run and achieving greater equality in earnings.[39]

A vastly more important restriction on kolkhoz investment concerns the supply of investment goods. As we saw in Chapter 3, after the abolition of the MTSs, kolkhozy were allowed (and indeed forced) to purchase and own machinery. At the same time, however, the state agricultural supply organisation selkhoztekhnika was given an exclusive monopoly on the sale of such machinery. The connections between the kolkhozy and the selkhoztekhnika have been a major source of conflict, and we shall return to this at length in Chapter 6. Recently the situation has also been further complicated by the creation of a similar organisation — the selkhozkhimiya — with responsibility for deliveries of fertiliser, feed additives and other chemicals. This will also be discussed in Chapter 6.

Let us now proceed to a presentation of the three different actors in our game, starting with the household. All three presentations will proceed along the same lines. First we present the rules of the game applying to that specific player, and then we define a strategy.

Households

The situation of the individual household in the kolkhoz is probably the most peculiar feature of all in Soviet agriculture, given the dichotomy of work on the private plot versus work on the communal fields. Our main emphasis shall thus be directed at defining a strategy for the household in deciding on its allocation of labour between the two sectors. In order to do so, we shall start by defining the rules of the game in terms of the main features of the private sector.

The Private Sector

'Economically it is backward, ideologically it is alien, politically it is suspect, and morally it stands in the way of the creation of the new Socialist Man.'[40] In spite of this condemnation, the private sector in Soviet agriculture still accounts for more than a quarter of total agricultural output, tilling barely 3 per cent of the land. How is this possible, and what do we mean by the 'private sector'?

Although we shall only be concerned with private plots tilled by kolkhozniks, it should be made clear that their contribution is only part of total private production. Apart from kolkhozy, private plots also exist for workers and employees in state organisations and enterprises (including sovkhozy), where the right to a plot may form part of the employment relationship. In addition to this form of production, which is called lichnoe podsobnoe khozyaistvo ('personal subsidiary farming'), there are also true private farmers, so-called *edinolichniki*, who are neither employed by the state nor members of a collective farm. However, their importance is minute, and they shall not be discussed here, although this is the category that is officially referred to as private production.[41]

In the overall private sector today there are around 35 million households, cultivating a little more than 8 million hectares.[42] Of these households, around 13 million are found on kolkhozy, 10 million on sovkhozy, and a further 10 million associated with other state organisations and enterprises. Although declining, the share of the kolkhozniks is still by far the largest. The average size of the kolkhoz plot is 0.31 hectares, compared to 0.21 and 0.07 hectares respectively for the other two categories.[43] The share of the private sector in the total sown area has been largely constant at a little over 3 per cent since the beginning of the 1960s. Its share in total output is declining, however, as can be seen in Table 4.2. Whereas the share of the private plot in total output is falling, its production in value terms is increasing. In 1978 it was 13.7 per cent above the 1961-5 average.[44] As can be seen from Table 4.3, however, part of this is a price effect which favours the plots.

Table 4.2: Share of the Private Sector in Total Agricultural Output (per cent, 1973 prices)

1960	1965	1970	1975	1979
35.6	32.5	29.7	28.3	26.5

Source: Shmelev (1981), p. 69.

Table 4.3: Private Plot Output (millions tons)

	Potatoes	Vegetables	Meat	Milk
1965	55.9	7.2	2.5	28.3
1970	62.9	8.1	4.3	29.9
1977	49.4	7.0	4.3	27.5

Source: Makarova (1979), p. 53.

The plots did expand during the first part of the Brezhnev period, and the cause of their falling share is simply that socialised production expanded faster. In recent years, however, there is an absolute decline as well, and this trend is becoming stronger.[45] The reason for the declining importance of the plot can be found in a comparison between conditions of work in the two sectors. Whereas massive investment has been poured into the collective, cultivation on the private plot is still medieval, chiefly relying on a simple hoe. There has been talk of the introduction of small-scale mechanised equipment on the plots, but nothing has happened.[46]

Furthermore, the structure of labour input is vastly different. In 1978, the share of able-bodied men in the total of labour performed on the communal fields was about half, while on the private plot it was 20 per cent. On the other hand, the share of retired women in communal work was less than 3 per cent, whereas their share in work on the plot was almost 25 per cent. A considerable part of the work on the private plot is thus performed by people who for one reason or another (old age, infirmity, mothers with small children, etc.) are unable to participate in the communal work.[47] It is obvious that with rising incomes from the kolkhoz, peasants will cut down on the arduous work on the plot. Although there have been times when food from the plot was crucial for survival, 73 per cent of household income today derives from kolkhoz pay and state transfers.[48]

The rules for private plot activities are laid down by the Kolkhoz Charter, which grants the use of a plot of land not to exceed 0.5 hectares, and regarding livestock: 'one cow with a calf up to one year of age, one heifer or bull up to two years of age, one sow with pigs up to three months of age, or two hogs that are being fattened, up to ten sheep and goats (combined), beehives, poultry and rabbits'.[49]

Actual possessions, are determined by the Charter of the specific farm, depending on local conditions and tradition. The plot may not be transferred for use by other individuals or be cultivated by hired labour, and the kolkhozniks may only own small agricultural implements. Finally, the household is given the right to use common pasture under 'established procedure'.[50]

Given these restrictions, the choice of output is seriously constrained. Capital- as well as land-intensive crops are ruled out, and labour input becomes of paramount importance. Cropping patterns are arranged accordingly. Grains are almost completely excluded, and the bulk of the land is given over to potatoes, vegetables and orchards.

The dominant activity is animal husbandry, which is borne out by the high share of potatoes to be used as fodder.[51] The extreme interest in animal husbandry is partly explained by the need to supply one's own family with eggs and dairy products, which are otherwise difficult to obtain, and partly by price differentials.[52] Price differentials that are sometimes 2-3 times those in the West have been cited for grains and meat.[53] This explains why peasants will go to any lengths to obtain feed, even to buying bread in state retail stores[54] or in the end resorting to outright theft. Consequently private holdings form a dominant part of total Soviet herds. In 1980 (end of year) the relative shares of the private sector in total herds were, respectively, cows 30 per cent, pigs 19 per cent, sheep 18 per cent.[55]

From this discussion, it should not be inferred that the private sector is in any way self-sufficient. On the contrary, there are very important interdependencies in production between the private and the socialised sectors. The household, on the one hand, is dependent on the kolkhoz to feed its livestock, and the kolkhoz, on the other, is dependent on the plot to meet livestock plans. Let us look at these two interdependencies.

While the major part of the plot is devoted to growing feed — above all potatoes — this is hardly sufficient. The household depends crucially on the kolkhoz for hay, pasture or other forms of feed. If feed were available for sale, households could specialise in high-quality products from the plot and purchase the sought-after fodder. This is not the case, however, and so trade with the kolkhoz becomes necessary. The terms of this trade have at times been used as a lever against the peasants,[56] and if we recall the importance to the households of animal husbandry, we can imagine what a threat of restricted feed supply will mean. Many kolkhozniks will prefer to work more than their required hours, not to earn more money, but to get feed as in-kind payment. Dependence works the other way as well, however. When compulsory procurements from the private plots were abolished in 1958, sales of livestock from households to kolkhozy rose markedly. Instead of letting the households freely dispose of their produce on the kolkhoz market, farms were encouraged to accept it for resale to state and co-operative agencies.

These intra-kolkhoz sales have since taken on substantial dimensions, but statistical evidence is scant — a fact about which Western as well as Soviet scholars complain — and their importance is difficult to assess.[57] The reason for the household to engage in such sales is obvious, given the restrictions on maximum stock. The reason for their selling to the kolkhoz, instead of on the free market, on the other hand, can be due either to coercion or preferential treatment regarding prices and fodder. The factors that account for the participation of the kolkhoz are equally evident. It offers a legitimate way to replenish or expand herds with young animals bought from the plots. For this purpose there is the above-mentioned system of contracts, kontraktatsiya, whereby the household agrees to breed and fatten young animals in return for the allocation of feed, and for the payment of a specified price at a specified date. Little is known about the extent to which such contracts are used.[58] Purchases that are made solely to meet procurement quotas fall within another category. These are the cases where extra high prices are paid, or where compulsion is used. Khrushchev was especially incensed at these practices when he found out that there were even 'people who purchase butter in the town and then deliver it as part of fulfilling their obligations'.[59]

The final aspect of the private sector to be examined is the very basis for its existence — the 'free' or kolkhoz markets.[60] Officially legalised in 1932, these markets are special parcels of land made available for this specific purpose in towns, at settlements, railway stations and landings, as well as in rural localities. They are equipped with certain facilities, and the peasants are charged a fee for trading there. In principle prices are formed according to the laws of supply and demand, and although there has periodically been interference in various forms, they are at present free markets in the true sense of the word.

Two important features of this 'free' trade should be noted. First, the right to trade is granted to all Soviet citizens who legally produce farm products on their private plots, i.e. trade is not restricted to kolkhozniks, which is a common misconception. Secondly, the operations of middlemen are strictly forbidden.[61] Every private producer must sell his products in person, no matter how small the quantity. This is a principle that was firmly established with the abolition of NEP and the so-called NEP-men, and has been firmly adhered to ever since, although with varying degrees of success.

In 1980 there were 5,700 of these officially registered markets, with a total of 1.5 million trading spots. Total turnover was 7.4 billion roubles which can be compared with 5.2 billion in 1975.[62] The share of these markets in total turnover of foodstuffs is insignificant however, accounting for less than 5 per cent throughout the Brezhnev period.[63]

The importance of the markets lies in very specific areas, such as fruit, vegetables and potatoes, since these are highly perishable and hence difficult for the official network to handle.[64] Quality differences between goods that are available on the market and those that are found in state stores are substantial, and sometimes they are so large that the produce might just as well be classified as two different goods.[65]

The attitude of the government to these markets and to the private sector in general has varied considerably over time, from outright hostility and attempts at repression to cautious encouragement. Currently it seems to be the latter, and at the May 1982 plenum Brezhnev said (in reference to the plots): 'As we all know their share in the production of meat, milk, poultry, and above all in potatoes, vegetables and fruit, is substantial. Further increases in the support given to these producers . . . can yield quick and important results.'[66] Let us now conclude our presentation of the household by defining its strategy in the game that it has to play against kolkhoz management.

Household Decisions

As we have seen above, the household derives income in two basically different ways, by work for the collective, and by work on the private plot.[67] Assuming that ideological factors are not important,[68] this becomes a simple maximisation problem. The household must allocate its time between leisure and the two types of labour so as to maximise private utility. By applying standard theory, we can derive optimum conditions, saying that the marginal utility of additional income should be equal to the marginal utility of additional leisure, as well as that the marginal remuneration for work should be equal between the two sectors.[69] Before we proceed we will comment briefly on the character of remuneration for the respective forms of work, starting with the plot.

To determine the form of reward for work on the private plot, we shall make three simplifying assumptions. First, given the restrictions in the Charter on the size of the individual plot, we shall take land to be a constant input. Secondly, given the same restrictions on the possession of implements and capital equipment, we shall take capital to be a constant input as well.[70] Thirdly, given the very basic prohibition against the use of hired labour, we shall take the input of labour to be limited to what the household can provide. From these assumptions it follows that private plot production will solely be a function of household labour.

Here we have the crucial difference between private and collective work. On the plot there is a direct link between effort and reward which, as we shall see below, is far from the case in collective work. If we assume further that the output from the private plot can be sold at given prices, i.e. that the households are price takers in the kolkhoz markets,[71] then the remuneration for work on the plot will simply be the value of the marginal product of labour (VMP) on the plot. Remuneration for collective work, on the other hand, is more problematic. Since 1966 kolkhozniks have received a fixed element of pay.[72] This is based on a piece-rate system, where rates are based on those prevailing in nearby sovkhozy. There is thus still one remaining difference between sovkhozy and kolkhozy, in that peasants on the former get a fixed monthly wage, whereas the kolkhozniks only get paid for work that they actually perform. The amount of work to be done in a kolkhoz is fixed via individual work quotas, and failure to fulfil these can lead to various forms of penalties, such as restricted feed supply or reduced plot size. The work quota is supposed to be the equivalent of full-time work, at least during peak periods, although it is not expressed in time units. In order to better understand how it works, let us take an example.

In the case of a tractor driver, the quota will be expressed in a number of hectares to plough. This creates some major problems. Since his pay is determined in advance, he will have a strong incentive to get things done as quickly as possible. This can be explained in two ways. First, his pay is only indirectly dependent on the *quality* of his work — via the end result of the entire collective — and thus he will not be too concerned with careful ploughing.[73] Secondly, the opportunity cost of his time, in terms of work on the plot, may be very high.[74] If we thus assume that the peasants minimise (given penalties, supervision, etc.) the time spent fulfilling their quota, we will get a fixed number of hours, and thus a given hourly wage.

To define household strategy[75] we shall need to assume on the one hand that the marginal return to labour on the private plot is known, and on the other that the fixed hourly wage in collective work is known, as outlined above. Given that the respective earnings possibilities are thus known, the household can make a labour-leisure decision, and here we arrive at the point that is of most relevance for our discussion.

Household strategy on the allocation of labour between the private plot and the collective will be to work the plot until returns have been brought down to the level of the collective wage. The remaining hours (recall that the total number of hours were determined via the income-leisure decision) will then be supplied to collective work. In Chapter 6 we shall return to the situation where a conflict between this household choice and the kolkhoz need for labour necessitates introducing compulsory labour quotas.

Control

The use of the Communist Party as a player in our game probably merits some explanation. Normally, a discussion of external control over agricultural production would require a study of the Ministry of Agriculture and its hierarchy and routines of administration. The special nature of the Soviet case, however, should be apparent from the historical framework of the previous two chapters. Ever since the birth of the Soviet state, party involvement in agriculture has been extensive and direct. The time has now come to use this historical experience in order to reveal party preference in matters of agricultural policy, i.e. we shall attempt to deduce party strategy in our game from its past behaviour. Before we do so, however, we shall look at the formal rules of the game for party activities.

Political Control in Theory . . .

The most fundamental principle of Soviet administrative theory is that of *edinonachalie* (one-man management and control), which should act as a guide to the activities of Soviet managers and administrators. According to Jerry Hough, this principle denotes three (and only three) things.[76] First, hour-to-hour and day-to-day decisions of a fairly routine nature are to be taken by a single person, the one-man manager. These decisions need not be cleared with party or other organisations. Secondly, important decisions can and must be cleared with other – notably party – organisations. Here it is repeatedly emphasised that party organs must work 'through' state organs, and not 'apart' from them.

This important principle was established as early as at the 8th party congress in 1919: 'The party should carry out its decisions through the Soviet organs . . . The party tries to lead the activities of the soviets, not to replace them,'[77] and in a classic article on administrative theory in 1951, the same principle is repeated; 'immediate direction of the economy must be in the hands of the state organs, and the party – as leader and director of the forces of the dictatorship of the proletariat – exercises its leadership through the state organs.'[78] Hence, party organisations cannot issue formal orders, but have to compel the relevant government official or agency to do it. The third and final meaning of edinonachalie is the established bureaucratic principle that employees are obliged to obey orders from formal administrative superiors.

From this it follows that the decision regarding what is important, and consequently a matter to be influenced by the party, will be a crucial one. Theory, however, is very weak on this point.[79] Slepov says that 'The leading role of the party is expressed in that not a single important *politicheski* or organisational issue must be decided without directives from the party.'[80]

The vagueness lies in the word 'politicheski', which is difficult to translate. Vaguely it means 'policy' or 'policy implication', but it can also denote 'political' in a general sense. If a party official believes that a managerial decision is 'politicheski', and is being decided incorrectly, he has a duty to intervene. Deciding when to intervene can be difficult, and an inquiry from lower officials can be given the answer 'It is impossible to give a recipe or some sort of catalogue.' This answer was given by the head of the 'Party Life' department at *Pravda*, who also further cautioned that some questions, which first appeared to be of minor significance, 'in reality should be raised to the level of important political significance'.[81] Against this background, it is easy to understand that party officials frequently consider it better to intervene once too often, rather than not enough.

The official attitude to party control depends very much on levels.[82] At the lowest level, the Primary Party Organisation (PPO), which is found on farms and in enterprises, has what is called *pravo kontrolya* (right of control). This, however, does not only mean a right to check and verify managerial decisions after they are made, but also to a certain extent to influence them before they are made. There is consequently a right to demand full information on an issue prior to a decision. Higher up there is not only the right of control, but also an obligation to take a more active stance, according to the principle of edinonachalie.

In exerting this party influence, terminology differs between *rukovodstvo* and *napravlenie*, a difference which is again hard to render in translation. It is chiefly a difference in flavour. While the former means 'lead, direct', the latter comes closer to direct administration. The official distinction is that the party 'directs' (*rukovodit*) the economy, but does not 'administer' (*upravlaiet*) it directly.[83] Thus it is once again emphasised that party control should be indirect.

... and in Practice

To understand the *informal* rules that govern actual party involvement in agriculture, we shall need to turn our attention to the historical experience of past behaviour, in order to reveal a strategy. Furthermore, we shall need to make a distinction between the top level, which we shall term *policy making*, and the local level, which we shall term *policy implementing*. Let us start with the former.

The bulk of the presentation in Chapters 2 and 3 was devoted to discerning an overall strategy, to which we shall now return. First, and foremost, we have the principle of administrative extraction, from which we can deduce all of the important institutions of control over production. We also showed that the policy reversal that followed the death of Stalin did not alter this principle. The only change was that material incentives were substituted for political repression, *within the same framework* of administrative extraction.

All the reforms attempted by Khrushchev were based on this principle, merely seeking to provide a better format for it, and the Brezhnev era also adhered to this very same principle, albeit in a rather discrete fashion. We shall thus argue that this constitutes party strategy, at the centre, in agricultural matters. It is up to the party to ensure that agricultural produce is extracted from the peasantry in sufficient quantities and without invoking market relations. It then becomes the responsibility of the party organisation at the local level to implement this policy.

At the local level, party influence is exercised through the raikom, the district party committee, and sometimes by the *obkom*, the *oblast* or regional party committee. Our main emphasis will lie with the former, which is the last in the chain of command, and which tends to be most important in running matters.

The raikom usually consists of 30-60 members, with widely varying backgrounds,[84] from professional apparatchiki to outstanding brigadiers, most of whom are purely honorific members. Real decision making lies with the raikom bureau. The first secretary of the raikom is also the chairman of the bureau, which otherwise includes the chairman of the raiispolkom (the executive committee of the district soviet), the local head of the KGB, a few other local apparatchiki, and maybe an outstanding kolkhoz chairman or sovkhoz director. The raikom bureau (henceforth only raikom) meets weekly, leaving day-to-day decisions to the secretaries and assistants. Consequently, the raikom first secretary, far from being a *primus inter pares*, becomes a key person in agricultural affairs. Apart from direct involvement in campaigns of various forms, the function of the raikom is to handle the important nomenklatura and to direct the Primary Party Organisations (PPOs).

The nomenklatura is a roster of important positions that cannot be filled without party consent.[85] Each party organisation keeps such a list with positions of importance relevant to that organisation's place in the hierarchy. Consequently, the Central Committee in Moscow will be responsible for the managers of major enterprises and organisations, whereas the raikom will be responsible for local kolkhoz chairmen, sovkhoz directors, and the like. Appointments to important positions in the raion will thus be closely monitored by the raikom, and here is one important way of exercising party control.

The other way of exerting influence is via the PPOs, and for this purpose the raikom is divided into different *otdely*, or departments. One is the *orgotdel*, the organisational department which is in charge of problems relating to the party apparatus as such, and another is the *agitpropotdel*, the department for agitation and propaganda, which has chief responsibility for implementing party policies and priorities.

Prior to Khrushchev's abolition of the raikom, there was also a separate department for agricultural matters,[86] but when the raikom was reintroduced in 1965, it was without this department. In this connection it should yet again be emphasised that the role of the party is to influence, rather than decide, and a standard Soviet textbook on administrative law explicitly denies that party directives have the force of law.[87]

To establish how the raikom actually operates, we shall turn to historical experience. Once again reality is far removed from theory. We shall observe two distinctly different modes of control, which — using Robert Miller's terms — can be called the *raikom mode* and the *politotdel mode*.[88] The former denotes the routine operations of the raikom, while the latter refers to its mode of operation under severe stress.

The name 'politotdel' derives from the political departments with the MTSs that were introduced by Stalin in 1933. We have discussed these departments above, and will limit ourselves here to recalling their most important feature, namely that of bringing party control to bear directly on agricultural production. The first politotdel lasted only two years, which can probably be largely ascribed to the basic philosophy of the 'production principle'. On the one hand it was held that political pressure could improve economic performance, and on the other that this pressure increased with the 'visibility' of the responsible officials. Consequently, party control was very direct and continuous. It is significant that the bulk of the heads of the politotdely were apparatchiki without experience of agricultural matters. Furthermore, it is also significant that every politotdel included a representative for the OGPU (the secret police), thus emphasising its punitive character.

During 1933, considerable time was spent on political investigations and arrests. Toward the end of that year, however, the purges were halted, and the politotdely more whole-heartedly turned their attention to proper production tasks. As they did so their ignorance of agricultural matters became more apparent, and their existence came under criticism. At the end of 1934 they were abolished.

In spite of this experience, the politotdel returned. It was used by Stalin in 1941-3 and in 1949-52, as well as by Khrushchev — although in a modified form — in his reforms. Each time it produced the same result and led the same short life. The heavy emphasis on political rather than economic matters created such disturbances that it had to be abolished.

One very important conclusion can be drawn from this experience. On the one hand, it can be inferred from the short-lived existence of the politotdel, as well as from its awkward position in the regular party hierarchy, either rivalling or replacing the raikom, that this is not a desirable mode of party control. Moreover, it is also in clear violation of all officially accepted theories on party control. Nevertheless, it has been repeatedly used on occasions when the party has been under severe pressure. We shall thus argue that this reveals a very basic philosophy behind party control over agricultural production: the 'production principle'.

After Brezhnev's succession, these dramatic forms of control ceased, and the party assumed a very low profile. Yet, the basic difference between the two modes of control remains, and for important reasons. As we saw above, the key figure in these matters is the raikom first secretary. He is directly responsible to his superiors for plan fulfilment, and this responsibility is of a very personal kind, according to the principle of edinonachalie. If something goes wrong, it will be on his head alone. Consequently he will take a very active stance during critical periods, to ensure that everything possible will be done. Delegation of tasks is very difficult, since he cannot delegate responsibility. Peak periods in agriculture form excellent examples of this situation, when he has to set everything else aside. Robert Miller gives a vivid account of this change of gear:

> At such times the raikom seems to shift gears, transforming itself into a managerial organ of particularly powerful type, with raion agriculture as its enterprise. Deluged with demands by their party superiors for reports on plan or campaign target fulfillment, raikom secretaries immerse themselves in the most detailed questions of production. Regular patterns of authority are often disrupted, as responsible officials from all walks of life in the raion centers — raikom instructors, agricultural officials, journalists, and even school principals — are dispatched by the secretaries as raikom *upolnomochennye*, plenipotentiaries, to individual farms, where they are expected to apply unceasing pressure for the attainment of the campaign goals.[89]

This is what Miller refers to as the 'politotdel mode' of party control. During normal times, control is of the 'raikom mode'. The party adheres to the law and works indirectly, via other organs. During times of stress, however, the 'politotdel mode' is reverted to, and this is a logical consequence of the system. The first secretary will be very reluctant to listen to complaints from a kolkhoz chairman if they endanger plan fulfilment, since he knows that his own superiors will take little interest in excuses for a failure to fulfil. They in their turn have their superiors, etc. Anyone who eases up on pressure downward will immediately run into conflict with his superiors, who will find it more difficult to fulfil their plan.

This conflict is obviously further sharpened if the issue is about short-run gains versus long-run damage, since nobody knows what next year's plan is going to be like, or for that matter where he himself will be posted. This produces the biased penalty/reward structure, where excesses leading to plan fulfilment will be dealt with leniently, whereas caution leading to a failure to fulfil will be dealt with harshly.

It is in this light that we should see the importance of the raikom first secretary. Party officials at higher levels can simply pass on plans and quotas to the level below them. These are merely paper decisions. The raikom, however, is at the end of the line. It is up to its first secretary to transform the papers into meat, milk and grain. This is why he is so important, and we shall return to the performance of these tasks at length in Chapter 5.

Management

The third, and final, actor in our game is kolkhoz management, to be represented by the kolkhoz chairman. Like the choice of the party, this probably also merits some comment. While the household and the party can both be regarded as true decision makers, the first deciding over individual supply of labour, and the second over agricultural policy, kolkhoz management is caught between these two actors, which inevitably complicates the discussion of management strategy.

Our discussion of the rules of the game for this player is also complicated by the fact that there is a considerable literature on the behaviour of co-operative organisations. We shall not attempt to make an exhaustive presentation of this literature, but rather deal only with those models that contain elements which are of interest for our purposes.

Existing Models

The seminal article in this field was by Benjamin Ward,[90] and the first application of the theory on the Soviet kolkhoz was by Evsey Domar.[91] The main approach of both these articles is to define a co-operative, the 'Illyrian' firm, and a profit-maximising counterpart, the 'capitalist twin', and then compare the behaviour of the two. The focus is on adjustment in the use of labour. Due to the way in which the Ward model is specified, it produces some rather curious responses to changes in variables like prices and rent. The 'Illyrian' firm, for example, will reduce output and employment in face of increased demand. The 'Illyrian' firm will also tend to use too little labour, compared to the 'capitalist twin'.

The problem lies in the assumption that relates to decisions on labour use. In the Ward model, the number of members is decided collectively, with the number of hours per member being fixed. The optimal membership is derived with the aim of maximising dividends per member. Supply of labour to the co-operative is thus implicitly assumed to be perfectly elastic. Domar sets out to modify this, which he refers to as the 'Pure Model', by incorporating a supply schedule for labour. Acknowledging the fact that the co-operative cannot admit and expel members at will, he assumes total membership to be fixed in the short run. Further, acknowledging the fact that peasant time has an alternative use, such as work on the private plot, work in town or on a nearby sovkhoz, or simply indulgence in the age-old custom of 'lying on the stove' and doing nothing, he derives an upward sloping supply schedule for labour to the 'public' sector in the co-operative. In so doing, he removes at least one seemingly perverse result in the Ward model.[92]

Something that both the Ward and the Domar models fail to discuss is the division of the kolkhoz into a private and a public sector. This problem has been dealt with by Walter Oi and Elizabeth Clayton.[93] In their model there is a collective crop and a private crop, produced by M identical members, each supplying a fixed, identical amount of labour, that is split between the two sectors. It is also assumed that total land holdings are fixed and divided between communal lands and private plots, where the size of the latter is institutionally determined. Given this analytical framework the authors proceed to derive conditions for the optimal allocation of labour, and for the optimal membership size.

A common assumption of all three models is that of collective decision on membership with a fixed individual labour supply. Domar takes half a step away from this by allowing for a supply surve for labour, but his derivation of individual labour supply is unclear, and his main interest remains with variations in membership. Ward and Domar focus on how the co-operative adjusts membership and output in response to various exogenous variables. Oi and Clayton are also primarily interested in variations in total membership, placing an additional emphasis on the allocation of labour between private and collective production. Nowhere are individual supply decisions introduced.

Since it is precisely these decisions that are at the centre of our discussion, the applicability of these models for our purposes is seriously limited. There are two features of interest, though. One is the mechanism of diverting communal lands to plots as membership increases. This is central to the Oi and Clayton model, and we shall return to it in Chapter 6 below, when we discuss the use of land in the kolkhoz.[94] The other is the impact on the kolkhoz of changes in membership. We shall not assume membership size to be a decision variable for the kolkhoz,[95] and will thus not be concerned with optimality conditions. However, membership will be affected by individual decisions to migrate, and in this connection it will be of importance to investigate the resulting consequences for the farm. We shall return to this model in Chapter 5 when we discuss the effects of migration. Here we will proceed to consider the problem that is of major interest for our purposes, that of individual decisions on labour supply.[96]

The paper that paves the way for 'breaking loose' from the Ward-Domar framework in this respect is by Amartya Sen.[97] He defines a co-operative with fixed membership and variable labour input by the individuals. The focus of the analysis is on the incentive structure that governs these decisions, and the approach is to compare the outcomes of two different systems of remuneration.

The first system is based on remuneration according to work. This is the Yugoslav model, where workers are not only paid wages, but also engage in some form of profit-sharing scheme. The other system is based on distribution according to need, which is some form of pure commune. To study and compare the two systems, Sen defines a social welfare function with interdependent utility functions. An important variable in the analysis thus becomes the individual's concern for others, or his social consciousness, in deciding on his labour supply. By assuming additive, cardinal utility functions, it can be shown that a system of centralised allocation of labour will lead not only to Pareto optimality but also to maximisation of social welfare.

The main emphasis of the article is on what will happen under a system of voluntary labour allocation. Here it is shown that a system based on distribution according to need will lead to an underallocation of labour, i.e. members will avoid work. On the other hand, it is shown that a system based on distribution according to work will lead to over-allocation of labour to the co-operative. Sen goes on to investigate under which conditions a mix between the two systems will lead to optimality, a path which will not be pursued here.

The most important part of the paper, for our purposes, is the discussion of voluntary labour allocation under a system of distribution according to work performed, which closely resembles the system used in the kolkhoz. To bring out the importance of the remunerative system, we shall compare three different models: a capitalist firm, a collective and a commune. Here we shall draw on an article by Dwight Israelsen.[98] In his model he assumes that the incentive for an individual to supply extra hours of work is simply the income that derives from that extra labour.

The first case is straightforward. In a *capitalist firm* under perfect competition, all workers will be paid the value of their marginal product (VMP), and the incentive to supply an extra hour of work will simply be the wage, or VMP.

The last case is straightforward as well. In a *commune*, the share of the single member is simply total revenue, less non-labour costs, divided equally by all members. Thus, if one member increases his supply of labour, the proceeds from this will be shared equally between all members, and the material incentive to do extra work becomes very weak.[99]

The case of the *collective* is more complicated. If we assume that distribution is according to work performed, then the income of the individual member will be dependent on two factors. On the one hand it will be dependent on *total* labour supply, which will determine the gross result of the collective and thus the value of each share (assuming that each hour of labour performed constitutes one share in the result of the joint efforts). On the other hand it will be dependent on the *share* of the individual in the total number of labour hours performed. Hence it can be shown that the incentive to supply an extra hour of work will be a combination of the marginal and average products of labour.[100] Let us summarise the incentives in these three different forms of organisation.

Capitalist:	VMP
Collective:	aVMP + (1−a)VAP
Commune:	VMP/M

Here VMP and VAP are the marginal and average products of labour. M is the number of members and a is the share of the individual member in total labour supply. From this we can see that the incentive will always be weaker in a commune than in a capitalist firm (given that the commune has more than one member).

The most important part of the model concerns the collective. Here we can observe two things. First, over the normal production range (where VAP is falling), the incentive in the collective will be stronger than in the capitalist firm. The reason for this is that the marginal hour will be paid more (VAP) than it contributes (VMP). This 'extra' pay will be at the expense of other members who find the value of their shares reduced. Secondly, we can also see that increasing the size of the collective will strengthen the incentive for the individual to supply more hours of work. This follows from the fact that increasing membership size will increase the weight on VAP by reducing the value of a, the share of the individual in total labour supply.[101]

From this discussion, Israelsen concludes that:

> The findings of this paper can be applied to two major criticisms of Soviet and other collective farms — that collective organizations are inherently inferior to others in providing individual economic incentives, and that the large size of some collectives exacerbates this problem. We have demonstrated that both these criticisms are misdirected.[102]

In Chapter 6 below, we shall return to this controversial statement, and argue that Israelsen's alleged refutation of these two important strands of criticism rests on a basic misconception of kolkhoz reality. Let us now conclude by attempting to outline a strategy for kolkhoz management.

Management Decisions

As we stated at the outset of this section, management is in a peculiar position of double loyalties. On the one hand, the chairman is elected by the members of the kolkhoz to which he himself belongs. Consequently he has a certain amount of loyalty to them. On the other hand, he is also a party member and thus has a responsibility for carrying out party policy. If there had been a large degree of common interest, this position would not have been difficult, but as we know this is not the case, and thus management has to operate a dual strategy. *Vis-à-vis* the *members*, it will have to operate a modified version of the extraction policy, applying quotas and using compulsion to fulfil them. The difference between the latter and party strategy is that management has to take a somewhat longer perspective. *Vis-à-vis* the *party*, on the other hand, it must operate a minimising policy. Since not only the results of the kolkhoz but also the personal income of the chairman depend on plan fulfilment, it becomes of crucial importance to get low plan targets, and for this purpose the chairman will engage in various forms of cheating and concealment.

Conclusion

This, then, concludes the presentation of the three players in our game. We have seen how the household is faced with the problem of deciding on the allocation of its labour between the plot and the collective. We have seen how the party is faced with the problem of maximising deliveries to the state of agricultural produce, and we have seen how farm management is caught in the middle between the other two actors.

We shall now proceed to investigate how the game is played. In *Chapter 5* we will start by looking at the game between the party and management with regard to prices, procurements and marketing. In *Chapter 6* we will continue with an examination of the game between the household and the party over labour allocation, and then return to the first game, in order to study the strategies employed regarding the use of land and capital in the kolkhoz.

Notes

1. Recall the account in Chapter 2, and see also further Male (1971), Schlesinger (1951), Taniuchi (1968) and Wesson (1963).
2. See Gsovski (1949), pp. 439ff, for an English translation.
3. The original text is in *Pravda*, 30 November 1969, and an English translation can be found in the *Current Digest of the Soviet Press*, no. 50 (1970), pp. 9ff.
4. Nove (1977), p. 138.
5. Schlesinger (1951), pp. 334ff, esp. notes 23-4.
6. For more details on this, see Miller (1970).
7. Joravsky (1970) is an excellent account of the impact of Lysenko on Soviet agriculture. See also Schlesinger (1949) for a briefer presentation.
8. Reference below will be made to the 1969 version.
9. Section 46, Article XI.
10. See section 48.
11. See sections 45 and 49.
12. Section 50.
13. We will return to the nomenklatura below. See in particular note 85.
14. See, for example, Belov (1956), p. 33f.
15. See further Stuart (1972), pp. 19ff.
16. This is not the entire truth. The kolkhoz can also earn revenue by allowing members to work on the outside and collect their earnings, or by engaging in other forms of operations, either on its own or in co-operation with other farms. To keep the presentation short, we shall ignore these forms of revenue.
17. For further details see *Spravochnik* (1972).
18. In the Western sense, a contract would imply some form of negotiations between equal parties. In the Soviet case this is not so. With reference to contracts

between the kolkhoz and the Ministry of Procurements, M.I. Kozyr says: 'Not in any way can there be talk about any form of equal bargaining strength. The kolkhozy are simply given the contracts to sign.' Khachaturov (1982), p. 55.

19. The contract proper includes provisions for some deliveries above the plan, amounting to a minimum of 35 per cent for grains, and a minimum of 8-10 per cent for livestock. See *Spravochnik* (1972), p. 141.

20. Apart from the institutional division into plots and communal lands, there is not much to say about land as a factor of production. We shall not be concerned with crop selection or rotation.

21. See Stuart (1972), pp. 61ff.

22. Ibid., p. 63, shows that this practice accounts for most, though not all, formations of complex brigades.

23. See Pospielovsky (1970) for a broad historical sweep and a wealth of reference to the considerable debate on this issue.

24. One explanation for this might be that in the early kolkhoz, which was usually centred on a single village, the zveno would consist of members of a family or a group of friends working together. See Schlesinger (1951).

25. Pospielovsky (1970), p. 413.

26. The reasons for this sudden change are obscure, but the results less so. At the end of February Andreev publicly admitted his mistakes in *Pravda*, and soon was succeeded by Khrushchev as spokesman on agriculture in the Politburo.

27. 5 October 1963. Pospielovsky (1970), pp. 415ff, attributes the re-emergence of the zveno to disastrous harvests. The last year of growth prior to 1964 was 1958, and 1963 especially was an unmitigated disaster. This view is also supported by evidence that the zveno had been quietly reintroduced already in 1958. An article in *Ekonomicheskaya Gazeta* (1 February, 1964) states that between 1958 and 1960 the number of links within brigades grew from 22,000 to 130,000. One interpretation, of course, is that following the events in 1948-50 the zveno never actually vanished but only went into hibernation, i.e. that it continued to exist in practice but officially was not recognised as such.

28. *Pravda*, 5 August 1964.

29. 7 August 1965.

30. See Pospielovsky (1970), p. 420 and especially note 23.

31. This problem is discussed by A. Yanov and G. Radov in two well known articles in *Literaturnaya Gazeta*, 7 August and 13 November respectively, 1968.

32. Ibid.

33. By 'zveno' we shall henceforth mean the *beznaryadnoe zveno*, or the 'unassigned link', which is given a piece of land to cultivate, and is then paid according to results. There are other versions as well, such as 'mini brigades' for example, but what is important are the principles of independent work, pay according to results, and longer-term tenure (to create incentives for land improvement), not so much names or shapes.

34. Pospielovsky (1970), p. 435.

35. Volin (1970), p. 354.

36. Khachaturov (1982), p. 27.

37. For details on internal accounting practices, as well as credits, taxes, transfers, etc., see *Spravochnik* (1972).

38. Volin (1970), p. 352.

39. Obviously this will only serve to aggravate income differentials in the long run, but as we shall see in the following chapters, such 'solutions' are common Soviet practice.

40. Wädekin (1973), p. xv. This is an English translation of Wädekin (1967), which is the *magnum opus* on the private sector in Soviet agriculture. It is also an expanded version, and reference below will be made to this rather than to the original. The quote above is from Gregory Grossman's foreword.

41. See Hill (1975) for closer definitions of the various forms of private production.

42. Kalinkin (1982), p. 64. 99 per cent of all kolkhoz households have plots, and 78 per cent of all plot land is located on either kolkhozy or sovkhozy.

43. Shmelev (1981), p. 68.

44. Ibid., p. 69.

45. Decreases in private plot output between 1971-5 and 1976-80 were as follows: potatoes 9 per cent, milk and eggs 5 per cent, meat and vegetables 2 per cent. Lazutin (1981), p. 96.

46. Obviously, the use of large-scale machinery, such as tractors and combines, is ruled out due to the small size of the plots, and since this is the only kind of equipment that is held by the kolkhoz, no help can be obtained from this quarter. What has been discussed is rather the use of intermediate-size implements, such as hand-tractors, reapers, etc., to free some of the much-needed labour from the plots at peak times. We shall return to this in Chapter 6. *Radio Liberty Research Bulletin*, no. 480/82, 1 December 1982, has a collection of letters that have appeared in the Soviet press, complaining about the lack of even simple tools and implements on the plots. Amongst other things it is claimed that there is only one scythe for every three households.

47. Kalinkin (1982), p. 67, puts this share at one-third of all labour on the plot.

48. Ibid., p. 63.

49. Sections 42-3.

50. There have been some important recent changes in these restrictions, but since they have not yet had any effect, we shall return to them in our final chapter, when discussing future changes in the agricultural situation.

51. In 1981, livestock and poultry accounted for 40 per cent of private plot output, milk for another 18 per cent and potatoes for 15 per cent. The plots also supplied two-thirds of the meat and 86 per cent of the milk consumed by the rural population. Kalinkin (1982), pp. 65, 67.

52. See Wädekin (1973), p. 56.

53. Ibid., p. 217, quotes examples of differentials ranging up to 1:20, and in a book on Khrushchev's crop policies, Naum Jasny says, amongst other things: 'Except for the USSR, where prices are fixed by ignorant people, there seems nowhere to exist a price of oats lower than the one which would correspond to the low content of digestible nutrients in them.' Jasny (1968), p. 238. He goes on to argue that corn and sugar beet have been over-valued in respect to feed content, whereas oats and leguminous hay have been under-valued, with consequent results for cropping patterns and feed balance.

54. Feeding foodstuffs from state and co-operative stores to livestock has been banned since 1956, but the ban seems to have had little effect. It should be noted that the reason for this practice, of course, is that the price paid for bread in the store is lower than that paid to the farm for an equivalent amount of grain.

55. *Narkhoz* (1981), p. 245.

56. The extreme situation is depicted by Dorosh (1964), p. 56f: 'Why does the kolkhoz prefer to burn the hay, rather than give it to the kolkhozniks? Why do you find potatoes left in the field, and grass unmown? If the peasant should take it he is a thief.'

57. See Wädekin (1973), pp. 232ff, for an attempt at an assessment of such sales.

58. Ibid., pp. 239 and 245ff.

59. Memo to the Central Committee (29 October 1960). Quoted by Wädekin (1973), p. 236f.

60. The *magnum opus* on these markets is Kerblay (1968). See also Wädekin (1973), Ch. 6.

61. The sole exception is the consumer co-operative, the tsentrosoyuz, which accepts produce for sale on commission basis.

62. Shmelev (1981), p. 70.

63. *Narkhoz* (1981), p. 452f. This is based on *actual* prices. If the comparison is made in state prices, the share is reduced from 4-5 per cent to 2-3 per cent.

64. There are many reasons for this, such as shortages of refrigerated storage and transport. We will return to these problems in Chapter 5.

65. Khrushchev himself observes that: 'Choice potatoes are on the market. Although they are cheap in the stores, a man has no desire to pay good money for a rotten thing.' Quoted by Wädekin (1973), p. 155.

66. *Pravda*, 25 May 1982.

67. There is also the opportunity to work outside the kolkhoz, but we will disregard this since it does not in any important way affect our argument.

68. Even if there once existed a true spirit of solidarity and devotion to socialist ideals in the collective farms, it should be obvious from our historical exposé that this spirit is long gone. Some even go so far as to say that the only reason for the kolkhozniks to stay is the right to the private plot.

69. A typical Lagrange maximisation problem.

70. Recall the failure to produce small-scale mechanised implements.

71. In essence these are free markets, and although there are periodic attempts at various forms of interference, this is not the rule.

72. Prior to 1966, there was no guaranteed element of pay. Remuneration was solely according to a fairly complicated piece-rate system (*trudoden*), and whether or not payments would actually be made at all depended on the results of the kolkhoz. Labour was a residual claim. See Wronski (1957).

73. This has given rise to the common Soviet joke about the helper telling the tractor driver: 'Plough deeper, the inspector is coming.' Variations on this theme are legion, and a popular target for *Krokodil* cartoons. *Radio Liberty Research Bulletin*, 456/81, 13 November 1981, has a collection of such anecdotes, reflecting the absence of incentives to supply effort.

74. Recall the structure of labour input on the plot.

75. See further Hedlund and Lundahl (forthcoming) for a more formal approach.

76. Hough (1969), p. 83f.

77. Quoted by Hough (1969), p. 82, note 10, from the protocol of the party congress in 1919.

78. Slepov (1951), p. 48.

79. Hough (1969), p. 83f.

80. Slepov (1951), p. 49.

81. Quoted by Slepov (1958), p. 49.

82. See further Hough (1965), pp. 220ff.

83. Slepov (1951), p. 47.

84. Miller (1970), pp. 198ff.

85. Voslensky (1980) is an invaluable source on this system.

86. In the 'Food Programme' it is suggested that this department should be reintroduced. See *Pravda*, 25 May 1982.

87. Vlasov and Studentkin (1950), p. 4.

88. See Miller (1970), Ch. 6.

89. Miller (1971), p. 78.

90. Ward (1958). See also Vanek (1970).

91. Domar (1966).

92. Ibid., pp. 742ff.

93. Oi and Clayton (1968).

94. Ibid., p. 40.

95. With regard to membership size, Hans Aage notes: 'This question is settled more or less administratively by forces partly external to the kolkhoz, and certainly not as a result of collective economic optimization.' Aage (1980), p. 131.

96. Other contributions to the 'theory of the kolkhoz' that incorporate such decisions are Bradley (1971, 1973), Cameron (1973a, 1973b), Bonin (1977), Putterman (1980), Aage (1980) and Israelsen (1980).

97. Sen (1966). See also Aage (1980).

98. Israelsen (1980).

99. It is precisely this fact that has been the Achilles' Heel of many co-operatives. Without a strong sense of solidarity, shirking will be widespread and the co-operative will break down.

100. If we define the share of the single member as the ratio of his labour input (h_i) and total labour input (H), times total output which is a function F of H, then we can find the incentive to work an extra hour by taking the partial derivative of this share with respect to his labour input as follows:

$$Y = (h_i/H)F(H), \text{ and } (\delta Y_i/\delta h_i) = (h_i/H)F'(H) +$$
$$(\,(H-h_i)/H\,)F(H) = (h_i/H)F'(H)+(1-(h_i/H))F(H)/H$$

where F'(H) is VMP of labour and F(H)/H is VAP of labour.

101. Follows from note 100 above, with a = (h_i/H), and from the assumption of a falling VAP.

102. Israelsen (1980), p. 118.

5 EXTERNAL CONFLICTS

In Chapters 2 and 3 we showed how the kolkhoz was gradually developed to become an integral part of the overall Soviet apparatus, first through its emergence as a part of the procurement system, and then through a strengthening of direct party control over production. We shall now turn to explore the significance of this incorporation into the overall machinery for the kolkhoz as a production unit. In this context we shall find that the word 'collective', in 'collective farm', has become largely void of content.

In this chapter we will focus on three important sources of conflict between the kolkhoz and its environment, i.e. between *management* and the *party*. First, we will see how the system of state procurements at centrally fixed prices hurts many kolkhozy by forcing them to deliver a range of products that they cannot possibly produce at a profit under the given prices. Secondly, the system of direct party control over production will be shown to lead to continuous disruptions and misallocations of resources.

Thirdly, we shall see how the continued existence of the 'free' markets, parallel to the official distribution system, forms an anachronism which illustrates in a basic way an important ambivalence in party attitude. On the one hand, these markets allow the official system to continue existing in spite of gross inefficiencies, simply by stepping in to cover up for the worst failures, such as in the case of perishables. On the other hand, although the markets are considered necessary, the authorities refuse to allow them to become efficient, and instead of promoting them, impose a number of restrictions.

An underlying assumption in the discussion in this, as well as in the following chapters, will be that things that apparently are due to mistakes, bad planning, or that simply 'go wrong', are actually logical consequences of decisions taken by rational actors faced with erroneous incentives.[1] It will thus be important to bear in mind the strategies and rules laid down in the previous chapter regarding the different players in our game. Against this background, let us now start our discussion.

Prices and Procurements

As a consequence of Stalin's policy that deliveries of agricultural produce to the state should constitute the 'First Commandment' of collective farming, these obligations today account for the bulk of kolkhoz sales. The consequences of this system are far-reaching. With quantitative targets accounting for the bulk of production, and with prices for deliveries fixed beforehand, with little regard to the costs of the individual farm, two important consequences will follow. First, farm income will be largely determined externally and, secondly, farm flexibility will be seriously circumscribed.

Whether or not this system is actually detrimental to the kolkhoz depends heavily on the role of information. If the Gosplan had possessed perfect information and virtually unlimited computational facilities, an optimal solution would have been possible.[2] In practice, however, it is a fact that the facilities of Gosplan are seriously limited, and that only very aggregated (and possibly distorted) data can be processed. This has led to the practice of so called 'ratchet' planning,[3] where the new plan is simply the old, plus x per cent.

Against this background, it is obvious that the system of prices and procurements will be detrimental to the bulk of farms. Even if the original position is optimal, inflexible prices will rule out adaptation to changing costs over time, and inflexible delivery quotas will prohibit the farm from shifting out of unprofitable lines of production.

We shall argue below that this system splits the farms into two groups, one with a favourable set of prices and quotas and one with the reverse. The first group will be locked into an upward spiral of increasing profitability, and the second into a downward spiral of deterioration. Our main interest will lie with the latter. Let us start our discussion by looking at the role of Soviet prices.

Soviet Prices

The development of Soviet price theory shows a rather confusing pattern.[4] Immediately following the revolution there were attempts to do away with money and prices altogether. The state budget should be 'money-free'. During the period of NEP, these experiments ceased and the market mechanism gained in importance, if only for a short while. After Stalin's takeover and the adoption of the first Five-Year Plan, command planning again replaced market relations, and the prevailing attitude was that of downgrading all existing 'economic laws'.[5] Prices were set by the central planners, and if they did not correspond with costs, subsidies would be handed out via the budget.

Over time the discrepancies between prices and costs grew, and the entire system of pricing came under debate. The relation of prices to the Marxian theory of value was of especial interest, and an important issue was whether or not the law of value could apply in a socialist society. While Stalin still ruled, the exchange of opinion was strictly controlled, but after his death it was widely recognised that pricing was arbitrary, and in 1956 a serious debate started on the concept of rationality with respect to pricing. Much of this debate would focus around the theory of value.

The opening signal came at the famous 20th party congress (1956) when both Mikoyan and Suslov openly criticised Stalin's economic doctrines, and called upon professional economists to revise them. Out of the ensuing vigorous activities, three different 'schools' emerged.[6]

The 'traditionalist' school wanted to preserve the existing structure, with marginal adjustments to improve its performance. This stance was backed by the bulk of planners, university and research economists, and ideological spokesmen. Their basic tenet was that price is the monetary manifestation of value, which is determined by the socially necessary expenditure of labour. They did acknowledge that in some cases prices could and should deviate from value, but also argued that in principle the existing system worked well. They refused to accept marginal cost or scarcity pricing, since it contravened the theory of value. Selective concessions to the market mechanism could be considered, but only where they were shown to be absolutely necessary. Prices should only be used to complement physical planning — not to guide resource allocation.

The 'surplus product markup' school attacked the 'traditionalists' on grounds that they lacked a general theoretical pricing principle, that pricing was on the basis of arbitrary rules of thumb. By introducing a general rule, the markup school argued that there would be a stricter adherence to the law of value. When it came to specifying the rule, however, there was a divergence of opinion. Some wanted a markup on the wage bill, others on average cost, and yet again others on working capital. We will not go into these details here, but it should be noted that proponents included celebrities like Strumilin, Kondrashev and Malyshev.

The third school was the 'opportunity cost' school, and this was by far the most radical, counting amongst its proponents famous economists like Kantorovich and Novozhilov. This school was heavily based on mathematical techniques, and advocated efficiency prices that would reflect relative scarcities and thus include charges for all productive factors, such as land rent and capital charges.

Ideally, prices would be formed as shadow prices, obtained from the formulation of an optimal plan by input-output and linear programming techniques. They recognised that neither data nor computational facilities were available for this, but argued that improvements could be made by going some ways along this path. Needless to say, they came under heavy attack for deviating from the theory of value, since their approach in essence advocated marginal cost pricing.

The first outcome of the debate was the 1963 revision of heavy industry prices.[7] The structure of prices was radically altered, bringing increases in extractive branches, and reductions in secondary ones, such as machine building and chemicals. The overall price level was not much affected, however, nor were the principles of pricing. The 'traditionalist' school had prevailed.[8]

The next price revision came in conjunction with a reform in industrial management. This reform had four important aims: (a) sales and profitability were to be the main success indicators, (b) a charge on fixed and working capital was introduced, (c) a larger share of profits was to be retained for investment and bonus payments, and (d) managers were to be given more authority over labour input. To supplement the reform, industrial wholesale prices were revised in 1966 for light and in 1967 for heavy industry.[9]

In spite of the emphasis on monetary targets the revision still did nothing to alter the *principles* of pricing. The only new element in the reform was an increase in prices to make it possible for enterprises to meet a 6 per cent charge on fixed and working capital. Prices were thus based on average cost, or *sebestoimost*, plus a markup on capital, which meant that the 'markup school' prevailed in the end.

Such cost-plus prices, however, exhibit the same problems as the old price system. They obviously do not reflect either utility or scarcity. They will not give the producer any indication of the consumer's valuation of the goods — in the case of output — nor will they give any indication of changes in the availability of different inputs. Consequently, prices will in no way help to change the resource allocation in accordance with changing conditions. Nor is this their purpose. The official position is that 'Market prices are in our view, alien to our economy, and contradict the tasks of central planning. It is . . . incorrect to imagine that prices should balance demand and supply. This balance is the task of the central planning organs.'[10]

Hence, marginal cost pricing was still rejected, and the only essentially new factor to come out of the debate on price formation was a 6 per cent charge on the use of capital. Prices still did not reflect relative scarcities and no rent on land followed the introduction of the capital charge. The 1967 price system thus performs little better than its predecessor of 1955, and after 1967 no further change has taken place. In Morris Bornstein's words: 'The planners will continue to be faced with the impossible task of regulating the 8-9 million prices in the Soviet economy.'[11]

Once again we are thus forced to note the continuity in basic economic principles. In spite of the awareness and the long debate over the problems caused by the present price system, in all important respects it is still intact. Although there is still a debate between the 'marketeers' (*rynochniki*) and the 'improvers' (*uluchshentsy*),[12] there is no indication that the basic principles of pricing are in for a change.

While these principles hold for producer prices, the situation for consumer prices is different. These are calculated separately, with an eye to clearing the market. The difference between producer and consumer prices is then made up of a turnover tax (although the Soviets deny that this is a tax, it is difficult to interpret a surcharge that goes straight into the budget as anything else). Since the market situation is different for different goods, however, the tax rate will also vary between goods.

Through this system of differential taxation the consumer is deprived of all possibility of influencing the producer. Any change in market conditions, which in a market economy would be signalled to the producer via a price change, will in the Soviet economy be fully absorbed by a change in the turnover tax, and the producer thus lives in splendid isolation from consumer preferences.

Furthermore, it should be noted that market pressure rarely leads to changes in consumer prices. Soviet policy is that shortages are preferable to higher prices, either on grounds of social fairness (to those who stand in line rather than to those with more money), or to create an illusion of what one could buy with the given income — if only the goods could be found.[13] There might of course also be an ideological block against rationing by price. Exceptions are cases where for other reasons it is desirable to increase (books) or decrease (vodka) consumption.

The most notable example of the policy of stable retail prices is that of foodstuffs. Food prices have acquired a very special status, and for good reasons they are politically highly sensitive. After the most recent increase in the retail price of meat (in 1962), there were persistent rumours of 'food riots' in some Soviet cities,[14] and the events in Poland in 1970 and 1976, and above all in the past few years, amply illustrate the risks involved in rationing by price.

The consequences of this policy are far-reaching. Faced with the necessity of continuous increases in producer prices, coupled with a commitment to stable consumer prices, something has to give and the difference has to come out of the budget. In the past decade, these budget allocations have grown rapidly, with livestock as the most notable example, since meat prices are particularly low in relation to procurement prices. In 1971 this livestock 'subsidy' was 9.3 billion roubles.[15] By 1977 it was up to 19 billion roubles,[16] and in 1980 it had reached 25 billion roubles.[17] These are huge figures, that should be compared to the gross value of total agricultural production and of total livestock production, which in 1980 were 120 billion and 67 billion respectively.[18] If this trend continues, the subsidy to livestock production will soon exceed 50 per cent of the total value of that production.

Moreover, there are other consequences apart from the strain on the budget. As we have seen above, the policy of low consumer prices also leads to absurd results like the feeding of bread to hogs, and above all it leads to notorious shortages. Let us now leave consumer prices and turn to agricultural procurement prices, which are of prime importance for our discussion.

Procurement Prices

Historically, two conflicting objectives have guided the setting of procurement prices. First, the relative prices for agricultural produce should be such that the peasantry was made to bear a more than proportionate share of the burden of industrialisation and, secondly, procurement prices should serve as an incentive to produce.[19] The relative weight of these two objectives changed drastically in the 1950s.

Between 1929 and 1953, the procurement prices for grain remained almost unchanged, and livestock prices, having doubled between 1929 and 1940, remained unaltered between 1940 and 1953. Over the same period retail prices rose manyfold, and in 1953 the retail price level was ten times that of 1940. Obviously, the lot of the peasantry was deteriorating rapidly under the pressure of the policy of 'super-industrialisation'. The picture was very uneven, however. Grain and livestock production were very unprofitable, and the price of potatoes did not even cover the cost of transportation to the delivery points. For technical crops on the other hand, procurement prices kept up with the general level of retail prices.[20] Following Stalin's death, however, there was a complete reversal of policy on this point. It was openly recognised that the policy of rapid industrialisation had been pushed too far. Low procurement prices had reduced profitability in agriculture to the point where investment was sadly neglected, and incentives to work seriously eroded.

From Chapter 3 we can recall that the most important part of the new policy was price increases, and from Table 5.1 we can see that during the Khrushchev period agricultural procurement prices quadrupled. It is an indication of the low initial level that this process of rising producer prices is still going on. Apart from the increases, it can also be seen from the same table that there was an attempt to correct the previous imbalances in relative prices. Grain and potato prices increased by three times the average, while those for cattle increased by more than five times the average for all agricultural products. Nevertheless, we shall argue that Khrushchev's programme failed to come to grips with the true causes of the problem, and thus failed to produce a cure.

Table 5.1: Agricultural Procurement Prices (1952 = 100)

Commodity	1952	1953	1954	1955	1956	1958	1962	1965
All agricultural	100	154	207	209	251	296	332	404
Grain	100	236	739	553	634	695	840	1024
Technical crops	100	115	111	117	147	143	143	174
Sunflowers	100	528	626	987	928	774	859	1046
Fruits	100	119	135	138	192	179	167	165
Potatoes	100	316	369	368	814	789	1043	1374
Cattle	100	385	579	585	665	1175	1523	1980
Milk	100	202	289	303	334	404	434	521
Eggs	100	126	135	152	155	297	339	342
Wool	100	107	146	158	246	352	246	379

Source: Bornstein (1970), p. 120.

Despite the substantial increases in prices, they were still too low to ensure the necessary profitability. It is commonly held that a profitability rate (*rentabelnost*) of 45-60 per cent of cost (sebestoimost) is essential. However, in 1966 the ratio of profit to cost in kolkhozy was only about 30 per cent, albeit with considerable variation between products, regions and individual farms,[21] and the situation was not to improve. Over the period 1964-77 the indices for prices and costs rose by 58 and 59 per cent respectively.[22] Table 5.2 illustrates the rapidly increasing costs of production in kolkhozy during the 1970s for some selected products.

Table 5.2: Costs of Production in Kolkhozy (Sebestoimost) (roubles/ton)

	Grain	Potatoes	Vegetables	Beef	Pork	Milk	Eggs (000)
1970	50	62	94	1,166	1,194	177	73
1971	53	64	101	1,266	1,231	185	72
1972	61	74	109	1,373	1,332	195	73
1973	51	66	93	1,336	1,297	197	70
1974	57	82	98	1,401	1,305	202	71
1975	69	80	111	1,574	1,487	217	74
1976	59	85	99	1,644	1,559	233	77
1977	65	92	108	1,639	1,505	235	76
1978	61	91	106	1,785	1,629	247	81
1979	77	93	119	1,981	1,855	268	85
1980	76	120	120	2,177	2,018	287	87

Sources: *Narkhoz*, respective years.

The most worrying feature, however, is the pattern of development, which as we recall showed initial success which subsequently turned into stagnation. Thus, in 1970-7 costs outgrew prices to an extent that profits were halved.[23] It is obvious that the cause of the problem is not that prices are too low, but that productivity is too low, and following the round of price increases in 1979,[24] Gumerov writes that 'We must realise that we cannot continually increase prices.'[25] One is tempted to repeat this warning after the new round of increases in 1983.[26]

It is not only the *level* of prices that is problematical. Although this is serious in terms of low investment and poor incentives to work, the structure of *relative* prices is probably more important, in terms of guiding resource allocation. Here it has long been the case that technical crops have had a favourable cost-price ratio, grains have been in the middle range, and livestock products commonly sold at a loss.

From Table 5.3 it can be seen that the above-mentioned attempt to rectify the price structure through, for example, a more than twenty-fold increase in livestock prices was not very successful. Animal husbandry at the end of the Khrushchev period was still not a profitable undertaking.

The official attitude to these obvious imbalances has been that they do not matter. The government has at its disposition other measures of compensation. First, losses from the production of unprofitable lines of produce will be compensated by profits from the production of more profitable ones (i.e. grains together with livestock). Secondly, budget subsidies can be paid out to unsuccessful farms and, finally, loans can be written off. As Meiendorf points out, however, these measures merely serve to sweep the problem under the carpet. They do not remove the fact that the farms have no incentive whatsoever to produce certain products (compare for example sunflowers and livestock products).[27]

Table 5.3: Kolkhoz Procurement Prices (1965) in Relation to Cost (1963-5 average)

Commodity	Price-Cost Ratio
Grain	184
Potatoes	153
Vegetables	99
Sugar beets	140
Sunflowers	589
Raw cotton	157
Milk	98
Cattle	109
Sheep	113
Pigs	104
Poultry	118
Eggs	83
Wool	134

Source: Bornstein (1969), p. 5.

Both Khrushchev and Brezhnev can thus be said to have failed to come to grips with the root of the problem, that of distorted prices. The situation in 1977 is only slightly better than in 1965, and given the government attitude that has been reflected above, any important change can hardly be expected.

From Table 5.4 we can discern the same rough division into three groups: technical crops, grains and livestock, in falling order of profitability.

The reaction of the kolkhoz to this price structure will of course be to devote maximum effort, in terms of slack capacity, investment, superior inputs and pure exertion, to favourably priced outputs, trying to ignore or get low quotas for unfavourably priced ones. Consequently, goods produced from technical crops (cotton textiles, cooking oil, etc.) are in adequate supply, bread is usually available, but meat is in chronic short supply. The failure of the system to supply a balanced output is largely a consequence of the distorted price system.

Apart from the *level* and *relation* of prices, regional differentiation also constitutes a problem. The rationale of zonal pricing is that of allowing for differences in natural conditions, i.e. to capture differential rent. In the West this problem is solved via market-determined levels of land rent which capture the difference between uniform prices and differential costs. However, land is not recognise as a productive input in Marxian theory, consequently land rent cannot be charged, and the problem has been approached via output prices.

Table 5.4: Kolkhoz Profits (Rentabelnost) from Various Products (per cent, 1977)

Commodity	Profit Rate
Sunflowers	+ 148
Cotton	+ 37
Tobacco	+ 29
Sugar beet	+ 17
Grain	+ 72
Vegetables	+ 11
Potatoes	− 18
Cattle	+ 11
Hogs	+ 2
Sheep and goats	− 1
Fowl	− 4
Milk	0
Eggs	+ 18

Source: Gumerov (1979), p. 86.

On this count, Soviet policy has not been very successful. Development has gone from a few very large zones, to an increasing number of smaller ones. Thus, for example, after the 1976 revisions, there were 199 zones for wheat prices, compared to 15 in 1964.[28] In the first case, zones were obviously much too large to be of any practical importance. Instead of a homogenous zone, you would find extreme variations in important factors, such as soil, moisture, temperature, growing season, etc., and the idea of zonal differentiation loses much of its appeal.

Over time, the refusal to accept the notion of land rent has been maintained and instead of direct charges, rent has been captured in a roundabout way via an increasing number of price zones. The result of this process has been that today 'prices paid to different farms for identical products now vary by several multiples, with lower prices paid to farms with lower costs, and higher prices to farms with higher costs'.[29] On the face of it one might be led to believe that this process has been beneficial, taking better account of differential natural conditions, than the early crude attempts at zonal pricing. However, we must remember that differentiation takes place not on the basis of differences in conditions facing farms, but on the basis of *actual* costs. Thus, the most inefficient farms — with the highest costs — will be paid the highest prices, irrespective of the conditions facing the particular farm.

The obvious result of this process has been that the relation between prices and opportunity costs has been seriously distorted, and Gray notes that 'Effectiveness studies suffer from the distortion of cost, income and profit data, caused by purchase prices that vary from zone to zone and even among contiguous farms'.[30] The reason for this, of course, is the refusal to accept land rent, and the concomitant absence of a standard whereby to judge differential conditions between farms. We will return to this problem in the final chapter.

The fourth, and final, line of criticism is concerned with the inflexibility of centrally fixed prices. First, the fact that prices do not vary *inversely* with the harvest means that farm revenue will fluctuate considerably, which will have a very destabilising influence. In the case of grain, this is further aggravated by the 50 per cent bonus price for above-quota deliveries.

The larger the harvest (above the quota), the larger will be the portion that is paid according to the higher price, and what we get is in essence a procurement price that varies *directly* with the size of the harvest but in the wrong direction. This of course further adds to instability and to inter-farm income differentials. Secondly, the fact that prices do not vary seasonally will remove all incentive to store products for off-season sales. This will be particularly true of perishables, where storage costs are high.

A Cumulative Process

Let us now try to summarise the impact on the individual kolkhoz of the system of prices and procurements. As we have seen above, prices are fixed centrally, and if we ignore for the moment zonal differentiation, they will be the same for all farms. So far there is no difference from the Western system, where individual farmers react to externally given prices. The Soviet case, however, exhibits two special problems. First, the given prices do not reflect marginal costs and, secondly, the individual farms have very little possibility of adjusting production to the given prices. Let us deal with these problems in turn.

Given that natural conditions vary geographically, and that different farms will have different levels of skill, technology and entrepreneurial ability, it follows that costs will vary considerably between farms. In the Western case this is not a problem, since individual farms will simply specialise in those products that offer the most favourable price-cost combination. In the Soviet case this is not possible, since the output mix of the single farm will to a large extent be centrally fixed. The individual kolkhoz will be given a set of prices and a set of delivery quotas, and there is nothing to say that these will bear any relation to actual costs and production possibilities.[31]

At this point one should be wary not to draw the conclusion that things could be put right simply by abolishing compulsory procurements. Given the way the price system works, some crops would simply not be produced at all. Compulsory quotas thus form a necessary complement to the system of centrally fixed procurement prices.

Given these premises, we now have all the ingredients necessary to analyse the impact of the procurement system on the kolkhoz. First, all farms will have different costs. Secondly, all farms will face the same prices and, thirdly, all farms will be compelled to deliver a wide range of output.

What we want to show is how this system creates vicious spirals for some farms and good ones for others, and to do so, let us assume that we have two different kolkhozy, with different costs, but facing the same prices. In the absence of a procurement system, they would choose an output mix according to the given prices and costs. This mix would be different between the two farms. Assume further that both kolkhozy at this stage show an equal and positive profit.

If we now introduce a system of forced procurements, and assume that both farms are given identical procurement plans, they will be affected very differently. One will receive a plan that is relatively close to the originally chosen output mix (assuming that prices remain the same). This farm will continue to be profitable.

The other farm will get a plan that is very different from the originally chosen output, and will thus be hurt by the quota. If we look at the biased structure of prices, and recall that plans allow for little specialisation, it follows that most farms will be in this category, where prices paid for their compulsory deliveries are unfavourable relative to costs. Furthermore, if we relax the assumption of identical plans, it follows that the differentiation between farms will be even stronger, as some have a bias towards technical crops, and others towards livestock products. Finally, if we take into account the growing differentiation of prices between farms, we will recall that this was due not to different conditions, but rather to different degrees of inefficiency. Price differentiation should thus be seen more as a way of covering up for inefficiency than as a way of correcting for the lack of correspondence between production plans and actual production possibilities. Differentiation might improve profitability for the farm, but in so doing it will only further encourage inefficiency.

This situation will create a cumulative process. Successful kolkhozy will realise high profits that can be used either to invest in land improvement and mechanisation, thus increasing productive capacity, or to increase labour bonuses, thus improving incentives to work. We have an upward spiral of improving profitability. For the other group of farms the process is reversed. Falling profitability causes disinvestment and erosion of incentives to work and we have a downward spiral of deterioration.[32]

Several factors influence these spirals. The practice of ratchet planning acts to preserve them, by prolonging the structure of plans, and the bonus price system acts to reinforce them, by increasing the rewards for successful farms. Most important, however, is the effect of these spirals on labour mobility, and in Chapter 6 we shall lift the restriction of a constant membership to investigate this problem. Here we shall turn to the practice of party control over plan implementation, and see how this creates an asymmetric system by checking the upward spiral of the potentially successful kolkhozy.

Plan Implementation

Starting from the premise, outlined above, that for many kolkhozy the given combination of prices and quotas will be unfavourable, it follows that these farms would prefer another output mix, and that it will be necessary to force them to adhere to given plans, in order to avoid imbalances in the central plan. (Recall the structure of prices which would in all probability have led to the virtual disappearance of certain products if the farms had been free to choose.)

What we have here is the most open manifestation of the basic conflict between the interests of the party in plan fulfilment, and the interests of the kolkhoz in revenue maximisation. Instead of resolving it via a formal penalty/reward system, built on *ex post* verification of achievement, we have seen in Chapters 2 and 3 how a system of detailed party control over routine matters has developed.

It is this system that we shall now proceed to analyse in terms of a game between the raikom and the kolkhoz, where the raikom first secretary represents the party, and the kolkhoz chairman represents the kolkhoz. Let us start by introducing the players.

According to the above-mentioned principle of edinonachalie (one-man management), responsibility for matters at the raion level rests firmly with one man — the raikom first secretary. It is he who is solely responsible for plan fulfilment within the raion, and as we shall see this strongly influences his behaviour. Furthermore, in terms of background, he will invariably be an apparatchik, a man of the party apparatus, with little or no knowledge of agricultural matters. In many cases he will also be one who views the post as raikom first secretary as a mere stepping stone to more important party nominations.

Most important, however, is the way in which his superiors can gauge his performance. Due to the very special nature of biological production, this monitoring problem has been greater in agriculture than in industry, and it has been necessary to develop a yardstick against which to gauge performance. This yardstick has been the various campaigns and priorities that are passed down through the party hierarchy. Khrushchev's rule in particular provided ample illustration of this mode of control. Certain crops became 'political', and were promoted at all costs. The situation for the first secretary depends more on meeting plan targets than on considerations for kolkhoz profitability. This is where you find fields of corn that have never had time to mature, and where the corn thus becomes useless, sometimes even for fodder.

Under Brezhnev, things were less spectacular, but the basic principle was unchanged. It is the *plan* that guides the first secretary. These factors taken together — little knowledge of agricultural affairs, a desire to move ahead, and a strong focus on short-run plan fulfilment — bring out the essentials in the character of the first secretary.

The other player, by the same principle of edinonachalie, is the kolkhoz chairman. Formally he is an elected official, who is himself a member of the kolkhoz. For his administrative duties he is rewarded according to a fairly complicated system, based on farm performance.[33] In practice, however, he is invariably a party member, who is chosen by the party for his post, and submitted to the kolkhoz general meeting for formal approval.[34] From this follows the difficult position of double loyalties — to the members and to the party — that was mentioned above.

Of equal importance to party membership is the changing educational background of the kolkhoz chairman. In 1953 only 18 per cent of all chairmen had higher education[35] and a main ingredient of Khrushchev's programme was to remedy this shortcoming.[36] Although progress was rapid at the level of the chairman, it remained slow at lower levels. Robert Stuart argues that one cause of the frequent conflicts between agronomists and management is not only that agronomic advice might go against the plan, but it might not even be properly understood.[37]

The picture that emerges is quite in line with the picture we have drawn of Soviet agricultural policy. Demands for persons with specialised skills in economics, accountancy and book-keeping will be small, since the bulk of effort will be devoted to routine completion of plan documents. Data that is compiled will also be of a fairly routine character, such as percentage fulfilment of plan targets. The underlying attitude is reflected in a statement by an agricultural economist, who said: 'Any little girl with no economic training at all could handle the job.'[38] If the basic policy is built on extraction, then complicated cost analysis will not be needed, and indeed under Stalin it was completely suppressed.

Naturally, since then policy has become more cost conscious, and training of various specialists has increased greatly. However, it is a slow process to transform the whole system from mere percentage reporting to cost analysis. In this respect, the hand of history still weighs heavily on the kolkhozy. Consequently we cannot expect agronomic evidence or cost calculations of any degree of sophistication to play any part in negotiations between the first secretary and the kolkhoz chairman.

A Complicated Game

Establishing exactly how this game is played, or how the 'negotiations' between the first secretary and the chairman are carried out, is of course impossible. No such accounts are found in Soviet sources, and we thus have a serious problem of documentation. To get around this problem, we shall have to use various forms of indirect methods.[39] One extremely rewarding approach is to rely upon Soviet fiction. During the thaw that followed Stalin's death, several authors used the agricultural scene as a background for their writings, and from this much valuable information can be gained.[40]

An excellent characterisation of the reactions of a first secretary under stress is found in a short story by Valentin Ovechkin.[41] Upon returning to his raikom after an interrupted holiday, first secretary Borzov finds to his dismay that, due to heavy rains, the raion has fallen seriously behind the plan for grain deliveries. He is further dismayed when his second in command informs him that the three best kolkhozy in the region have already fulfilled their quotas, so that nothing more can be obtained from them.

Borzov's reaction is typical. With resignation he looks at his second, Martinov, and says: 'So you first say to the chairman: "Have you fulfilled?" God, Petr Illarionych, how much do I have to teach you? Where is the list over the kolkhozy?'

He then proceeds to transfer the three farms in question to the highest procurement group, thereby extracting more grain from them, and thus he saves the raion procurement plan. Extremely satisfied with himself, he exclaims: 'There my boy! Don't you know how to take their grain?' Martinov objects, saying that the good kolkhozy are being taxed extra on account of the backward ones, and asks on what grounds the quotas have been increased. Borzov simply replies: 'On the grounds that the country needs bread' ('strane nuzhen khleb').[42]

This episode captures the essence of the situation of a raikom faced with the risk of not being able to fulfil its plan. In the ensuing discussion, Martinov criticises their way of sending out directives, requiring impossible feats, and Borzov's reply is again typical: 'And don't we ourselves get the very same telegrams from the obkom (the regional party committee)? Don't they sometimes call us, asking why we are not sowing, when we are knee-deep in snow?'[43]

The raikom does not make decisions. It is a cog in the machinery. Decisions are taken higher up and passed on down through the hierarchy, and the reason why we focus on the raikom first secretary is that he is at the end of the line. It is he who will have to confront the farms with impossible tasks, and somehow see to it that they are carried out.

According to the principle of edinonachalie, there is little excuse for him if he does not deliver. If any of his superiors should allow him to reduce his plan targets, they in their turn will have to answer to their superiors for not fulfilling their plan. Given these premises, Borzov's reaction was a logical one. After all, the country did need bread and there was no other way for him to get it.

It would not be correct, however, to assume that the first secretary always reacts in a simply mechanical fashion. His personality will be of some importance. Ovechkin's Martinov is an example of an official who is 'good' from the kolkhoz point of view. He will listen to reason, and he will not force one farm to make up for the deficiencies of another. On the other hand he will not be 'good' for the system, since he will leave grain that could have been taken. Even if such an attitude might be healthier in the long run, we must emphasise the extremely short-run nature of the game. If you do not fulfil the present plan, it will not help to promise that the next one will be overfulfilled. There are no incentives or rewards for taking decisions that are beneficial in the long run, if they are costly in the short run.

An example of an official who carries this philosophy to the extreme is found in a short story by Efim Dorosh.[44] His first secretary, Fetisov, has a habit of bragging that when he had finished procuring, 'mice would break their necks in the barn, looking for a single grain'. This attitude is also borne out by a comment from one of the kolkhozniks: 'Leaving the children without milk, his hand wouldn't even tremble — he wouldn't leave a drop.'[45]

Given the short-run character of the game, this type of secretary will be the ideal choice from Moscow's point of view. He can be counted upon to always be giverned by the plan, disregarding if at all possible virtually every obstacle to plan fulfilment. In Russian this mode of behaviour is described as 'blestnut pered nachalstvom', 'to shine in front of your superiors', and it illustrates not only the typical behaviour of Soviet officials in general — 'licking upwards and kicking downwards' — but also the only sure way of getting promotion.

As we have stated above, there is little else but plan fulfilment that can be used to gauge performance of party officials. Furthermore, it will not be the entire plan, but rather those parts that are currently receiving priority that will be of interest. Consequently certain crops become 'political', an acid test of the political reliability of local officials. The prime example of this of course is Khrushchev's campaigns, but there are also numerous other minor examples, such as an incident in a story by Fedor Abramov,[46] where the kolkhoz chairman is accused of 'political underestimation' of silage.

Against this background, it is easy to understand that there are numerous examples of complaints about party secretaries who act purely as procurement agents. One such example is an incident in a story by Leonid Ivanov where the kolkhozniks complain that 'they even took away our concentrates as above-plan deliveries'.[47] On occasions this behaviour can become quite absurd, such as the case where the secretary ordered delivery of all grain, then having to take some of it back again, using scarce trucks and manpower during peak harvest time.[48] Although this behaviour is absurd in the macro sense, it must be emphasised that it is a logical consequence of the structure of incentives. The official who chooses not to behave in this way will suffer personally.

The philosophy of close party control over agriculture, which we have tried to bring out above, clearly necessitates an intensity of supervision, for which the raikom staff proper is hopelessly inadequate in numbers. Thus, during peak periods, such as sowing and harvesting, when the raikom moves into what Robert Miller calls the 'politotdel' mode of control, staff increases will be necessary. These are brought about by appointing people from the outside as upolnomochennye or plenipotentiaries.

These people are sent off to the farms with the full authority of the raikom, and with very clear directives — fulfil the plan. The sheer size of the recruitment task makes it obvious that they will not all be agronomists, but pretty much whoever is available and has some standing in the community, such as schoolteachers, for example. Nor will any qualifications be necessary. It is all a question of making sure that nothing is hidden from the procurement agents, and that if possible there will also be above-plan deliveries.

Again, this phenomenon is not the result of tyranny on behalf of the raikom secretary, nor is it something that is resorted to in emergency. It simply has to be carried out in this way. If you order farms to deliver produce at prices that hardly cover costs, or perhaps are outright loss-makers, they will naturally try to avoid it, and if you do not have a man on the spot, there will be ample room for concealment and faulty reporting.

The plenipotentiary is the man who, in Alec Nove's words, 'crude and brutal though he may be, if sent to a district with some kind of a concrete task to perform, will run himself into the ground, raise up the living and the dead, but he will carry out his orders'.[49] Just as in the case of campaigns, it is of paramount importance that directives are clear-cut and leave no room for choice, simply because the plenipotentiary has no qualifications to make other decisions than 'more'.

Yu. Chernichenko gives an excellent account of the attitude of a plenipotentiary. On this occasion he comes straight from the capital, and descends on officials and kolkhozy alike.[50] The scene is a meeting that is attended by *kraikom* and raikom officials and by kolkhoz chairmen. The plenipotentiary immediately interrupts the raikom secretary to ask why the delivery schedule is not being kept, and when the secretary makes a reference to the weather, his reaction is typical: 'Did any communists remain in the raion centre? If so, why? What right did they have to stay behind when the fate of the grain harvest was being decided?' When the secretary replies that these were officials belonging to the post, the railway and other administrations, who did not really have any business in the field, the man from Moscow explodes, shouting: 'How can such a capitulator still be on the raikom? Get rid of him! What do you fear? In Tula we removed countless people until we found the right man! His likes should be chased off! Who gave you the right to be so liberal?'

The plenipotentiary's contribution towards solving the grain problem consisted of shouts like: 'When will there be a plenipotentiary with every combine? Take communists from wherever they might be, send them to the machines! Make them stay there all the time! Let them be

personally responsible for the threshing! A thousand combines? Then —
a thousand plenipotentiaries! If two thousand are needed, we will send
them!' The attitude of the chairmen to this help from the party is
reflected in the words of one of them: 'The plenipotentiary only
wanted one thing; that this very day, the day of his arrival, grain should
be arriving at elevators and storage dumps. No matter what quality, dry
or damp, intended for sale or delivery (later we found out that he had
left Novosibirsk oblast without seed that autumn)'.[51]

Two important conclusions can be drawn from this account. First,
it is an excellent illustration of what we have called the basic philosophy of Soviet agricultural policy. There is a very strong belief that
political pressure can be successfully substituted for improved agricultural techniques and inputs, and against this background the most
important rationale for the introduction of the kolkhozy can only
have been to facilitate procurements. Secondly, it also forcefully
illustrates the position of local officials. It is not up to them to make
decisions or judgements. If they do not fulfil the plan, excuses will not
help.

If we now turn our attention to the kolkhoz chairman, we will find
much the same problems plus the additional one of double loyalties.
We will thus expect to find chairmen that are 'good' from the point of
view of the members and those that are 'good' from the point of view
of the party.

An example of the former is Demian Openkin, chairman of one of
the good kolkhozy in the above-mentioned story by Valentin Ovechkin.
In a conversation with the second secretary of the raikom, Martinov,
he explains why his farm is doing so well: 'It is because the kolkhoz is
well off, because there is pay for work done, both in kind and in money.
With us, the most severe punishment is to be cut off from work for
three days.'[52] This type of chairman will take a genuine interest in the
lot of his kolkhozniks. He will visit the raikom frequently, and maintain a running battle to try to improve the situation from the point of
view of his peasants. Although it will often end in the same way as
when Borzov returned, he will sometimes be successful.

Another important fact that is brought out by Ovechkin's story is
the link between effort and reward. If the peasants clearly perceive the
gains, their attitude to work will be completely transformed. A classic
example of this is found in a short story by Fedor Abramov. One
evening, faced with a situation where haymaking is so slow that the hay
threatened to rot in the fields, the kolkhoz chairman (admittedly with
the help of some vodka) promises the kolkhozniks a 30 per cent share

in what can be saved. The following day he finds the job done, not only with lightning speed, but under singing and cheers. At the conclusion of the story we find the chairman on his way to the raikom representative to account for his actions.[53]

Here, the chairman has flagrantly violated the rules, and he will be severely reprimanded. The account amply illustrates the split situation of a kolkhoz chairman. He can take a stand for his kolkhozniks and, gambling with his own situation, he might be successful. However, he might choose to take the opposite stand as well, and aim at 'shining' in front of his superiors. An excellent example of this attitude is found in another story by Efim Dorosh. Here the newly appointed chairman 'feels an irresistible urge to free the peasants from their petty property instincts', and thus orders them to transfer voluntarily all their cows to the kolkhoz, promising all but free milk. Just to make sure that nobody fails to volunteer, however, he withdraws both hay and pasture.[54]

Other examples of this promotion-oriented behaviour are found in an article by A. Sharov from the same period.[55] In one instance a chairman acquires large quantities of mandarin duck, which are subsequently killed by pike in their pond. His motivation is significant: 'Who will be surprised by potatoes or garlic? But a mandarin duck, that's different! They will write in the papers about the ducks.'

In yet another example, a sovkhoz director decides to plough up a hillside, causing many a tree to fall, all in order to exceed 100 per cent of the ploughing plan. His motivation of course: '100 per cent, that is just average. With average indicators one will work on indefinitely. No one will notice.' As long as the current party preference was for expansion of the sown area, this would be the right thing to do. The director's position would not be greatly affected by the resultant destruction of trees, nor by low yields on the hillside.

Dorosh is very indignant at the position of the peasant in this drama.[56] 'If we were to reach an agreement with the peasants to give them part of the hay, they would perhaps cut it all. Then both the kolkhoz and the kolkhozniks would have hay, and maybe you would even find the peasants voluntarily handing their surplus over to the kolkhoz.' This is precisely what Abramov's hero did, and of course it is an anti-Soviet act. Better let the hay rot in the field. Dorosh goes on to wonder: 'Why does the kolkhoz prefer to burn the hay, rather than give it to the kolkhozniks? Why do you find potatoes left in the field, and grass unmown? If the peasant takes it, he is a thief. Is he master of his own kolkhoz, which is indeed implied by the words *kollektivnoe khozyaistvo* [collective economy]?' When he proceeds to answer these questions, Dorosh becomes particularly vitriolic: 'then perhaps it is better to burn the hay, and indeed in this way work is credited to those who set the fire, perhaps it is better for old women to exhaust themselves, dragging trash from God knows where, to use as manure bedding. After all the interests of the state, that is some obscure dogma, are preserved in this way.'

His attitude can be summarised in some further remarks: 'It is odd . . . that when in the raion centre, and also in the oblast, the discussion enters agricultural matters, the talk is about amalgamations, about sending new chairmen, about using corn for fodder, . . . and it does not enter everybody's heads to wonder how much the kolkhoznik earns, would he earn more from amalgamations or new chairmen, and what does he think about things in general?'

Sharov would seem to be in agreement with the essence of this critique, when he condemns the bulk of officials and chairmen as 'half-educated guardians of the infallibility of pamphlets'. He also elaborates on this attitude of extreme belief in panaceas by drawing parallels with mighty feudal lords, who preferred alchemy to chemistry, and astrology to astronomy, because the former avoided the tedious path of trials and experiments. They too wanted quick results.[57]

It would not be correct, though, to say that there will always be hostility between the chairman and the kolkhozniks. Sometimes it will be realised that the chairman is powerless, as in a story by Leonid Ivanov. Following some particularly absurd directives from the raikom, 'there was not a single reproach for the chairman. In the words of the youngest pigminder, Nadia: "He takes good care of us, but . . . sometimes they will just not let him do it right." '[58]

The point does not concern so much the intentions of the chairman as his actual opportunities for action. Even with the best intentions, he will still be highly constrained by party supervision. There is scope for manoeuvre, however, and if sufficiently shrewd and unscrupulous, a chairman can accomplish quite a lot. A brilliant example of such behaviour is found in a short story by V. Tendriakov.[59] The hero of this story, Artemi Bogdanovich, is in a constant battle with the raikom, and receives numerous reprimands, which he accepts, simply noting: 'A reprimand is not a tuberculosis. You can live with it.' His general attitude towards working with the raikom is: 'A wise man does not climb a mountain, he walks around it.'

Under this slogan he meets the threat of the corn programme. First he makes speeches to the 'queen of the fields', and then he announces that all his corn has been killed by frost, and requests permission to resow the fields with oats and barley. Predictably the raikom does not accept this at face value, and when they come to inspect, the first thing that meets their eyes are fields of beautiful growing corn. When confronted with this, Bogdanovich clasps his hands and replies: 'This is all we managed to save. We put all our forces to it, to save what we could. God knows we tried. God knows we tried. We put together a team of elite cornworkers.'

What he did not reveal was that the team consisted of one person, and that the amount of 'saved' corn was more like 2 than the stated 5 hectares. The result was that he got another reprimand, but also permission to sow oats and barley, and come fall there was plenty of feed grain. This would not have been the case if the fields had been sown with corn, which was a highly unsuitable crop for the area.

In the same way all future threats are countered — lying shamelessly when possible and playing along just long enough to avoid major trouble. Naturally, numerous reprimands are accumulated, but the damage to the kolkhoz is kept at a minimum. This necessity for the kolkhoz chairman to engage in lying and deceit to survive is a well known fact. In the words of Dorosh: 'The chairman of a kolkhoz finds himself more frequently than any other manager in the economy, in a position where it is necessary to twist and turn, and if not to break the law outright, at least to evade it.'[60]

Consequently, relations between the kolkhoz and the raikom will be based on anything but economic analysis. Ivanov illustrates this: 'What then were the grounds for doubling our sowings of corn and sugar beet? Was this not solely intended for the report? Without insight or thought about the consequences, without any form of economic analysis.'[61]

Dramatis Personae

What picture then, emerges from the above excerpts, with regard to the *dramatis personae*? The raikom first secretary is the last in the chain of command in the party hierarchy. It is his responsibility, and his alone, to make sure that the raion meets its plan. Penalties and rewards will accrue to him alone. Above him in turn, the first secretary of the obkom finds himself in a similar position. Should he let the raikom off the hook, he will be confronted with the same trouble as if the raikom had let a kolkhoz off the hook. If the quota is reduced for one, it will have to be increased for another, and this might prove difficult. Such juggling of quotas will entail more increases than reductions.

The first secretary will thus be extremely reluctant to follow the theory of party work, operating indirectly through the primary party organisation in the kolkhoz. Since there is so much at stake, he will prefer to take on a strong personal commitment during that part of the year when the agricultural scene is very busy. He will set everything else aside, and despatch plenipotentiaries as his extended arms. His prime concern will be the plan, or more specifically that part of the plan which is currently in focus in Moscow.

Finally, he will have a marked tendency to disregard long-run costs in favour of short-run benefits. He will not show much hesitation in adjusting the quotas for successful farms upwards if this saves his plan. After all, even if this does cause long-run damage to the raion agriculture, it is not very likely that he will be there when the costs materialise.[62] It is important to emphasise that the first secretary is a rational economic agent, who acts according to given incentives. If his behaviour is detrimental to the system, the blame should not be put on him as a person.

The kolkhoz chairman presents a less homogeneous picture. Personalities will vary, from Dorosh's promotion-oriented 'procurement agent' to Tendriakov's 'manipulator' and Abramov's 'hero'. The common denominator, however, is that there is always some scope for manoeuvre. The kolkhoz will always have some slack capacity that can be used at the discretion of the chairman, and it is the size of this slack that will be his prize in the game.

By concealing capacity a low target can be obtained, and the released capacity can then be used either for over-fulfilling that target, or for some other purpose. It is important to note that in this respect all categories of chairmen will stand to gain from playing against the raikom. The hard-liners will gain by getting low quotas, thus increasing their possibility of over-fulfilment and promotion, and the soft-liners will gain by being able to increase the welfare of their members.

Party Control Today

Needless to say, party control today is far removed from what it was during the time of Stalin. Outright violence is no longer part of relations with the peasantry and the extraction of produce with complete disregard for peasant welfare is also a thing of the past. The change in practice is one of degree rather than one of principle, however. The basic attitude of party control over agriculture has not changed. The principle of 'closeness to production' is still there. Every farm operation down to the most minute detail is subject to party scrutiny and approval, exercised by the raikom secretaries. The difference is that it is no longer subject to the full impact of an extremely unwieldy bureaucracy.

Let us illustrate this situation by quoting from a letter written to *Izvestia* in 1981 by a group of three outstanding kolkhoz chairmen.[63] They start by noting the importance of the plan as a link between the state and the working collective in agriculture, emphasising its important function of 'educating people, of teaching them responsibility, of mobilising creativity and of stimulating initiative.' They then go on to wonder:

> Is it always the case that the planning meets these demands? Not at all! The farms — up to this day — still have not been freed of the petty tutelage of higher organs, in spite of the fact that such behaviour has long since been condemned in party and state documents.

Kolkhozy are still handed detailed plans over sown area, and over holdings of cows, pigs, goats, etc., and chairmen are still held responsible for failures to sow the right quantities of potatoes and sugar beet. Sometimes this tutelage is carried to such an extent that the authors refer to it as 'outright stupidities'. Furthermore, they ask: 'Who can know better than local specialists and agriculturalists where, what and when to sow?' and conclude by demanding that 'It is time to take a firm stand against regimentation and petty tutelage in agricultural planning.'

The Soviet press abounds with similar criticism. In a letter to *Pravda* in 1981,[64] for example, an agronomist complains that instead of doing what he has been trained for, his day is filled with petty supervision of tractor drivers and other field workers and writing long reports about operations that he would be better spending his time actually performing. He is especially incensed at the relation to various extension services, and claims that for every agronomist in the field, there are three or four directing him from above, all commanding that *he* write long reports on *their* visits.

The same situation is also brought out by a zoo-technician in a similar letter to *Pravda* in 1980.[65] He complains about the time lost in writing reports that are not required by the central authorities, but by all kinds of local organisations on which the farm depends. Apart from such reports, which can sometimes contain 40 tables and more, substantial amounts of time are also lost in various meetings and conferences. According to the author, during the first nine months of 1979 alone, his farm received 562 such calls, with the chairman taking the lead at 131 summons. It is easy to understand the frequent complaints about the lack of specialists in Soviet agriculture, although it is hardly the *numbers* that are too low.[66]

Perhaps most illuminating, however, is a letter to *Pravda* in 1980.[67] from a sovkhoz director. He summarises his situation as follows:

> I cannot find it normal that a sovkhoz director should be surrounded on all sides by innumerable and often contradictory instructions, orders and targets. One would think that it should be like this: 'Here are the targets for deliveries to the state, and now it is up to you — the director — to see to it that these targets are met.' But what is the real situation? In practice, the raikom determines what and where to sow, how much to spend, etc., etc. What remains for the agronomist and the zoo-technician to do? See to it that people show up for work?

The reasons for this continuous interference in the internal affairs of the kolkhozy are to be found at the very roots of Soviet administrative practice. Central control and local initiative are at loggerheads, and the latter is firmly discouraged. Local initiative might not only upset the central plan, but it might also lead to increased power for local officials, which is definitely not desirable.

From Chapters 2 and 3 it will be recalled that this form of interference has a long history, and it will be shown that the 'Food Programme' envisages no change on this account. At the same time we should again note the difference between *Homo faber* and *Homo agricola*. Practices that can be harmful to industry can sometimes be disastrous to agriculture. Where time is of paramount importance, such as in harvesting, transport of perishables, etc., the system of administrative control can have very serious consequences. A shipment of tomatoes, for example, that is held up at a railway siding for a few days will hardly be fit for human consumption. Soviet authorities are no doubt aware of this problem, but there appears to be no indication that anything will be done to correct it. Let us now try to summarise our argument so far concerning the impact on the kolkhoz of the system of fixed prices and procurements.

Consequences

In the first section of this chapter, we showed how the system of centrally fixed prices and procurement quotas affected different farms in a highly differential fashion, creating virtuous and vicious spirals, depending on the price-cost-quota combination of the individual farm. If this had been the end of it, damage might have been contained by various *ex post* measures such as subsidies and writing off debt.

In the second section, however, we showed further how the procurement system is accompanied by the habit of constant party interference in routine matters, which seriously aggravates the problem. First, the constant disturbances, and the considerable amounts of time spent in meetings and report writing, waste resources across the board and reduce efficiency for all farms alike. Secondly, the habit of local officials of shifting quotas between farms, and adding on to the quotas of successful farms, creates the game situation that was described above.

For his part, the chairman knows that satisfactory performance this year will mean higher quotas next year,[68] and he also knows that good performance this year might mean that he will be assigned additional delivery quotas during this same year, in order to make up for the shortcomings of other farms.[69] Given that quota deliveries form the least profitable activity for the farm, the chairman thus has a double incentive to conceal his productive capacity. Moderate performance is fine, but a certain slack capacity must be kept. 'A wise director fulfills the plan by 105, not 125 percent.'[70]

The raikom first secretary, on the other hand, is fully aware of the same facts, and will thus view all protests from the chairman as an attempt to cover up in order to get easier quotas. From this it follows logically that the chairman in his turn simply cannot be honest. He is forced to engage in deceit since it is expected from him and already discounted.[71]

The outcome will be a game that is built on very little agronomic evidence. Instead it adopts as its point of departure plan figures that are frequently seriously distorted. The actual outcome for the individual kolkhoz will to a large extent depend on the skill of the chairman as a player. Some might significantly improve the position of their kolkhoz,[72] whereas others might not. It all depends on the circumstances.

One thing that is certain is that this type of party control is detrimental to the economic viability of the entire system. It distorts the basis of planning, it makes for a built-in waste and misallocation of resources, and above all it hampers innovation, since:

> The introduction of a new method involves risk and, as in all gambling, capital is needed. Risk involves the possibility of loss, does it not? Yet, even if a director is given the capital, just let him take

a gamble — and not win![73]

The extreme risk aversion of Soviet officials is intimately linked to the system, where local initiative is firmly discouraged. At the same time it also seriously hampers productivity improvements. The Soviets are no doubt well aware of all these facts, and have repeatedly denounced them. Yet, they are well embedded and not very likely to be dislodged. The system that originated as a means for controlling agriculture, appears to have become an end in itself.

Free Markets

Before we conclude this chapter, we shall look briefly at the role of the free markets, which absorb whatever agricultural output is neither sold via the official purchasing network nor consumed on the farm. We shall see that the existence of these markets is a striking illustration of a very basic ambivalence in party attitude to agriculture and to the peasantry.

The very concept 'free market' is slightly vague. It can refer to un-official market-places, such as roadsides, railway stations and ferry landings, or it can refer to the officially recognised permanent markets. This distinction goes back to 1932 when the black market was legalised. Free trade was only to occur at specifically designated places and these developed into what we know today as the 'kolkhoz market'.

The trade that has continued outside these places has remained illegal in theory, but in practice has been largely tolerated. Regarding the importance of this trade, we can only refer to G. Shmelev, the authority on the private sector in Soviet agriculture, who says that: 'What is sold there, and in what quantities, is unknown even to the Central Statistical Authority. We the consumers, however, know that it is a lot, especially in times of harvesting gardens and orchards.'[74]

There are better statistics for the official markets,[75] and in Chapter 4 we showed that while their importance has decreased greatly over time,[76] they are still important, above all in perishables.

Purchases of fruit and vegetables are the responsibility of the con-sumer co-operative, the tsentrosoyuz, which does not do a very good job. This type of trade forms an insignificant part of its overall activi-ties, largely because of the difficulties of handling. Consequently, there is a shortage of purchasing points and of equipment for refrigerated transport and storage, and there are even examples of purchasing agents flatly refusing to accept perishables.[77]

It is simply a matter of incentives. In the case of a refusal to accept, the loss will be borne by the producer, who will have to see his tomatoes spoil in the field.[78] If, on the other hand, the produce is accepted and found rotten or otherwise damaged when it reaches the outlet, the loss will be borne by the consumer, who — given the shortages — will have to buy anyway, and at the given price. In neither case will the tsentrosoyuz suffer. Premiums and bonus payments to its officials will not be affected, and there is thus no tangible incentive for them to strive for more efficient handling.[79] Similar problems affect the handling of other foodstuffs as well, but the consequences are most serious in this case.

Thus far, two important conclusions can be drawn regarding the role of these markets. First, they fill an important function in covering up for the shortcomings in the official distribution system, and this accounts for their specialisation in certain products. Secondly, they illustrate an ambivalent attitude of the party towards trade in general. When food supply threatened to break down completely in 1932, private trade was legalised, but only within certain narrow confines. It was allowed to exist because it was necessary, and the same holds for the 'illegal' trade — it is needed, so it is tolerated. This attitude of 'merely tolerating' still very much applies.

When it comes to preventing a total breakdown of the official system, the markets are successful. Information on differences in supply and demand is spread quickly and kolkhozniks are swift to react. The fact that co-operative retail prices are sometimes 25-30 per cent lower than market prices is an indication of the superior quality of the goods that are found on the latter.[80]

Fulfilment of this cover-up function is a mixed blessing, however. If the official distribution network were to assume full responsibility for supplying the population with foodstuffs of all kinds, pressure for increased efficiency would be great. As things are today, this pressure is partly removed by the efficient working of the private markets, leaving the official system to continue as a highly inefficient, resource-devouring colossus.

Unfortunately this is not all. If the free market were truly free in the Western sense of the word, it might completely take over the role of the official system, leaving the latter as a sad curiosity. However, the free markets are far from free. They are surrounded by various restrictions that limit their operation, and in order to illustrate these restrictions we shall look at the second function of these markets, that of acting as an outlet for the produce of the private plot.

About a quarter of the part of private plot output which is marketed goes to state purchases, a further quarter goes to state and co-operative trade (i.e. outside the procurement plans), and about half is sold via the kolkhoz market.[81] The important point here is that the role of co-operative trade is declining, both in terms of direct purchases and in terms of commission sales.

Between 1970 and 1977, these had fallen by 5 per cent for meat and vegetables, by 8 per cent for potatoes, by 20 per cent for eggs and by 50 per cent for milk.[82] Kolkhoz households are thus forced increasingly to rely upon going to the market themselves, and here they are given very little assistance. The prohibition against middlemen forces each single household to take its own produce to market, and although farms are encouraged to provide help with transportation, the need usually arises at times when farm transport is already seriously overstrained. The kolkhozniks thus have to travel to town in whatever way they can,[83] and the costs are tremendous. It is estimated that 200 million man-days are lost annually in this way.[84] Part of this will be foregone leisure but a lot will be lost labour, since marketing of household produce usually coincides with the harvest, when kolkhoz demand is at its peak.[85]

This refusal to exploit obvious economies of scale, which is the most obvious sign of an ambivalent attitude towards the private markets, is also reflected in other aspects. One way to obtain major savings would be via the so called 'trade bureaus', *buro torgovlya*, that exist at some markets. These will accept produce for sale on a commission basis, or directly purchase produce for resale, and it is obvious that an expansion of their activities would benefit both households, via a saving in time, and consumers, via lower prices.

It is estimated that the annual saving in time from the existing bureaus is around 260,000 man-days. In 1977, however, there were only 717 of these bureaus in some 6,000 markets, and it is symptomatic that they were not to be found in any of the 28 permanent markets of the capital.[86]

The pattern is consistent. Investment in the markets has been neglected. Health officials complain about health standards.[87] Only 4 per cent of the markets are covered, only one-third have cold storage facilities, only one in seventeen has overnight facilities, etc.[88] One is given the impression that these markets are not really desirable features of Soviet life, and a survey made by *Izvestia* in 1981[89] confirms this picture. Numerous examples of arbitrary and illegal interference by local party officials were given.[90]

In spite of these shortcomings, the free markets still perform better than the official network, which says something about the overall efficiency of Soviet distribution. The situation is far from ideal, though, and by way of conclusion we would concur with Shmelev's verdict: 'Instead of reductions in prices there have actually been large increases, and the consumer at the free market has been forced to pay, not indirectly but in a very direct way, for the short-sighted policy of the authorities.'[91]

Conclusion

The most important conclusion to be drawn from this chapter concerns the role of *markets*. The function of markets in the Western sense is to provide *information* on what to produce, and to provide *incentives* to produce in the most efficient way. Both these functions are handled by the price system. Producers are given information on surpluses via falling prices, and on deficits via rising prices. Based on this information they will adjust their output so as to iron out differences in supply and demand. Furthermore, given output prices, producers are under pressure to keep costs down, in order to make a profit.

In the Soviet case both these functions are largely suppressed. The procurement quotas account for the bulk of kolkhoz production, and for this allocation of resources to be optimal, the optimal requirements at the centre are formidable and not likely to be fulfilled. Instead the planners 'spread their eggs' by letting each farm produce a wide variety of output, and by largely duplicating last year's plan. Change, and particularly specialisation, requires information that is only available at the local level, and local initiative, as we have seen above, is not accepted. Exploitation of economies of scale by specialisation is thus not possible given the present structure. That part of kolkhoz productive capacity which is not accounted for by the procurements can be used according to the comparative advantages of the specific farm. Here there ought to be scope for some market adjustment. However, two problems arise.

First, the signals that the farms should react to might be seriously distorted. If capacity is used for further sales to the state, which might be tempting at above-quota bonus prices, there is nothing to ensure that this allocation of resources will be the socially optimal one, since the prices do not reflect relative scarcities. The only field where kolkhoz production might be adjusted to the needs of the consumer is via sales on the free market, but the possibilities of exploiting this are limited by the factors discussed above.

The second problem concerns the implementation of plans. As we have seen above, the raikom holds considerable power over kolkhoz production decisions, and it is doubtful whether the unplanned capacity is actually at the free disposal of the farm. Ambitious party secretaries will make sure that 'their' kolkhozy fulfil their plans. This is especially the case with 'political' crops, or crops that are currently being given priority in Moscow. If this should mean interfering in kolkhoz decision making or forcing the farms to produce output that is not profitable, then so be it. After all, it is the hope of the secretary that he will not be there when the negative effects materialise.

Finally, the problem of lacking incentives to improve efficiency is notorious. If the kolkhoz should succeed in improving efficiency and hence in raising output, the immediate result will be raised procurement quotas.[92] Since state procurements are definitely not profitable to the farm, it becomes a very delicate matter as to how much of your production function should be revealed to the authorities.

Hidden capacity can be used for over-fulfilment and thus lead to bonus payments. However, if you reveal your true capacity, quotas will be adjusted accordingly, and you will only have derived a one-off benefit. Furthermore, if your quotas are adjusted upwards you are stuck at this level, and there is thus a very strong incentive to keep a certain slack as a buffer against misfortunes.

After all, it is not the *level* of production that counts, since there is no profit to be made from state procurements. The real gains lie in over-fulfilment, but this is a risky business since if you do not manage to sustain the higher level of production, you will be left with impossible delivery targets. The best bet will be to play safe, to keep a certain slack and not to gamble with innovations.

What we have is a production system with a built-in inefficiency, and with no obvious mechanisms whatsoever for guiding the resource allocation towards a social optimum. Furthermore, we have a system where the individual farm can do very little to influence its own position. Its total revenue is largely determined via the system of fixed prices and procurement quotas, and if it gets an unfavourable combination, it is very likely that this will lead to a vicious spiral of falling profitability, falling productivity and losses of skilled labour. The problems of such farms, which the Soviets call 'backward', or *otstoyaschii*, are mounting and there appears to be little to be done. We will return to this in the final chapter.

Notes

1. See Nove (1977), p. 9.
2. See Lange (1938) and Lerner (1944).
3. See above all Voslensky (1980), pp. 157ff, for an account of how this system works in practice. He also touches on the problem of 'padding', i.e. of inflating reports by adding products that have never been produced.
4. See Malafeev (1964) for a historical survey.
5. The attitude to economics at this time is reflected in a statement from the famous economist S.G. Strumilin in 1927. He says that 'Our task is not to study economics but to change it. We are bound by no laws. There are no fortresses which the Bolsheviks cannot storm. The question of tempo is subject to decision by human beings.' Quoted by Susiluoto (1982), p. 135.
6. See Bornstein (1970), p. 113.
7. For further details, see Bornstein (1963).
8. The new price list encompassed millions of prices, published in 679 price handbooks. See Schroeder (1969), p. 466.
9. Ibid.
10. *Ekonomicheskaya Gazeta*, no. 6 (1968), p. 10f.
11. Bornstein (1970), p. 137.
12. Krylov (1979), p. 20. These are nicknames given by the respective opposition schools. The first refers to the tendency of finding market solutions, and the second to the traditional opening phrase of government decrees in the 1960s: 'On the improvement of . . .'
13. Nove (1977), p. 188.
14. Ibid., p. 187.
15. Protsenko (1971), p. 65.
16. *Pravda*, 8 February 1977.
17. Lokshin (1981), p. 85.
18. *Narkhoz* (1981), p. 206.
19. Bornstein (1962), p. 81.
20. See further Bornstein (1970), pp. 119ff, Karcz (1957) and Nimitz (1959).
21. Bornstein (1969), p. 3. Kolkhoz profitability (rentabelnost) is defined as the profit (*pribil*) from sales (actual money income less non-labour cost), in relation to the value (sebestoimost) of sales (non-labour cost less various overheads), expressed as a percentage. 'Profits' will be used to cover labour costs as well as to pay taxes and social security transfers. What is left will be spread over various internal funds in the kolkhoz. See further *Spravochnik* (1972).
22. Gumerov (1979), p. 86f. If we separate our livestock production, however, we find that its price index rose by 84 per cent, while its index of costs rose by only 55 per cent, which reflects the increased emphasis on that sector.
23. Buzdalov (1979), p. 65.
24. Prices were increased at an estimated annual cost to the government budget of 3.2 billion roubles. Gumerov (1979), p. 86.
25. Ibid., p. 86. He also states that a 1 per cent reduction in costs equals a saving to the budget of 0.8 billion roubles.
26. This time the estimated annual cost of the price increases is 16 billion roubles. *Pravda*, 25 May 1982.
27. Meiendorf (1982), p. 79. Gray (1981), p. 46, also notes that 'procurement quotas for products that are nonremunerative are often "spread around" among a number of farms, irrespective of their comparative advantage in producing these products'.
28. Gray (1981), p. 44. Regarding the early period, Bornstein (1970), p. 125, quotes an example of a price zone that stretched from the shores of the Arctic

into southern Siberia, comprising an area 10.3 times that of France.

29. Gray (1981), p. 44. It should be noted that the possibility of differentiation extends to taxes as well. Durgin (1964), p. 395. There is no evidence, however, that the latter is actually done.

30. Gray (1981), p. 46.

31. See Oi and Clayton (1968), p. 44ff, for a formal approach to the problem
of procurement quotas.

32. Suslov (1982), p. 24, gives some evidence on the outcome of this process.
The table below shows the distribution of kolkhozy according to gross revenue
per 100 hectares of cropland (000 roubles).

−5	5-10	10-15	15-20	20-30	30-40	40+	
16.4	15.9	12.5	11.2	14.9	8.5	20.6	(%)

The top fifth of the farms thus has more than eight times the revenue per hectare
than the bottom fifth, and according to the author there is a distinct regional
pattern. The profitable farms are found in the Baltic republics, on irrigated land
in middle Asia and the Caucasus, in some parts of the Ukraine and White Russia,
and in areas close to the urban centres of the RSFSR. This is obviously a manifestation of the failure of the price system to extract differential rent. Furthermore,
we shall see below that the regional pattern is reinforced when we take into
account the effects of internal migration.

33. Nove (1963) and Stuart (1972), pp. 78ff.

34. This practice had long been the same (see Belov (1956), p. 35). What
changed was the strength of the party grip. The proportion of farm chairmen
who were also party members rose from 79 per cent in 1952 to 90 per cent in
1956, and 95 per cent in 1960. Stuart (1972), p. 174.

35. Stuart (1972), p. 81f.

36. Between 1953 and 1966 the proportion of kolkhoz chairmen with higher
and specialised secondary education increased from 18 to 70 per cent. Ibid.,
p. 175.

37. Ibid., pp. 181ff, goes further into this problem.

38. Quoted by Durgin (1964), p. 406.

39. See further the Appendix to Chapter 1.

40. Alec Nove has used this approach in two articles, from which we shall
draw much reference. Nove (1964b, 1967).

41. Ovechkin (1952).

42. Ibid., p. 209f.

43. Ibid., p. 212.

44. Dorosh (1964).

45. Ibid., p. 67.

46. Abramov (1963).

47. Ivanov (1963), p. 186.

48. *Pravda*, 26 November 1964.

49. Nove (1967), p. 66.

50. Chernichenko (1965), p. 182.

51. Ibid., p. 206.

52. Ovechkin (1952), p. 206.

53. Abramov (1963), p. 137.

54. Dorosh (1962), p. 13.

55. Sharov (1965), p. 170.

56. Dorosh (1964), p. 56f.

57. Sharov (1965), p. 163.

58. Ivanov (1963), p. 186.

59. Tendriakov (1965), p. 103f.

60. Dorosh (1962), p. 24.

61. Ivanov (1963), p. 186.

62. It is a well known fact that high turnover amongst Soviet officials is a major problem. The situation is brilliantly illustrated in a *Krokodil* cartoon (no. 16, 1982) showing a conveyor belt with stern-looking, briefcase-carrying men in trenchcoats being rapidly shifted past an office desk, papers flying. The official term is *tekuschestvo*.

63. *Izvestia*, 29 September 1981. One was a delegate to the Supreme Soviet and another a 'Hero of Socialist Labour', which indicates some of their weight.

64. *Pravda*, 18 August 1981.

65. Ibid., 16 Janaury 1981.

66. A more humorous illustration of this deluge of paper is a *Krokodil* cartoon (no. 7, 1983) showing a peasant spreading papers, with the word 'Instruction' written on them, over a field. By the side of the field a man in a suit is observing his behaviour. The caption reads: 'What do you want me to do? If instead of fertiliser and implements to spread it with they keep sending me instructions.'

67. *Pravda*, 11 October 1980.

68. Belov (1956), p. 191.

69. Recall the fate of chairman Openkin in Ovechkin's story.

70. Nove (1958), p. 4. Quoted from *Kommunist*, no. 1 (1957), p. 49.

71. Recall the statement by Dorosh on this (cf. note 60 above).

72. Recall the behaviour of the chairman in Tendriakov's story (cf. note 59 above).

73. Nove (1958), p. 8. Quoted from *Zvezda*, no. 5 (1957), p. 155.

74. Shmelev (1979), p. 2.

75. See Karcz (1964a) for a discussion of the quality of these statistics.

76. In 1950 they accounted for 30 per cent of the total turnover in foodstuffs. In 1965 it was down to 10 per cent (Shmelev (1979), p. 2) and in 1980 to 5 per cent. Shmelev (1981), p. 70.

77. Voronin (1980), p. 121.

78. It is against this background that we should view information that in some regions 30-40 per cent of the vegetable harvest ends up as animal fodder every year. See for example *Kommunist*, no. 11 (1982), p. 7.

79. Voronin (1980), p. 121.

80. Ibid., p. 120.

81. Ibid., p. 119.

82. Ibid., p. 120.

83. A common road sign in the Soviet countryside is a peasant holding a stick with a potato on top, indicating to passing truck drivers that if they give him a ride into town, there might be a bag of potatoes in it for the driver.

84. Voronin (1980), p. 119.

85. A brilliant illustration of this problem is found in a *Krokodil* cartoon showing a row of stern-looking peasants selling vegetables at a market, and in front of them a man on his knees, hands clasped against the sky. It is the brigadier trying desperately to get his kolkhozniks to come back in time to save the harvest. *Krokodil*, no. 30 (1977).

86. Shmelev (1979), p. 2.

87. *Literaturnaya Gazeta*, 6 May 1981.

88. Shmelev (1979), p. 2.

89. *Izvestia*, 24 May and 27 May 1981.

90. In one example private motorists were stopped by police patrols out to confiscate potatoes, to be counted against the raion procurement plan. See *Radio Liberty Research Bulletin*, no. 353/82, 8 September 1982, for a collection of such letters of complaint that have been published in the Soviet press.

91. Shmelev (1979), p. 2.
92. There are examples where the reward for increased productivity actually has been a *reduction* in income. See *Pravda*, 20 September 1980.

6 RESOURCE UTILISATION

We shall now turn to perhaps the most fundamental of all problems facing Soviet agriculture today — that of a wasteful utilisation of resources. As we have repeatedly indicated above, it is not the *volume* of resources allocated to agriculture that is inadequate. On the contrary, Soviet agriculture of today increasingly gives the impression of a 'Black Hole', capable of swallowing everything that comes in its vicinity. The problem lies in the *utilisation* of given resources.

In this chapter we shall present evidence as to the magnitude of the problem, as well as attempt to explain its underlying causes. For clarity's sake, we shall use the traditional division of factors of production into labour, land and capital. First, we will examine the conflict between kolkhoz management and the household (over the allocation of labour), and will subsequently deal with two cases of conflict between the party and kolkhoz management (in terms of external restrictions on the utilisation of land and capital).

Unwilling Workers

A notorious and increasingly acute problem for the kolkhozy is that of labour shortages at times of peak demand for labour. The very nature of agricultural production gives rise to an inevitable seasonal variation in labour demand. However, we shall argue that in the Soviet case this basic problem has been aggravated by problems in the present incentive structure.

One reason for the labour shortages is the persistently low level of mechanisation,[1] or rather the low level of accessibility to existing machinery, due to frequent breakdowns and a severe lack of spare parts for repairs. We will show in the final section of this chapter that such problems are also intimately linked to the incentive structure. In this first section, however, we shall start by investigating how incentives to work affect the utilisation of given labour resources in the kolkhoz.

There is no lack of ample documentation on the acute nature of the labour shortage. Millions of people are brought in from outside to help out during the busy periods, and an increasing reliance is being placed on the over- and under-aged segments of the farm labour force. The inevitable conclusion from parallel trends of growing labour intensity and growing labour shortages, with stagnating output, must be that productivity is falling, and in 1981 E. Manevich stated bluntly that the productivity of labour in Soviet agriculture was lower than in any other form of activity in the Soviet economy.[2]

An important part of the explanation of this falling productivity of labour is the changing structure of the kolkhoz labour force, caused by the departure of the most productive people for the cities. In conjunction with an explanation of the causes of this migration, we shall also examine the impact of the auxiliary labour that is brought in from the outside each year. The most important explanatory factor, however, must be the utilisation of existing labour in the kolkhoz, and this will be our starting point.

Decisions of the Individual Household

In Chapter 4 above, we outlined the strategy of the individual household in determining the allocation of its labour time between the private plot and the communal fields. Our assumption was that this decision is taken with a view to attaining equality between the marginal remuneration for labour in the two sectors, i.e. the last hour worked on the plot should yield the same revenue as the last hour worked for the collective. We shall now proceed to see how this strategy comes into conflict with kolkhoz labour requirements, and how this leads to the imposition of compulsory labour quotas.

In Chapter 5 we saw how the system of compulsory procurements of a wide range of products, usually at unfavourable prices, led to a serious constraint on kolkhoz profitability and in some cases also to the creation of a vicious downward spiral. From this position, the kolkhoz has to compete with the private plots for labour, and although capital intensity will be higher on the communal fields, the kolkhozniks will have the benefit of selling their output at free market prices, usually realising a considerable bonus for superior quality, in spite of inferior technology. Kolkhozy which are thus unable to compete for labour will still have to meet their delivery quotas, and will thus be forced to rely on compulsion. This will require the introduction of labour quotas.[3]

While the quota will lead to an increase in hours worked for the collective (assuming that it is binding), the effect on hours worked on the plot is indeterminate, since the household's labour-leisure decision will be affected. One possibility is that there will be a reduction in work on the private plot, and another is that there will be a reduction in leisure. Where the extra hours will come from will depend on the household's marginal valuation of income versus leisure. The outcome that tallies best with historical evidence is the latter. During large parts of kolkhoz history, peasants have been forced to work long hours on their private plots — on top of their labour for the kolkhoz — simply in order to secure subsistence for their family, given the low level and sometimes virtual absence of pay for collective work. We shall see below that today the situation has been reversed. With continuous improvements in kolkhoz pay, peasants enjoy more leisure and work less on the plot.

The point at issue here, however, is that the labour quota will be uniquely damaging to the household, in terms of a reduction in leisure, or a reduction in income, or both. From this it follows that in all kolkhozy where the quota is binding,[4] there will be a built-in aversion towards collective work, an aversion that is reinforced by the historical experience of times when it was necessary to work long hours on the plot simply in order to secure subsistence.

Decisions of Several Households

Our second point with regard to household decisions is of more fundamental importance. In order to establish this point it will have to be taken into consideration that kolkhozy consist of several households, and that labour does not only have a quantitative dimension, but also a qualitative one. Households must not only decide on how many *hours* to supply, but also on how much *effort* to expend. In addition, the system of remuneration for labour makes it necessary to consider actions taken by other member households as well. These additional considerations will be of crucial importance for the understanding of kolkhoz reality.

In Chapter 4, we presented an argument by Dwight Israelsen that kolkhozy might not only exhibit stronger incentives to work than other forms of organisation, but also that these incentives might be strengthened as the kolkhoz grows in size.[5] We are now prepared to look more closely at this controversial statement.

Israelsen's first conclusion rested on the assumption that an extra hour of labour was paid more (VAP) than it contributed (VMP). This assumption is critical in three ways. First, it ignores the fact that kolkhozniks are paid a fixed piece-rate, which in the case of loss-making farms will be paid out of state credits. Only in the longer term will the kolkhozniks be affected by variations in kolkhoz profitability, and then via changes in the provision of public goods within the farm. Secondly, it ignores the existence of the private plot, which is a highly important competitor for the labour of the kolkhoznik, and, thirdly, it ignores the difference between *hours* and *effort* in labour supply. Let us see how the addition of these dimensions will improve our understanding of the kolkhoz.

The most important point is the existence of the private plot. In the case of, say, a lemon-growing household in Georgia, the plot will be a highly profitable undertaking and the discussion of the form of incentives to perform collective work becomes rather complicated. Given the nature of lemon production, where the trees manage themselves most of the time, competition for labour between the plots and the collective will not be a daily matter. The problem arises when the kolkhozniks need to go to town in order to market their lemons. Since this need will coincide in time with peak kolkhoz demand for labour, a very tangible conflict arises. It will be impossible for the kolkhoz to pay the peasants for not going to town, and few chairmen would be prepared to prohibit them from doing so, with the resultant spoiling of the private crop. The conflict is further aggravated by the need of the kolkhozniks to go to town in order to buy things that are not available in local shops. The joint pull of these two motives makes it virtually impossible for the kolkhoz to compete, and it will be forced to see a large part of its labour force vanish at the busiest period of the year. The result will be the 'cries for help' that each year send millions of urban dwellers into the fields to help out with the harvest.

The conflict is yet further complicated if we consider private plots that produce more labour-intensive crops, such as tomatoes, for instance. Here there will be a daily need to spend time on the private plot, and the kolkhoz will thus fight a running battle for the kolkhozniks' time − on top of the loss of labour due to marketing activities. If it is the case that plot production is very profitable, then the kolkhoz will not be able to compete, and will instead have to rely on labour quotas in order to meet procurement plans.

A more interesting situation arises in the case of, say, a cabbage-growing household in Tambov province. Here the plot will not be quite so profitable, and work for the collective might become a real option. Let us assume for the sake of argument that the kolkhoz is able to pay a wage that is competitive. At this point we shall need to turn our attention to the real crux of the matter, the link between *effort* and *reward*.

Soviet agriculture today is plagued not so much by an inability to elicit an adequate number of hours, as by a deficient quality of work. This is brought out by numerous articles in the press, as well as by numerous cartoons in the satirical periodical *Krokodil*. In Chapter 4 we saw that the root of the problem was the formulation of work assignments in purely quantitative terms. A tractor driver will be given a number of hectares to plough, a lorry driver a number of tons of grain to take to the elevator, etc. Once the kolkhoznik has met his assignment, he is free. At no point will he be credited for the *quality* of his work.

Furthermore, supervision of performance is made difficult not only by the sheer size of the farms, but also by the fact that the peasants are shifted around between different fields and different tasks. Thus, if the harvest should be a failure in one particular field, it will be virtually impossible to assign guilt. It could be due to poor ploughing, poor sowing, poor harvesting, etc., and this holds for most farm operations. If a tractor breaks down it will be difficult to tell whether it was due to poor maintenance or poor handling. As the peasants are not directly credited for quality, and as management is faced with a supervision problem,[6] the stage is set for trouble.

The really crucial dimension lies in the way in which the kolkhoznik decides to tackle his work assignment. Here there are two alternatives. He can either decide to *minimise the time* spent working for the collective, as in the case of a tractor driver who ploughs at a shallow depth in order to increase the speed of his tractor, or he can decide to *minimise the effort* expended, such as when the tractor driver rests in the shade of his tractor. In the first case, *time* will be released that could be used to increase the number of hours worked on the plot, while in the second case, he may either conserve energy in order to increase the effort put into work on the plot, or he may simply enjoy leisure while carrying out his assignment. The *common denominator* is that, by shirking, the kolkhoznik will be able to realise important benefits, not only in terms of an easier work pace and more leisure, but, more importantly, in terms of increased income from private plot production. The opportunity cost to the kolkhoznik of expending time and effort in carrying out his work assignment might be substantial. This possibility is underlined by the structure of labour input on the private plot, where able-bodied labour, released from the collective, might be substituted for or complement that of women, children and the elderly.

While the private benefits from shirking are thus both tangible and probably substantial, the costs are less so. If one individual decides to shirk, it is obvious that the kolkhoz will be hurt via a reduction in output, but how will it affect the shirker? In the short run he will not be affected at all (other than by detection and penalties), since he receives a fixed piece-rate. In the longer run he *might* be affected by a general deterioration in kolkhoz living conditions, but only in the case of profitable kolkhozy. In the case of the large number of backward (otstoyaschii) farms,[7] further deterioration will simply lead to more subsidies, more credits, more written-off loans, etc., and the losses caused by the shirker will be shared equally by all Soviet citizens, via the state budget.

In the more successful farms, where shirking will actually hurt the kolkhoz proper, there might arise a Prisoner's Dilemma situation.[8] The individual will know that while the benefits to him from shirking are substantial, the costs will be shared by all members alike and will thus be negligible. In all probability, all members will react in the same way and the kolkhoz is faced with a dead-weight loss, resulting from the absence of a link between effort and reward. It will be a Prisoner's Dilemma, however, only in the case where by co-operating in devoting more time and effort to the communal tasks, the kolkhozniks will be able to increase their income. This may hold in our 'Tambov case'. It will not hold in the 'Georgia case'. Here the form of remuneration for collective labour is irrelevant, since it can never compete with private labour.

In summary, then, we can see that the kolkhoz labour problem derives directly from the structure of the system. It is either a result of a low *level* of remuneration relative to private earning opportunities — the Georgia case — or a result of the *form* of remuneration — the Tambov case. Israelsen's conclusion on the strength of incentives *may* be valid in the latter case, but only with respect to the supply of hours. By increasing kolkhoz pay, members can be induced to work long hours. There is nothing, however, to induce them to supply more effort. His second conclusion, regarding the strengthening of incentives in relation to the increasing size of the kolkhoz, is obviously false. An increased membership will only serve to aggravate the supervision problem and to worsen the potential Prisoner's Dilemma, by reducing the prospects for successful co-operation.

It is precisely these problems that are at the focus of the debate around the *beznaryadnoe zveno*[9] (the unassigned link), and they will be discussed at length in Chapter 7. The next section of this chapter deals with the long-run consequences of the labour problem for the kolkhoz, as the size of the membership is allowed to vary. In order to do so, we shall first briefly study the problems of migration, and of the 'auxiliary' labour that is sent from the cities at times of peak demand for labour.

Migration

Soviet rural-urban migration is becoming an increasingly serious problem, due to the rapid drain of agricultural manpower. If the migration out of rural areas had been accompanied by an offsetting growth in agricultural labour productivity, there would not have been a problem, since production could have been maintained while labour was released for industry. This, however, has been far from the case.[10]

Today the drain is substantial. Over the period 1970-9, annual migration out of rural areas was 3.1 million people, while migration into rural areas amounted to 1.5 million. There was thus a net annual loss of 1.6 million people, or over 15 million over the decade.[11] This rate of net rural out-migration was excessive.

Given the role that agriculture has been assigned in the national economy, it is estimated that net migration out of rural areas cannot be allowed to exceed the population growth, which for the entire USSR is below 1 per cent. In some areas this limit was exceeded several times. Given social-environmental ambitions, it is estimated that the population density cannot be allowed to fall below 7-8 persons per square kilometre. In practice some areas have been left virtually desolate, and special programmes have been initiated to deal with these 'dead villages'. Finally, the demographic pattern has been seriously distorted, leaving some areas with a heavy bias towards women and the elderly. To combat these problems, migration must be reduced by a third, to a net loss of about 1 million during the 11th Five-Year Plan (1981-5).[12]

On closer scrutiny, the migration problem shows a distinct regional pattern. A classification of regions into five categories shows annual net migration varying from -3.6 to +0.7 per cent.[13] Regions experiencing an inflow are characterised by a well developed infrastructure, closeness to major cities, favourable climatic conditions and a relatively low cost of living. Examples are the Moscow region, the Baltic, Moldavia and the southern part of the Ukraine. Regions that suffer a heavy outflow, on the other hand, are characterised by a predominance of women and elderly, falling birth rates and a low level of education. There is thus clear evidence for the existence of cumulative vicious spirals. Areas that suffer a loss of the most productive parts of the population will experience falling productivity and thus further reduction in attractiveness, whereas favoured regions will attract migrants not only from other rural areas, but perhaps even from urban areas.

What then are the causes of migration? Here evidence is scant. In a book on migration from 1975, V.I. Perevedentsev devotes a chapter to urban-rural migration, from which reference can be made to certain findings.[14] The burden of work is obviously an important variable, and a study from 1963 indicated important urban-rural differences.[15] A male worker put in 53 hours per week (employment and housework) on average, while a male kolkhoznik had a working week which extended to 75 hours. Their female equivalents put in 70 hours and 88 hours, in the latter case more than a twelve-hour work-day. Work on the private plot accounts for much of the heavy work-load on the kolkhoz. In 1964 the plot consumed 23 per cent of labour time (excluding housework) in the RSFSR. The corresponding figure for women was 34 per cent. During the busy summer months women had on average only 7.8 hours of leisure time per *week*.[16]

Another important variable is pay, and in spite of substantial relative improvements, kolkhoz pay is still the lowest of all sectors of the economy.[17] In a study of migrants from Western Siberia, it was shown that after the move three-quarters of the migrants had improved their weekly pay by more than 30 roubles, half by more than 50, and one-third by more than 70. It should be added that average weekly pay for the entire USSR was 81 roubles in 1960, and 96 in 1965. Migration to the cities has thus been a profitable undertaking, and although income differentials have shrunk, this is still the case.

A further important determinant is housing standards. The urban housing problem is still enormous, but we know very little about the rural situation. Although Perevedentsev complains about the absence of data, he simply states that conditions in rural areas are even worse.[19]

Although the data cited above are far from recent, the problems remain the same. In a recent study, T.I. Zaslavskaya claims that the most important determinants of migration out of rural areas are: 'unpleasant conditions of work, impossibility of receiving a specialised education, difficulty coupled with necessity of tending the private plot, unfavourable climatic conditions, and unhealthy social-psychological climate'.[20] Rural areas are still characterised by heavy work, poor pay and poor opportunities for education and cultural activities. Hence, it is not surprising that it is chiefly young people who leave.

A comparative study shows that the determinants of migration are fairly stable.[21] Pay together with conditions of work are the dominant causes; 23.2 per cent gave this as a reason in 1967 and 20.7 in 1977. Problems of training and education persist as well (11 per cent at both times). Certain changes can be observed, however. Sharp rises in the number of people who indicate the growing burden of the private plot, and increasing problems with the social-psychological environment (alcoholism, deteriorating moral standards, increasing bureaucratic interference), show that the problem is taking on more of a social nature, although it is significant that pay is still the dominant reason in spite of substantial relative improvements. Young people are becoming increasingly dissatisfied with the old way of rural life. They refuse to take part in the arduous work on the private plot, and demand more social and cultural activities. When they cannot fulfil these demands they move, and the population left behind will experience falling productivity and a further deterioration in economic as well as social conditions. A vicious spiral has established itself.

The only thing that appears to be able to break this spiral (which of course does not affect all areas — as we have seen, some rural areas even attract migrants), short of radical changes in rural life, is a deterioration in urban living conditions. Zaslavskaya appears to have found some evidence for the latter.[22]

From the early 1960s to the mid-1970s, net migration out of rural areas was slowly rising. However, in 1976 there was a sudden drop and thereafter the level has stayed about the same. This can be partly explained in demographic terms. Large groups of young people reached working age, and thus deprived migrants of employment opportunities. However, a factor of greater importance was that it had become increasingly difficult to find foodstuffs in the cities. Together with the increasingly unpleasant rhythm of city life, this accounts for the growing desire to be 'close to nature'.[23] Although this development might reduce the outflow from the countryside in the short run, it is hardly a viable long-run solution. Policy must be directed towards making life on the farms appear more attractive, or the vicious spiral in which some areas find themselves cannot be broken. Such a policy, however, must be built on increasing the economic viability of the kolkhoz, a subject to which we will return in Chapter 7.

Auxiliaries

In an attempt to compensate for the loss of labour, millions of people are sent every year from the cities to help on the farms. In 1978 15.6 million people were involved, which was 2.4 times higher than in 1970.[24] The problem is rapidly deteriorating. Another indication that the problem is growing serious is the recent so called 'labour and rest' schemes whereby pensioners from the cities are given a small plot of land and maybe an abandoned house on the farms in return for whatever labour they can contribute on the collective fields.[25]

The problem with the 'auxiliary' labour is obviously that of low productivity. People sent on to the fields will be pretty much whoever is at hand when the need arises, from Komsomol youth to industrial workers, and there can hardly be said to be much voluntariness involved. E. Manevich claims that this type of labour is twice as expensive for the kolkhoz as that of its own members, and that their productivity in agriculture is only one-quarter of the level prevailing in their normal line of work.[26] There are thus considerable costs involved. If each person spends one day travelling in each direction, which is probably an understatement, the losses 'on the road' are equivalent to around 100,000 full-time employees.

Furthermore, if about half of those involved are industrial workers, and each spends a month on the farm, the loss in industrial production alone corresponds to more than half a million full-time workers. For industry, the situation is further aggravated by the fact that these operations are rarely well planned, but rather built on 'cries for help' from local party organs, who find that their farms are unable to cope. To guard against such disruptions, industry will generally attempt to overstaff, which of course further increases the cost of production. Moreover, it serves to aggravate further the shortage of labour in industry as a whole. Against these losses[27] in production – either from overstaffing or from losses of productive manpower – what can be put in terms of increased agricultural production?[28]

To answer this question we require a picture of the activities of these helpers, and here we are aided by a survey carried out by the *Literaturnaya Gazeta* in 1978.[29] The first impression that this survey provides is one of general disorganisation. When people arrive on the farms there are frequently no facilities for either feeding or housing them, and when after a couple of days they can start working, they are poorly equipped. Instances are quoted where people have been found digging potatoes with their bare hands. Furthermore, the quality of the helpers may not be so good. Some will be industrial workers who may never have been on a farm before, and others will be Komsomol youth and similar volunteers, who may have a lot of enthusiasm but little practical knowledge. The result will be poor handling of machinery and equipment, with resultant excessive wear and tear. Instances are quoted where the kolkhozniks simply leave for town when they see the 'auxiliaries' coming. All in all, we can only infer that the productivity of these people is not very high. Combined with the fact that the use of their labour is increasing rapidly, this must be taken as a powerful indication of the growing seriousness of the labour problem in the kolkhoz.[30]

A Labour Problem

In this section we have tried to establish that the real root of the kolkhoz labour problem is to be found at the very foundation of the kolkhoz system as it emerged under Stalin. First, the difference in profitability between the private and the collective sectors is largely a consequence of the procurement system. This creates a situation where the collective cannot compete with the private plot for labour, thus necessitating compulsory labour quotas, which in turn leads to a hostile attitude towards collective labour. Secondly, the absence of a direct link between effort and reward in remunerating labour is a consequence of the need to make labour a residual claimant in the kolkhoz in order to facilitate the extraction of produce. This was seen to create an incentive for the kolkhoznik to shirk his communal tasks, either by minimising effort or by minimising time spent working for the collective. Under certain circumstances, there might also be a Prisoner's Dilemma.

In the long run, the consequences of these problems will be further aggravated by an outflow of labour, which serves to reinforce the vicious spiral of falling profitability. To see how this works, we will start by recalling, from Chapter 5, how the procurement system for some farms created a vicious spiral of falling profitability. The compulsion to deliver a range of products at unfavourable price-cost combinations started the spiral, which was then fed by the resultant disinvestment and eroded incentives to work. The long-run effects of the losses in manpower that result from this spiral will now be analysed in a Domar framework,[31] where all members are identical, and are paid according to the value of their average product (VAP).

The fact that kolkhozniks are paid a fixed piece-rate instead of VAP does not change our argument, since in the long run they will be affected by reduced kolkhoz profitability in terms of a reduced quality of kolkhoz infrastructure (housing, schools, cultural activities, etc.). Neither is it important that membership size is not determined by the kolkhoz, since what we want to show is the impact of *uncontrolled* out-migration following a deterioration in profitability.

This reduction in profitability can be interpreted as a fall in kolkhoz distributions to the members (VAP). The reaction of the kolkhozniks to this fall in 'pay' will be to reduce the supply of labour to the collective, indicating a stronger preference for leisure or work on the plot. With this reduction in labour supply, however, it will not be possible for the kolkhoz to meet its delivery obligations, and it will have to impose a compulsory labour quota. The introduction of forced labour will cause some kolkhozniks to leave, which will only serve to aggravate the labour shortage. Given the inflexibility of the system, procurement quotas are unlikely to be adjusted downwards, which means that as people leave, the burden of forced labour will increase for those remaining. This in turn will speed up the outflow of labour, and a cumulative process has established itself.

Furthermore, if it is the case that it is the most productive parts of the labour force that leave — and there is much evidence to this point — then the labour outflow will not only lead to a direct loss of labour, but it will also lead to a fall in average labour productivity, which will lead to a more than proportionate deterioration in the labour problem.[32] There appears to be nothing to break this vicious spiral.

Within the present framework, it only remains for the government to bail out the ailing kolkhozy via increased procurement prices, increased subsidies and written-off loans. This is also precisely the pattern that we have observed under Khrushchev, under Brezhnev, and presently under Andropov. We have seen how wage payments have absorbed a larger and larger share of farm income, and how indebtedness has increased dramatically.

We cannot emphasise enough, though, that such measures constitute a 'non-solution', leading only to an increasing strain on the state budget and to a continued deterioration in production performance. In the final chapter we will return to see if there are possible ways out of this spiral. Let us now turn our attention to the remaining two factors of production, starting with land.

Free Land

There are two important points to be made with respect to the utilisation of land in the kolkhoz. First, the total size of land holdings is fixed, partly by the fact that no more idle land is available, and partly by the prohibition against buying or renting land. There is thus no way for the individual kolkhoz to expand, except by way of an amalgamation, which we will disregard here, since it is not relevant to our argument. Secondly, the internal division of land between private plots and communal fields is institutionally determined by the provision for the individual households to receive private plots of a given size. Thus, as kolkhoz membership expands, land will be diverted from the collective sector to plots, and *vice versa*. With a constant membership, the division of lands between the two sectors cannot be influenced.[33]

Both these restrictions are consequences of early agricultural policy. The removal of land from the market was one of the very first actions taken by the Bolsheviks after the revolution, and land can still be neither sold nor mortgaged, nor does there exist any land rent in official terminology. As the market mechanism was suspended, land was and still is distributed by administrative allocation.

The chief problem lies in the reaction to market signals. The Western farmer is constantly and acutely aware of the opportunity cost of the land he uses, and is consequently continually engaged in a search for its best use. This is not so in the case of the Soviet Union. The Soviet system was never intended to, nor needed to, react to price signals. However, today other factors are showing an increasing mobility and the failure to carry out corresponding reallocations of land when other things change will lead to a serious misallocation of resources.

In a competitive system, a change in prices, for example, will lead to a reallocation of resources in such a way that, at the margin, all factors of production yield the same return in all uses.[34] In the Soviet case this adjustment process is seriously hampered. Let us take the case of procurement prices. The introduction of forced procurements at low prices, combined with the existence of free markets with higher prices, leads in practice to a two-price system. The same good will be paid different prices depending on whether it originates in the private or in the socialised sector. The resultant adjustment process will be a transfer of labour from the latter to the former, and this will continue until returns to additional labour on the private plot have been brought so low that it corresponds to the difference in prices. While this is rational from the point of view of the *kolkhoznik*, it is less so for the *kolkhoz* as a producer. Since it is the same good, the marginal product of labour ought to be identical between the two sectors. However, this will not be the case, since this ratio will correspond to the ratio of prices. An erroneous price signal triggers an adjustment process that leads to a reduction in overall efficiency.

This seeming failure provides a perfect illustration of an important ambivalence. If the transfer of labour could have been prohibited, the failure would not have arisen, and if the system had been consistent there would not have been any transfer of labour. The ambivalence lies in the fact that one factor of production — land — is guided via administrative allocation, while another — labour — is guided via market signals. Ideally, labour should be allocated in the same way as land, and no doubt this was the original intention. The fact that peasants were not generally issued with internal passports until 1975, and thus had to rely on military service and other drastic measures to leave the farm, shows that the regime has reluctantly conceded the principle of controlling the allocation of labour. Let us use an example to illustrate the consequences of these conflicting mechanisms of resource allocation.

In the case of a kolkhoz that is faced with a reduction in membership, for unspecified reasons, a reallocation of land will take place within the farm. As we have seen above, each member household has the right to a private plot of a given size, and as the number of households is reduced (we assume that a decision to leave applies to the entire household), land will be returned to the socialised sector. This will lead to two different results.[35] First, the reduction in total labour will raise the marginal product of labour on the communal fields, while the plots will not be affected, since we assumed that there was a reduction in the number of *units*. Secondly, the reallocation of land will reduce the marginal product of that factor in the socialised sector, while again the private sector is unaffected. As a result, relatively too much labour will be used on the plots and too much land in the socialised sector. In order to restore an efficient allocation of resources, it would be necessary to transfer labour from the plots and land from the collective. However, such an adjustment will not take place. The transfer of land is blocked by institutional restrictions, and the transfer of labour will only take place as a reaction to a change in earnings opportunities, which will not occur given the fixed wage. This mechanism will thus further add to the vicious spiral of unsuccessful farms.

If we turn now to the successful farms that manage to attract labour, we find the same process working in reverse. As new member households are admitted, land will be diverted to private plots. Assuming again that factor intensities are unaffected in the private sector, this will lead to a rise in the marginal product of land and a fall in the marginal product of labour in the socialised sector. A necessary adjustment *within* the kolkhoz would be to transfer labour to the plots and land to the collective. However, for reasons outlined above, this adjustment will not take place. More serious is the situation *between* farms. The successful kolkhoz will be left with abundant labour and a scarcity of land, while the reverse is true for its less successful neighbour. If land could be sold or leased, this problem would not arise.

In conclusion, then, we have here another example of a conflict between two systems. Under the early system of extraction, administrative allocation ruled, and labour mobility was controlled via the issue, or rather refusal to issue, passports to the peasants. Today, however, passports are freely issued, and labour mobility is not controlled.[36] We thus have a situation where one factor, labour, is allocated via the market, and another, land, via administrative control. Such a system will necessarily lead to the complications we have described above. Successful farms will attract labour, but will be unable to expand their land holdings, and will thus find themselves with an abundance of labour but with a shortage of land. Unsuccessful farms, on the other hand, will lose labour and find themselves with idle land and a severe labour shortage. The crux of the matter is the absence of a market for land. If households could rent idle land to expand their plots, this would improve the situation of unsuccessful kolkhozy. Furthermore, if successful kolkhozy could buy or rent land that is idle or extensively used from less successful neighbours, then this would not only aid further expansion of successful farms, but also improve the overall allocation of resources in the economy.

Today's Soviet agriculture thus suffers from a built-in misallocation of resources, within farms as well as between farms. To remove this problem would mean either controlling labour mobility or allowing land mobility, neither of which seems a likely way out. What we have is thus yet another system-related dilemma, the solution of which will necessitate a policy reversal. We will return to this in the final chapter. Let us now turn to the final factor of production, capital.

Difficult Partners

As we saw in Chapter 3, the most important part of Brezhnev's programme was a rapid increase in agricultural investment, which, with the Food Programme, has brought that sector's share in total investment up to a record high of one-third. Table 6.1 illustrates this development, in terms of both roubles and percentages.[37]

Table 6.1: Agricultural Investment

	1965	1970	1975	1980
Billion roubles	12.3	19.4	30.8	35.9
Share in total	22	24	27	27

Source: *Narkhoz* (1981), p. 340.

From the table we can see that a path of rapid expansion was replaced by stagnation in the latter 1970s, a pattern which we have repeatedly observed in previous chapters. What is more striking, however, is the change in the relation between capital investment and output in the kolkhoz. Table 6.2 below shows the growth in kolkhoz output and capital stock.

Table 6.2: Capital Stock and Gross Output in Kolkhozy (billion, 1973 roubles)

	1965	1970	1975	1980
Capital stock	42.3	60.0	91.7	109.8
Gross output	35.4	42.3	42.0	41.5
Capital/output	1.19	1.42	2.18	2.64

Source: *Narkhoz* (1981), p. 254.

The problem that begs explanation is why these massive increases in agricultural investment have not been accompanied by a corresponding increase in output. While the capital stock in kolkhozy has increased by some 160 per cent, output has increased by less than 20 per cent. Part of this discrepancy can be explained by reductions in other factors. Over the period indicated above, kolkhozy experienced a decline in sown area by 10 per cent, and in labour force by 26 per cent.[38]

However, these reductions only go a small way towards explaining the slow growth in output. In particular the reduction in the labour force — from 18.6 million to 13.3 million people — should be viewed against the approximately 15 million urban dwellers that now 'help out' at the harvest every year. The explanation must thus be found in the process of transforming financial capital into physical capital. Table 6.3 provides an indication of the problem. Stocks of the major types of equipment are given, with the corresponding *annual* flows in parentheses.[39]

Table 6.3: Equipment in Kolkhozy (000)

	1965	1970	1975	1980
Tractors	756 (240)	942 (309)	1,064 (370)	1,057 (348)
Grain combines	224 (79)	292 (97)	298 (92)	300 (118)
Trucks	426 (94)	479 (157)	520 (269)	529 (268)

Source: *Narkhoz* (1981), pp. 217-18, 254.

It can be seen from the table that the volume of capital invested in kolkhozy has greatly increased. In relation to output the volume of capital has grown even more substantially. However, the stocks of available equipment have been little affected by these increases. The only possible explanation for this apparently contradictory evidence is that there has been a drastic fall in the return to capital. The cause of this decline can be found in the relations between the kolkhozy and the organisations that supply investment goods.

Partners

Another reflection of the suppression of market forces is the replacement of private trade by administrative allocation of inputs. Enterprises and administrations responsible for the production and allocation of agricultural machinery and equipment will consequently have great influence over kolkhoz production possibilities. In this section we shall argue that the operation of such organisations is detrimental to kolkhoz production.

One of these is the *Minselkhozmash* (Ministry of Agricultural Machinery), which is responsible for production. The dominating problem here is a lack of what in Russian is termed *kompleksnost*, a lack of co-ordination. This is the situation where one hand does not know what the other is doing, and the best illustration is perhaps the rapid increase in fertiliser production without a corresponding increase in the production of equipment to spread it.[40]

Complaints of such imbalances are frequently found in the press. Recently a new all-round heavy-duty tractor was introduced, designed to be used with 33 different types of implements. So far only 4 types have been produced.[41] Farms that have invested in these new tractors, which are then used in the same way as the older and simpler versions, have found that their expenditure is doubled without any resultant increase in output.[42] Many similar examples can be quoted.[43] In the case of potato production, for example, only 14 out of 51 planned implements have actually been produced. The bulk of equipment is thus obsolete, and planting takes place in much the same way as 25 years ago.[44]

One reason for these problems is the extreme risk aversion of Soviet managers, which makes the introduction of new products a very slow process.[45] Another reason is found in the system of industrial planning. Production targets will inevitably be highly aggregated (tons of nails for example). As a result, managers are able to choose the combination of output which makes it easiest to meet plan targets (such as 10-inch nails only). Usually this means large-scale equipment, and the most obvious manifestation of the problem is the notorious shortage of spare parts. These are simply too costly to produce, and if the industrial manager were to cater to the needs of his customers, he would suffer himself by being unable to meet his plan targets.

A typical example of such industrial supply constraints is that of small-scale machinery and equipment, chiefly intended for use on the private plots. A debate on the merits of such things as weeders, cultivators, etc. has been going on in the Soviet press for years. The focus of attention has been on the introduction of a minitractor of 3-5 hp, and in 1977 and 1979 *Izvestia* carried two long articles on the matter.[46] Following the first article promises were made by responsible officials, and the second article is highly critical of their failure to deliver.

In 1968 the Minselkhozmash was ordered to investigate the matter, but little has been achieved. At enterprise level, development is presently at the third-generation prototype, but no production has taken place. The Ministry refuses to allocate the necessary funds, arguing on the one hand that large-scale machinery for the kolkhozy must be given priority, and on the other that demand for the minitractor would be insufficient. However, *Izvestia* claims that in Belorussia alone, ten to twelve thousand tractors could be sold at the suggested price within the first year alone. In conclusion, the reporter became very indignant, claiming that the Ministry has done everything to ward off all discussion of the matter, and demanding that 'The time has come to answer for this breach of government discipline . . . It is after all not a question of wishes, but of firm demands.'[47]

The minitractor is a typical example of the Soviet producer's isolation from consumer demand. In spite of pressure from the very top, nothing happens. The bureaucracy simply stalls. Brezhnev personally complained about this inability to control the apparatus. Other examples apart from the minitractor can be quoted.[48]

However, it is not only the production side that is a problem. Further problems have arisen in the distribution of agricultural inputs, which is also a state monopoly, ranging from poor service to outright fraud. The *Goskomselkhoztekhnika* (State Committee for Agricultural Machinery) is responsible for the supply of agricultural machinery. This agency is responsible not only for the sale of machinery and equipment, but also for repair and maintenance.[49] It is probably the most heavily criticised body in Soviet agriculture. The most frequent target for complaints is repair. Machinery sent to the local selkhoztekhnika facilities will remain there a long time,[50] and repairs performed will be of poor quality. As a result, a large part of kolkhoz machinery and equipment is constantly idle, awaiting repair. To combat this problem, many farms have been forced to set up their own workshops. However, all spare parts are allocated to the selkhoztekhnika and orders have to be made through this organisation, which creates formidable difficulties. Some activities can even be classified as outright fraud. A 12.5 per cent surcharge for delivery and assembly is included in the price paid for machinery. This is charged irrespective of the distance to the farm.[51] It is also charged even in cases where machinery arrives in kits, perhaps to farms without specialised workshops. Complaints have also been made about charges for repairs that have never been carried out.[52]

This state of affairs is common knowledge, and is a frequent target for *Krokodil* satire. There is the mechanic sliding under a brand new combine, where the caption reads: 'In these cases you do look a gift horse in the mouth.'[53] There is the truck dumping a pile of different-sized crates in a farm yard, where the caption reads: 'Here is the combine you ordered.'[54] Such cartoons appear regularly, especially with regard to the lack of spare parts.[55] Sometimes they are also accompanied by a highly ironical discussion of the responsible agency's way of handling things. The problems are thus well known to the authorities, but still nothing happens. Even when it comes to fraudulent charges, officials admit facts but claim that they have to do so in order to meet their plans. It is thus the same story again. Selkhoztekhnika operates in complete isolation from the needs of the farms that it is intended to serve, making plans according to objectives that rarely coincide with those of its clients.

The consequences for agriculture are considerable. Large portions of machinery and equipment stand idle, awaiting repair. Others are scrapped to be used for spare parts. New machinery is delivered with parts stolen in transit.[56] Machinery that is repaired by the selkhoztekhnika rapidly breaks down again, etc., and it should be emphasised that these are all logical consequences of the existing structure of incentives. If officials involved were to cater more to the needs of their customers, they would suffer themselves, in terms of reduced plan fulfilment and reduced bonus payments. Until incentives for producers can be brought in line with the interests of the consumers, the present state of affairs will continue, and, since it is a seller's market, the kolkhozy will absorb the direct costs.

Much the same kind of problems apply to another state organisation, the *Goskomselkhozkhimiya*, which is responsible for the supply of chemicals to agriculture. An article in *Sovetskaya Rossiya* from 1981 summarised the situation with regard to mineral fertiliser.[57] Annual losses in transit amounted to 626,000 tons. Losses within the selkhozkhimiya (storage and handling) amounted to 1.9 million tons, while losses on the farms amounted to 6.5 million tons. All in all, over 9 million tons of fertiliser, or 10 per cent of total output, is lost every year in transport, storage and handling.

These losses can be partly explained by the inadequate transport system. A shortage of covered trucks and railcars increases the amount that is simply blown off in transit. These losses are compounded, however, by a lack of co-ordination. Selkhozkhimiya is not supplied with plastic bags for shipment (this is the responsibility of the Ministry of Chemical Products) and thus has to ship fertiliser bulk in open railcars. Furthermore, prices include delivery to the farm, but frequently fertiliser is just dumped at railway sidings due to the inadequate transport of the selkhozkhimiya.[58] In both cases rain will rapidly turn fertiliser into concrete. In other cases fertiliser is delivered, but the wrong kind and thus useless. Returning the shipment is just not to be considered.

Once again these are well known problems, which are frequent targets for *Krokodil* cartoonists. There are the men with pneumatic drills, carving out large blocks of stone for a nearby construction site, where the caption reads: 'Rains have turned the fertiliser into concrete, so we have decided to use it to build a store for fertiliser.'[59] There is also the train that has stopped beside a small hill. There is no caption, but the engineer is looking in astonishment at a telegraph pole at the foot of the hill. The pole has started sprouting.[60]

The conclusions are the same. The problems are well known, but there is no obvious solution. The selkhozkhimiya is paid for the volume that is shipped. Whether or not it reaches the farms, or in what condition, is immaterial. In a system which is a seller's market and where all costs of inefficiency are borne by the consumer, there is no obvious solution to these problems. The losses are the logical consequences of a system that, for example, can double the output of fertiliser without producing any more equipment with which to handle it.

In summary, the utilisation of capital in kolkhozy is seriously constrained by the conflicting objectives of external suppliers. The farms have very little opportunity to influence these constraints. They can try to lobby the Minselkhozmash into producing the equipment and machinery that is needed, but they have no sanctions at their disposal. Since there is only one supplier, farms cannot 'vote with the rouble'. Producers receive bonuses for the total value of their sales, irrespective of the usefulness of their output, and after all it is better to get poorly suited machinery than no machinery at all. In a similar vein, kolkhozy can lobby the selkhoztekhnika into improving its service or into supplying badly needed spare parts. Again, however, there are no sanctions. Farms cannot order machinery straight from the producers, and even if they set up their own workshops they will still be dependent on the selkhoztekhnika for spare parts.

The latter is paid according to the deliveries that it makes and the repairs that it performs (or claims to perform), irrespective of distance and of quality of repairs. This also applies to the selkhozkhimiya. The quality or type of fertiliser delivered will not influence the supplier, only the farm.

As long as incentives diverge, all of these effects will be built into the system. The only way to remove them is by making the 'partners' dependent on the success of the kolkhozy, i.e. by penalising them in some form for faulty deliveries, poor repairs, etc. One way of doing this would be by introducing competition between suppliers, and allowing the farms to choose. Such market arrangements have been tried successfully in Hungary, but there are no indications that they will be introduced widely in the Soviet Union. Hence it remains to look for improvements *within* the system of administrative allocation. However, such attempts have a poor record. The centre has little ability to apply direct sanctions to local managers, whereas the latter have numerous opportunities simply to stall, in a bureaucratic manner, all attempts by the centre to effect any change. This is borne out by the vigorous but largely ineffective criticisms that appear regularly in the press.

However, these problems are not the only ones. They are compounded by poor maintenance and rapid wear within the kolkhozy. An example from Mogilev province will serve to illustrate the magnitude of the retirement problem.[61] During one year 2,500 tractors were delivered and simultaneously 1,821 written off, 502 combines were delivered and 673 written off, 488 potato harvesters were delivered and 430 written off, etc. The result, of course, is that large parts of the total stock of machinery will more or less constantly be out of order, and it is against this background that the high figures for new deliveries should be seen. One reason for these high retirement rates is neglect and sheer incompetence in handling. This problem is aggravated by the rapid turnover of skilled manpower. In 1975 the output of qualified technical personnel, so-called mechanisers, from various technical schools in Mogilev oblast was 2,730. Simultaneously 2,732 left their jobs on the farms. Similar figures are quoted for following years.[62]

The most important explanation, though, is related to infrastructure. Poor roads cause frequent breakdowns, and a lack of garages and shelters increases detrimental exposure to the elements. In the words of one mechaniser, upon leaving his farm: 'How do you expect us to carry out repairs in the open with 20°C frost?'[63] Much of this machinery will be written off within one season. Let us take a closer look at the problems embedded in a seriously underdeveloped infrastructure.

Infrastructure

When country people meet and talk, there are three common topics of conversation: international events, tomorrow's weather and local roads. International events, that's well known to all, and tomorrow's weather, that's unknown to all, but roads — that's like a headache. It concerns everyone. It besets you, and makes you suffer, and there is no getting rid of it.[64]

This is the introduction to a long *Izvestia* article attempting to penetrate the deplorable state of the Soviet network of rural roads. Let us quote some facts.

The annual cost to the Soviet economy from the *bezdorozhe* (roadlessness), i.e. when roads without hard surface are turned into impassable mud, is estimated at between 5 and 7 billion roubles. On average, every vehicle is out of commission for 40 days. Five per cent of the grain harvest is lost under the wheels of vehicles traversing fields. Forty per cent of available operating time is lost on the roads to elevators, reception points and the like. Seventy per cent of all accidents and breakdowns are caused by bad roads. During the mud season, 60 per cent of all tractors are used to tow or recover other vehicles, as well as for transporting produce. Premature harvesting of sugar beet motivated by the need to avoid the bezdorozhe reduces the sugar content by 1.3 per cent, causing losses of hundreds of thousands of tons of sugar. Migration from rural areas is significantly higher in areas affected by the bezdorozhe than in other areas. In the Moscow region alone, reduced speed on the roads causes losses of tens of millions of hours, or the equivalent of more than 10,000 vehicles. Transport costs in areas of bezdorozhe are 5-10 times higher than elsewhere, and on average accounts for 40-7 per cent of total cost, while in some farms it even surpasses total revenue from procurements.

Hence the problem of poor roads is massive, not only in economic terms, but also in reduced welfare. Inaccessibility greatly constrains the availability of films, cultural activities and the variety of consumer goods in the stores.

The dominant explanation for this state of affairs is clearly a long-term neglect of investment. The Soviet economy today is paying off debt on past policy. In the last thirty years total freight loads have increased by over forty times, while the total length of hard-surface roads has only increased fourfold. Only 7 per cent of total freight is handled on the roads, whereas 65 per cent of total transport resources are consumed in the process. In the RSFSR, only 21 per cent of major and less than 1 per cent of minor roads have a hard surface.

These facts are well known to the authorities, and research indicates that returns to investment in this sector would be high. For each rouble invested, 2 to 3 would be returned. Increasing the length of hard-surface roads from 1 to 3 or 4 km per 1,000 inhabitants would reduce the need for other capital investment by 5-15 per cent, given the same output. A doubling of the volume of repair and construction would reduce the need for trucks by 150,000 and for manpower by 200,000 people annually.[65] Given that 30-40 per cent of all farm labour is spent on loading, unloading and transporting produce, increased mechanisation and road improvement could lead to labour savings of 15-20 per cent.[66]

Needs, however, are enormous. Eighty-three per cent of all farms lack hard-surface access roads, which means that during the mud season they are virtually isolated.[67] To alleviate the worst problems, the volume of road construction would need to increase by more than 2.5 times,[68] and the volume of repair work by 10-15 per cent.[69]

If the problem were simply one of a shortage of investment, it would hardly be worth discussion.[70] This, however, is not the case. The system exhibits many imbalances and diseconomies.

Roads without hard surface are destroyed within less than three years, and sometimes within a season. Yet the bulk of investment goes into such roads. Many roads are still constructed on an old standard of supporting maximum loads of 6 tons, although today most loads are considerably heavier. Road improvement units usually spread out their operations over large areas, thus lengthening completion time, increasing disruptions and failing to accomplish continuous stretches of good roads. Construction of hard-surface roads is slowed down by supply constraints in the cement industry, etc. Other examples can be quoted, and the common denominator is that of a distinct lack of co-ordination and interest. Nobody seems to be willing to assume responsibility for tackling the problem. Meanwhile funds that are allocated often come to poor use.

The Minister of Roads in the RSFSR characterises the situation in the following manner: 'We are like the poor man of old days who, living in his miserable hut, cannot bring himself to build a new one, although well aware of the fact that his discomfort is increasing, and that the time and money continuously spent on repairs long since has exceeded the cost of building a new home.'[71] He then goes on to say that the difference is that the Soviet state today has both the means and opportunities of finding an economically suitable solution, but that unfortunately it is not obvious to everyone that the present state of affairs cannot continue much longer. His explanation is that the root of the problem is neither of an economic nor of a technical, but rather of a psychological, nature. Both planners and other officials have simply grown used to the problem of the bezdorozhe, considering it as an unpleasant or almost fatal unavoidability.

This problem is reminiscent of the policy of 'superindustrialisation', where the construction of large industrial complexes had priority over virtually every other activity in the economy. It is well known that many elements of this policy still linger in various aspects of Soviet life, and when it comes to improving rural areas, it is probably especially pronounced. Unless such priorities can be changed, the road problem is there to stay. The long and vigorous, but largely fruitless, criticisms in the press indicate that this might very well be the case.

Another, related, aspect of infrastructure is that of storage. There is an overall shortage of storage space for agricultural produce, as well as a misallocation of existing facilities. While the former is of the same character as that of an inadequate road work, i.e. simply a lack of funds, the latter is more serious. Instead of allowing on-farm storage, virtually all grain is first taken to central elevators, and then a large part of it is shipped back to the farms as the need arises.[72] This completely absurd policy cannot be explained in any other terms than as a remnant of the old policy of extraction. When force was used to make kolkhozy deliver, on-farm storage could not be allowed, since this would be tantamount to concealment.

The consequences of this policy are far-reaching. The distance from farm to elevator can sometimes be in the vicinity of 100-150 km (for one district an *average* figure of 130 km is quoted).[73] Given that harvested grain has to be stored as quickly as possible, and given the state of roads and availability of transport, the losses that are *induced* by this policy are tremendous. Produce is left to rot in piles on the fields, while scarce trucks are standing in line for hours at overcrowded elevators, after having been towed for hours through virtually impassable mud by equally scarce tractors.

Once again, these are well known facts.[74] In spite of criticism, however, nothing is done to solve the basic problem. The standard cure is more funds but no institutional change. Consequently, the annual addition in elevator capacity has risen from 1.7 million tons in the 1966-70 period, to 3.3 million in the 1971-5 period, and 3.7 million in the 1976-80 period.[75] Yet the problem remains.

Gosplan estimates that about 15-20 per cent of the total potato harvest is lost every year in the process of procurement, storage and distribution, and figures for the RSFSR indicate that as much as a third of all potatoes harvested are simply left in piles in the fields (for some regions as much as 60-5 per cent).[76]

Part of this, of course, is due to the overall shortage of storage, but the problem is exacerbated by the policy of centralised storage. Due to the great haste in loading and shipping, newly harvested produce is inadequately cleaned, and some shipments contain as much as 20-30 per cent dirt and soil. Annually, tens of thousands of tons of soil are removed in this way, which not only overloads scarce transport, but also reduces the fertility of the soil, since the best layer is taken to the cities.[77]

Soviet sources estimate that by allowing on-farm storage, transport costs could be reduced by three-quarters.[78] For example, during harvest time in Georgia, every day 250 refrigerated railcars ship 4,000 tons of mandarins out of the province. If farms were allowed to cater only to current needs, shipments could be reduced to 1,000 tons per day, and the demand for refrigerated transport could be spread out over the year, as produce was retained on the farms for future shipment.[79] On average, it is estimated that around 70 per cent ought to be stored on the farms, instead of virtually none, as today.[80]

The reason for the persistence of this seemingly absurd situation is simple. Although the economy as a whole would benefit from a solution, no single decision maker would derive any benefit. For the kolkhoz, on-farm storage would be a loss. As they are paid the same procurement price throughout the year, they would incur storage costs that they could not recoup.[81] Enterprises that are responsible for constructing elevators, on the other hand, are paid per ton of storage capacity added, and will accordingly incur considerable losses from the construction of a number of small facilities. This is amply illustrated by the massive development programme for the non-black-earth zone.[82] To meet their plans, enterprises construct stations with individual capacities of 130,000 to 140,000 tons, which should be compared to an annual addition of 3.3 million tons from 1971 to 1975, and of 3.7 million tons from 1976 to 1980. As long as the present structure of incentives remains unchanged, the problem cannot be solved. Even direct pressure from the centre will have little chance of success, since change would damage all the parties directly involved. On the one hand a solution would necessitate seasonal variations in prices to provide incentives for the farms, and, on the other hand, a change in enterprise incentives to make it profitable for them to cater to the needs of their customers. This, however, is a tall order and it is likely that the problem is there to stay, particularly with regard to its long history.

Conclusion

In this chapter we have analysed the internal utilisation of resources in the kolkhoz, and while we showed the labour problem to be largely the result of a conflict within the farm, other problems were seen to have external causes. In all cases, conflicts arise from divergent incentives for different actors, and they were seen to be of such a nature that they seriously hamper the efficiency of present agricultural policy. Continued increases in the flow of resources into agriculture will result in continued decreases in returns. Hence, a change in the structure of incentives is required. However, before we turn to this discussion, let us briefly summarise our findings so far.

The *labour problem* in kolkhozy was seen to have three different dimensions. First, low profitability, which is to a large extent caused by the procurement system, results in an outflow of labour from rural areas, and frequently in an outflow of the most productive segments of the labour force. Secondly, differences in the relative remuneration for communal and private labour, caused by the difference between procurement prices and free market prices, creates a bias in labour supply in favour of the private plot. Finally, the system of remuneration for communal labour creates an incentive for the kolkhozniks to shirk which results in a very low productivity of kolkhoz labour.

All these factors seriously affect the allocation of resources. The first necessitates sending millions of people from the cities to help out with the harvest. The second causes a misallocation of labour between private plots and communal fields, and the costs of the third are obvious. All these factors are built into the system. They are remnants of the former policy of forceful extraction of agricultural produce. Compulsory procurements were necessary, given the low prices, which in turn were necessary to fuel the industrialisation drive, and from this followed the residual character of labour remuneration. Although *policy* is built on creating incentives, we have seen that the *system* is still built on compulsion. The conflict is obvious.

The *land problem* was seen to be largely one of a lack of transferability. Institutional restrictions prevent the shifting of land between different uses. Within kolkhozy, there may be highly profitable plots that are unable to expand in spite of the existence of idle communal land. Between kolkhozy there may be highly successful farms that are unable to expand, in spite of the fact that others have lost so much labour that they cannot fully utilise their own land. Both of these are consequences of the early removal of land from the market. If land cannot be sold or rented, then there will not be any mechanism to guide it towards its optimal use. While it should be pointed out in the context that today most kolkhozy actually operate with idle land, and that thus only part of the problem actually materialises, it is important to note its existence, as related to the system.

The *problem of capital* was also seen to have two dimensions. One is the external restriction where kolkhozy are dependent on 'partners' who have no incentive to cater to the needs of their customers, and the other is the seriously underdeveloped infrastructure. Both of these are also remnants of the old policy. The lack of power on behalf of the kolkhoz is a necessary consequence of a system that is built on administrative allocation and extraction, while an underdeveloped infrastructure is a necessary consequence of a policy of maximum short-run extraction. With the change in policy towards a stronger reliance on incentives, this system becomes a serious constraint. Declining returns to investment in kolkhozy will in no way affect their suppliers, nor will the latter be hurt by infrastructural problems. All costs will be borne by the farms (or eventually the consumers), who lack the power to influence their environment.

Let us now draw together the threads of our argument and see what possible change lies ahead in Soviet agriculture.

Notes

1. *Sotsiologicheskaya Industriya*, 1 October 1982, claims that out of 5.2 million people engaged in crop cultivation, 3.2 million rely chiefly on horses and on their bare hands in carrying out their work.
2. Manevich (1981), p. 60.
3. See Hedlund and Lundahl (forthcoming) for a formal approach to this problem.
4. The definition of when the quota is binding is somewhat vague. Bradley (1971), p. 349, quotes a Soviet source which states that 'in 1965 . . . members would not work on the collective at all in the absence of minimum work requirements', but Stuart (1972), pp. 118 and 128, claims that most kolkhozniks put in more hours than the minimum necessary. The reason for this is that livestock is the most important part of private production (Hill (1975), p. 494) and that the peasants are dependent on obtaining fodder and pasturage rights for their animals. Thus, in a sense, work beyond the minimum is compulsory as well. We may think of the quota as consisting of two parts, where the second part entails a somewhat higher payment per hour.
5. Israelsen (1980).

6. See Bradley and Clark (1972) for a discussion of these problems.

7. In 1978 tax regulation was changed so that 73 per cent of all kolkhozy were exempted from paying tax. Garbuzov (1978), p. 16. One reason for the rapid deterioration in the financial situation of the kolkhozy has been the large increases in wage payments. While kolkhoz gross income fell from 22.8 billion roubles in 1970 to 19.6 billion in 1980, over the same period wage payments increased from 15.0 to 18.6 billion. Thus the share of wage payments increased from 66 to 96 per cent of gross income. Suslov (1982), p. 27. Furthermore, differences between 'strong' (*krepkie*) and 'backward' (*otstoyaschii*) farms are so great that while wage payments in some of the former account for only half of gross income, in some of the latter they exceed it by half. *Izvestia*, 17 September 1981. Here is one obvious reason for the heavy indebtedness of the kolkhozy.

8. The Prisoner's Dilemma is a situation where two men are apprehended following a bank robbery. The police are certain of their guilt, but have no evidence. To elicit confessions, the District Attorney puts each man into solitary confinement and puts the following proposition to him: 'If you confess and your partner does not, you will be released immediately as State's Evidence and your partner will be sentenced to 10 years. If both confess, this will be regarded as a mitigating circumstance and you will both be sentenced to 8 years. If nobody confesses, you will both be sentenced to 2 years on petty charges.' The obvious dilemma is: 'Can your partner be trusted?'

9. Recall the discussion of this system in Chapter 4.

10. Simon Kuznets observes that relative product per worker (full-time equivalents) in Soviet agriculture declined continuously over the period 1928-50, and after 1950 increased only slowly, which is in sharp contrast to Western development where agricultural productivity has kept up with that of the rest of the economy. Kuznets (1963), p. 350. Our account in Chapter 3 also shows that the large increases in agricultural production during the Khrushchev and Brezhnev periods have been chiefly due to increased inputs.

11. Zaslavskaya and Korel (1981), p. 42.

12. Ibid., p. 43.

13. Ibid., p. 44.

14. Perevedentsev (1975).

15. Ibid., p. 143.

16. Ibid., p. 145.

17. Ibid., p. 135. It should be noted that figures on relative earnings are not quite comparable. On the one hand kolkhozniks have a shorter working year than in industry, and thus would realise a lower annual income even if hourly pay were the same (which it is not). On the other hand, however, they supplement this income with produce from the plot.

18. Perevedentsev (1975), p. 137.

19. Ibid., p. 140. *Kommunist*, no. 11 (1982), p. 7, claims that 80 per cent of the rural housing stock is substandard.

20. Zaslavskaya and Korel (1981), p. 47.

21. Ibid., p. 47f.

22. Ibid., p. 48.

23. Ibid., pp. 48ff. It should also be noted that there is a growing aversion amongst young people towards the arduous work on the private plot.

24. Manevich (1981), p. 60.

25. These schemes are obviously also highly interesting for the pensioners, who are thus able to secure scarce vegetables and potatoes for their urban households. See *Literaturnaya Gazeta*, 3 June 1981, and 20 January 1982.

26. Manevich (1981), p. 60.

27. One factory in Gorky, for example, reports a loss of 20,987 man-days

during the first 9.5 months of 1977, which gives something of an indication of the magnitude of disruptions that are caused in industry. *Literaturnaya Gazeta*, 11 January 1978.

28. This strain is further aggravated by the fact that a number of kolkhozniks have full-time jobs in the cities, and thus will be travelling as well, only to be replaced by the 'auxiliaries'.

29. *Literaturnaya Gazeta*, 26 July, 23 August and 13 September 1978.

30. Another indication is an example from Estonia, where farms daily drive buses into the urban market, picking up anyone who is willing to do a day's labour in return for some produce. *Literaturnaya Gazeta*, 8 February 1978.

31. Domar (1966), p. 743.

32. An important objection to this argument is that the reduction in labour and the freeing of plot land for communal use will both act to shift the VAP schedule upwards by increasing the productivity of labour in communal work. However, this objection is not serious. First, it is mostly young people who move to the cities, leaving the older generation behind. Since plots are allocated to the household, there will not be any reallocation of land in this case. Secondly, even if plots are vacated, their small size and usually awkward location close to the home-steads will make their addition of limited use to the communal sector. Finally, and most importantly, if it is the most productive segment of the labour force that leaves, this depressing effect on productivity will most likely outweigh the positive effect of increasing the endowment of land per remaining worker, and particularly so if the continuous out-migration has a demoralising effect on those left behind.

33. See further Oi and Clayton (1968), p. 38f.

34. For full efficiency in production, we require that for each factor of production, the ratio of its marginal products in different uses should equal the ratio of output prices. If we assume that there is only one crop, that is grown in both sectors and sold at different prices, and that there are only two factors, land (T) and labour (L), then this condition can be expressed as below:

$$\frac{P^p}{P^c} = \frac{MPL^c}{MPL^p} = \frac{MPT^c}{MPT^p}$$

where P^p and P^c are output prices for the private and communal sector respectively, and where MPL and MPT are the marginal products of labour and land respectively.

35. An increase in MPL^c and a decrease in MPT^c (given that factor intensities in the private sector are unchanged) will lead to a distortion in the equilibrium condition as follows:

$$\frac{MPL^c}{MPL^p} > \frac{P^p}{P^c} > \frac{MPT^c}{MPT^p}$$

36. One remaining obstacle is the difficulty of obtaining a residence permit, a *propiska*, in the major cities.

37. Emelyanov (1979), p. 3, claims that out of all agricultural investment undertaken between 1918 and 1977, 72 per cent took place after the March 1965 plenum on agriculture.

38. Suslov (1982), p. 24.

39. *Kommunist*, no. 11 (1982), p. 6, claims that out of all new deliveries of machinery and equipment to agriculture, 87 per cent are replacements.

40. Between 1970 and 1979 the deliveries of mineral fertiliser increased from 45.4 thousand tons annually to 76.3 thousand, while the deliveries of fertiliser spreaders decreased from 55.8 thousand to 50.2 thousand. *Narkhoz* (1980), pp. 236, 262.

41. *Pravda*, 7 January 1982.
42. Ibid., 5 January 1982.
43. Ibid., 20 June 1981, has a long list of such 'wanted' equipment.
44. Ibid., 26 October 1981.
45. A *Krokodil* cartoon entitled 'Happy Ending' will serve to illustrate this problem. In the first part we see a young engineer proudly presenting blueprints for a new grain combine. The second part shows a middle-aged man being congratulated on the first prototype of his combine. The third part, finally, shows a grey and bent old man being given flowers in celebration of the first of his 'new' combines to leave the assembly line. *Krokodil*, no. 6 (1983). Of course we shall not disregard the sheer weight of bureaucracy as an obstacle to introducing new products. *Pravda*, 7 January 1982, claims that this requires 450 signatures and stamps, and that officials and technicians are employed full-time just filling out forms.
46. *Izvestia*, 12 January 1977 and 15 August 1979. That this is not a recent debate can be seen from *Radio Liberty Research Bulletin*, no. 115/67, 20 February 1967.
47. *Izvestia*, 12 January 1977.
48. *Pravda*, 24 June 1982.
49. The repair stations of the former MTS network have been taken over by the selkhoztekhnika.
50. Complaints about substandard work and long delays are legion. Just taking 1982, examples of critical articles can be found in *Pravda*, on 15 February, 16 and 30 March, 2, 9, 20 and 29 June, and 3 August, in *Ekonomicheskaya Gazeta*, no. 34, and in *Krokodil*, no. 27; many more examples can be cited. The criticisms contain nothing new, and they have been appearing for years. Yet they seem to have little effect.
51. *Pravda*, 2 October 1978.
52. Ibid., 2 February 1978.
53. *Krokodil*, no. 25 (1982).
54. Ibid., no. 26 (1982).
55. Again, a *Krokodil* cartoon will provide an illustration. A number of people are shown encamped in front of a selkhoztekhnika station. At the front door there is a sign saying: 'No spare parts'. In the foreground there is a man with a megaphone addressing the people, who seem to be well installed, with tents, campfires and even portable television sets. The caption reads: 'Those who have waited longer than three months must apply for a residence permit.' *Krokodil*, no. 8 (1983).
56. *Pravda*, 26 October 1979, claims that the volume of machinery that is stripped in transit doubled in 1975-7, and *Selskaya Zhizn*, 14 May and 18 April 1980, complains about premature write-off of machinery that is butchered for spare parts.
57. *Sovetskaya\Rossiya*, 30 May 1981.
58. We will return below to the problems of transport.
59. *Krokodil*, no. 20 (1982).
60. Ibid., no. 11 (1980).
61. *Izvestia*, 18 March 1980.
62. Ibid.
63. Ibid.
64. *Izvestia*, 10 October 1982.
65. Ibid.
66. Amosov and Marunchenko (1978), p. 55.
67. Ivannikov (1978), p. 65.
68. Amosov and Marunchenko (1978), p. 53. Other authors claim that their

estimates should be regarded as minimum. Ilychev (1978), p. 138.

69. *Izvestia*, 10 October 1982.

70. This is not intended to reduce the importance of lacking investment. Allocations to investment are still lower than the total losses from poor roads. *Izvestia*, 10 October 1982.

71. Ibid.

72. *Pravda*, 9 December 1981.

73. *Izvestia*, 16 June 1981.

74. On one *Krokodil* cartoon you see a long row of trucks fully loaded with grain. In the distance is an elevator, and on a field beside the road some men are sowing. The caption reads: 'To prevent the grain from going to waste, we decided to sow and reap another harvest while we are waiting.' *Krokodil*, no. 22 (1982).

75. *Narkhoz* (1981), p. 330.

76. *Izvestia*, 2 December 1981.

77. Ibid.

78. *Izvestia*, 16 June 1981.

79. Ibid., 2 December 1981.

80. It is hardly a rational policy where you have to ship grain back to the farms for seed.

81. The procurement price for potatoes is 10 kopek/kg, and the storage cost is estimated at 3 kopek/kg. *Izvestia*, 2 December 1981.

82. See further Chapter 1.

7 FUTURE PROSPECTS

We have now presented a picture of those problems that are the chief causes of the present crisis in Soviet agriculture, and the colours we have used have been rather sombre. We have shown how the system of state procurements at centrally fixed prices forces some farms into a vicious spiral of ever falling profitability, and we have shown how the system of continuous interference by local party officials not only causes harmful disruptions across the board, but also directly stifles potentially expansive units by forcing them to conceal their true capacity.[1]

In this connection we have also shown how an ambivalent attitude to the free markets leads to a reaping of the worst of two possible worlds. On the one hand they cover up the worst deficiencies of the official distribution system, thus allowing it to continue operating in a grossly inefficient manner. On the other hand these markets are subject to restrictions and interference to such an extent that it becomes impossible to reap obvious economies of scale. Thus, they too are reduced to inefficiency.

Turning to the internal working of the kolkhoz, we have further shown how the low level and the form of remuneration for labour have caused not only falling productivity, but also a large outflux of labour, thus aggravating the vicious spiral of falling productivity. We have shown how the absence of transferability of land creates distortions in factor allocation, and finally how the dependence of the kolkhoz on various external 'partners' — for the supply of investment goods has caused a rapid fall in returns on investment.

The underlying assumption throughout our exposition has been that all these problems are intimately connected with the basic structure of the agricultural production system as it emerged during Stalin's reign, and that all subsequent attempts at correcting the problems left by Stalin have failed, largely because of a conflict between *changes* in policy and a *continuity* in the basic structure of the institutional framework. What remains to be investigated in this final chapter is the most likely future course of Soviet agricultural development. Here we shall argue that the present policy, as outlined by Brezhnev in May 1982, chooses to ignore the fundamental problems and instead attempts to buy more time by devoting ever increasing amounts of resources to the agricultural sector. We have likened the present situation to a chain that is being subjected to an ever increasing strain. Eventually one of the links in the chain must break, and it shall be our endeavour now to identify the critical links, and to speculate as to where the break might occur. First, however, we shall take a closer look at the Soviet view of the problems.

The Soviet View

There is no doubt that the Soviet leaders are worried about the situation. The May 1982 plenum on agriculture took place in the middle of a plan period, when very little could actually be done, and it was followed by intensive coverage in the press.[2] In an article in the economics journal *Voprosy Ekonomiki*, academician V. Tikhonov explains that

> Many newspapers and journals in the West have taken this decision [the adopted Food Programme] if not as an admission of the critical state of food supply in the Soviet Union, then as a symptom of some form of crisis. Not only professional journalists and propaganda makers have participated in the newspaper campaign, but also a few economists. This demands a thorough discussion of the causes and symptoms of the current agricultural problems in the Soviet Union.[3]

He then goes on to state that there are no grounds for talking about a 'crisis'. The daily calory intake of the average Soviet citizen is 3,443 kcal, which should be compared to 2,590 kcal for the world as a whole and 3,378 for Western European countries. The risks of starvation and malnutrition have thus been eliminated.

This line of argument is typical of the Soviet attitude of ignoring the real problem. As we stated at the outset of our study, the 'crisis' is definitely not one of malnutrition or pending starvation. It is rather a question of the breakdown of traditional Soviet development strategy.

On the one hand, the rapid growth in household incomes has not been matched by corresponding increases in consumer prices, nor by corresponding improvements in kolkhoz profitability. For the kolkhoz this has meant that today virtually all revenue is paid out as wages, which leaves the state to cover other costs via credits. For the kolkhoz household it has meant that the utility of money has fallen rapidly, since there has been no corresponding increase in the production of consumer goods. This vastly inflated consumer demand is one side of the crisis. On the other hand, the traditional, extensive development strategy has now come to an end. In the past, increases in agricultural production have largely been obtained via increases in agricultural inputs. Today these inputs have run out. There is no more land, no more capital and no more labour.[4] This is the other side of the crisis.

The real problem, as we see it, is thus the rapid deterioration in the food situation, a deterioration which derives partly from over-inflated demand, and partly from constraints on the supply side. The seriousness of the crisis derives from the political implications of a failure to find a cure in the near future.

The Soviets themselves admit the *manifestations* of the problems. They acknowledge the growing gap between demand and supply, and they recognise the mounting problems on the supply side. To illustrate this, we shall give some further evidence from a *Kommunist* editorial that has been cited above.[5]

For example, due to a lack of co-ordination in production, only half of the types of machinery and equipment that would be needed in integrated systems is actually produced. Because of poor handling and poor repair of machinery, 87 per cent of all new deliveries are needed as replacements. A poor nutritional balance increases the need for feed by 40-50 per cent in milk production and by 25-30 per cent in meat production. An underdeveloped infrastructure causes losses during procurement-transport-storage, amounting to 15-20 per cent of the harvest. As a result, in some areas as much as 30-40 per cent of the total output of scarce vegetables end up as fodder. Eighty per cent of the rural housing stock is considered substandard. An underdeveloped 'social infrastructure' causes a large outflux of people from the villages. 'Partners' such as the selkhoztekhnika take no interest in the end result of the kolkhoz. Profitability is too low, etc., etc.

There is thus little difference between the Soviet view of the situation and that which has been presented above. The Soviet leaders are very well aware of both the magnitude and the nature of the crisis. Their view of what should be done, however, differs considerably from ours.

More of the Same

The measures to be taken were outlined in the Food Programme that was presented at the May 1982 plenum,[6] and as we have already presented the details of that programme in Chapter 1 above, we shall merely recall the most important features here.

To improve profitability, procurement prices were to be raised at an estimated annual cost of 16 billion roubles. To bail out 'backward' kolkhozy 9.7 billion roubles in debt were to be written off, and a further 11 billion rescheduled. To check the outflow of labour from the farms, the 'social infrastructure' (schools, housing, kindergardens, etc.) was to be improved, at an annual cost of 3.3 billion roubles. Furthermore, the supply of draught power and chemical fertiliser was to increase substantially, and the same holds for the area under irrigation and drainage. The main impression of the 1982 programme is that history repeats itself.

Khrushchev's programme[7] which followed upon the September 1953 plenum, featured increased investment, improved financial conditions and an expansion of land under cultivation. In the first three years, there was a sixfold increase in procurement prices for grain and livestock, taxes were lowered, arrears written off, and over the whole period, about 35 million hectares of Virgin Lands were added. Results were impressive. Over the period 1950-65 agricultural production increased by 70 per cent.

However, if we take a closer look, the picture is less favourable. More than half of the whole period's growth fell between 1956 and 1960, and on an annual basis, growth rates were highest in 1954-5. Average factor productivity grew by 25 per cent during the period 1950-65, but *all* of this occurred before 1959. The result of the programme was thus a short-lived boost in output, and to sustain this, continuous increases in inputs were necessary.

Brezhnev's programme[8] which followed upon the March 1965 plenum, included very similar features. Procurement prices were increased, a tax reform lowered the overall tax pressure, and arrears were again written off. Particular emphasis was laid on increased investment. Deliveries of machinery, equipment and fertiliser were to double. One difference between the two programmes was that Brezhnev did not have the option of expanding cultivated land. This limit had been reached, and the emphasis thus had to be on investment, in physical capital as well as in land reclamation. Another difference was the restoration of administrative order, in lieu of Khrushchev's campaigning.

The results, however, were similar. Initial rapid expansion turned into stagnation. Between 1966 and 1975, one-third of the increases in output were due to improved productivity, and *all* of this occurred during 1966-70. Consequently, after 1970, all growth in agricultural production has been solely due to increased inputs. Between 1971 and 1975 average factor productivity *fell* by 0.4 per cent annually.

Against this background, one cannot but take a pessimistic view of the prospects for the *'new programme'*. Its main features are precisely the same as before — increased procurement prices, increased investment, written-off debt, etc. — and it can hardly be expected to produce different results. On the contrary, it might even prove worse.

In 1953 kolkhoz income was very low and increased prices had a powerful incentive effect. Today household incomes have doubled and the main problem is *finding* something to buy, rather than how to afford it.[9] In 1965 investment had long been neglected, and the initial increases yielded high returns. Today it has surpassed all-time records, and returns are very low.

What is required is thus a policy that comes to grips with the real problems, and by now it should be obvious that such a policy cannot rest on continuous increases in the flow of resources into agriculture. Instead, a policy is needed that improves the yields from the already massive resources at the disposal of the agricultural sector. It is our opinion that this can only be done via changes in the structural framework — i.e. the chain must break — and we shall now turn to see where that break might occur. Let us start by identifying the critical links.

Critical Links

Since much of the discussion in the remainder of this chapter will revolve around possible breaks and changes in the present system, maybe we should start by defining our understanding of the term 'impossible'.

The distinction between 'possible' and 'impossible' has many dimensions. Some things may be impossible simply because they are against the laws of nature, but few of the things that concern us here are of that absolute character. Other things that are impossible in the short run might be possible in the longer run. Many of the problems that face Soviet agriculture, and particularly those that relate to adverse natural conditions, are of this kind. Gigantic projects, such as the reversal of Siberian rivers or the draining of marshlands in the non-chernozem zone, may in the long run overcome unfavourable odds. Our presentation, however, rests on the assumption that the present crisis is acute, and this type of measure will thus not provide a feasible solution.

Instead we shall be concerned with solutions that are workable in the short run, and here we enter another dimension. While choice between different alternatives is normally made on the basis of what is economically feasible, there might be yet another restriction in terms of ideological feasibility. Things that are physically and economically possible might still be impossible, simply because they are contrary to an underlying ideology, religion or other such conviction. In the Soviet case such restrictions are of particular importance and they will be at the focus of our attention.[10]

We shall portray the present Soviet leadership in a situation where the only 'possible' solution to the crisis is one that runs counter to basic principles of the system, and thus becomes 'impossible'. On the other hand, we shall also see that a continuation of the present policy will have such far-reaching consequences for the legitimacy of the regime that this too becomes 'impossible'. There would thus not appear to be any way out, but obviously this too is impossible. Something must happen, and we shall now proceed to look at some of the more critical points.

The Price System

The *low level* of agricultural procurement prices was seen to be consistent with the old policy of maximum extraction of produce from agriculture, in order to support the industrialisation drive. We have also seen that this policy has undergone a drastic change. Farm incomes have increased considerably, the kolkhozniks have been granted pensions, etc., and there can be little doubt that there is a *willingness* to improve kolkhoz profitability via increased procurement prices. The problem lies in whether it will be *possible* to do so.

Increased producer prices will have to be matched by either increased consumer prices or increased budget subsidies. Both pose problems. The former is politically sensitive. The last wave of substantial increases in consumer prices (in the early 1960s) was rumoured to have brought food riots in some cities, and recent Polish experience must have brought this threat very much alive to the Soviet leaders.

On the other hand it will not be possible to absorb much more via the budget either. As we have seen above, the gap between consumer prices and producer prices is growing at a dramatic speed, above all in the case of livestock products. The most likely outcome is thus that improvements in kolkhoz profitability must come from reductions in costs rather than from further increases in procurement prices.

The problem of *relative prices* is even more difficult, since this is intimately linked to the economic system as such. The outcome of the debate on pricing, which was referred to in Chapter 5, shows that the

Soviet planners are neither prepared to accept marginal cost pricing, nor to recognise land as a factor of production.This means that prices will continue to be based on some form of historical average cost concept, with little if any relevance to the present situation. It is obviously impossible to revise prices continuously in order to reflect changes in costs. This would thus appear to be another firm link in the chain. Use of the price system for the purpose of allocating resources does not seem likely in the near future.

This leaves us with the role of the price system in *distributing income*. The fact that farms face very different natural conditions, from the famous black earth to the Siberian tundra and the southern steppes, need not be a problem. In the West, where individual farmers face given prices just like their Soviet counterparts, different natural conditions are compensated for by the extraction of differential rent. Furthermore, the differences are partly compensated for by choosing that output mix which is locally most feasible.

In the Soviet case, both these options are closed. Land rent does not exist, nor is there any degree of freedom for the kolkhoz to choose a suitable output mix. Consequently, income differentials between farms are large and growing, and measures such as merging weak farms with their more successful neighbours, transforming weak kolkhozy into sovkhozy, or forcing successful farms to invest more in order to reduce wage differentials between farms, can only be seen as a way of covering up the problem rather than solving it.

It is thus obvious that a real solution will have to be found to close the widening gap between 'weak' and 'strong' kolkhozy. One such has been sought in the system of zonal pricing, but for reasons outlined above this has not been successful. Another attempt has been the provision for differentiation of taxes between kolkhozy. Here it should obviously be possible to obtain a certain positive effect, and the fact that this provision has not been used to any extent can probably be partly ascribed to bureaucratic lethargy.

A very real practical problem that lies in the way, however, is the absence of a workable *kadastr*, or land survey. Without such a survey it will not be possible to extract land rent on the basis of differing natural conditions. All attempts to do so will necessarily lead to the problems described above regarding the differentiation of procurement prices. With a kadastr it would be possible to introduce uniform prices — thus avoiding the distortion of cost and profit data — and to extract rent via differentiated taxation.

Development, however, has not gone in this direction. As Kenneth

Gray points out, 'just as a mammoth Soviet land-cadastre effort [begun in the 1950s and intensified in the 1960s] was bearing fruit, the single-price idea was not only not realized, but prices are now differentiated even more for most agricultural products by zone and sometimes even by groups of farms'.[11] He further quotes a Soviet source, saying that 'there is no single method of evaluation [of land quality] that is generally accepted in agricultural practice',[12] and concludes that 'the existing cadastral results cannot provide a satisfactory basis for setting direct taxes that would extract land rents'.[13]

It would thus not appear that the Soviets are prepared to give up the old practice of 'patching-up' (price differentiation based on different actual costs) in favour of a solution to the real problem (uniform prices with differentiated taxes based on a proper kadastr). Indeed, the November 1981 plenum takes a further step down the very same road by authorising local officials to introduce price supplements for 'farms that find themselves under adverse conditions, making losses or realising low profits'.[14] From our discussion above we can infer on what basis these price supplements will be introduced.

The final problem with the price system is that of *rigid prices*. As long as prices do not vary seasonally, it will not be profitable to store produce on the farms. As we saw in Chapter 6, the resultant costs are considerable, in terms of added strain on transport and central storage. Yet, this hostility to on-farm storage can only be seen as a remnant of the old policy of forceful extraction, where on-farm storage would be tantamount to concealment. If this policy is no longer operational, we must look for other explanations.

One such explanation is the difficulty of making construction enterprises build small local facilities. As we have seen above, they are primarily interested in large scale. Another difficulty lies in adopting prices. Neither of these need to be insurmountable. Inter-farm enterprises are presently developing that could be allowed to carry out construction and seasonal prices can still be fixed centrally. The real crux of the matter lies in whether available options will actually be *allowed*, i.e. if they are 'possible' in the sense we have discussed above. With regard to the price system, some links in the chain are firm, such as the principles of pricing and the absence of land rent. Others — differentiated prices and taxes, seasonal variation, etc. — are weaker and they become interesting. As we recall from Chapter 5, it is explicitly stated that sometimes deviations from the value-based price can be motivated, i.e. a certain amount of 'patching-up' is accepted, and this is precisely what our 'weak links' represent. There is no basic change in the system

— it is only eroded a bit. Let us now proceed to test the other links, within this framework of 'possibility'.

The Procurement System

State procurements of agricultural produce are one of the most basic principles of Soviet agriculture, stemming from the very first post-revolutionary policies. The principle that the state should have this important trade monopoly has been upheld ever since, and Stalin sometimes referred to it as the 'First Commandment' of collective farming. Apart from this ideological commitment, we have also seen that there is a more tangible problem involved. If procurements were abolished, without a change in the price system, chaos would result. As Kenneth Grays points out:

> Although farm's suggestions about the quantities of various products they would themselves like to sell do reach the officials who set the quotas, they often cannot be accepted because disequilibrium prices cause these quantities to differ from the quantities 'needed' by the government. Much of the information obtainable from farm suggestions is then necessarily ignored in setting quotas because of the requirement that the supply be balanced with the demand for each farm product.[15]

Thus, if the price system is one firm link in the chain, the procurement system as such is another. Farms will remain under compulsion to deliver a range of products, at fixed prices with little regard to local conditions. As with the case of the price system, however, there is a weaker link as well. Kolkhozy have recently been allowed to count sales on the kolkhoz markets against their procurement quotas.[16] Here one would be tempted to think that this is the end of the procurements, as the kolkhozy would simply divert their output to the free market. Again it is important to consider to what extent they will actually be *allowed* to do so, i.e. it remains to be seen to what extent this is 'possible'.

The real core of the problem of procurements is the behaviour of local party officials. If farms had been given firm quotas and left to get on with it, without interference, many problems could have been 'patched up'. Yet we have seen that the raikom and other organs exercise very detailed control over the kolkhozy, and not to the benefit of the latter.

Out of this grows the game situation that was described in Chapter

5. It is up to the raikom to see to it that the raion procurement plan is fulfilled and in so doing it will be necessary to get as much as possible from each farm. For the kolkhoz this means that it will be necessary in the short run to avoid unprofitable quotas, and in the long run to conceal capacity in order to avoid higher quotas in the next period.

The outcome of this game will be that the raikom constantly interferes in the internal affairs of the kolkhoz, to prevent concealment and evasion, and consequently that the kolkhoz will be forced to engage in these activities since they have already been discounted. The only point where the interests of the two players coincide is in the padding of reports. Overstating harvest figures will benefit the kolkhoz, in terms of higher income, and the raikom, in terms of political prestige derived from over-fulfilment of the plan.

One seemingly obvious solution would be to monitor kolkhoz performance *ex post*. However, this might not be such a simple matter, since there are considerable vested interests in the present system on the part of local party organs. A system that was based on self-determination for the kolkhoz would remove one highly important function from the raikom, and thus considerably reduce the power of its first secretary. He can thus be expected to put up fierce resistance to any attempt at change in this respect.

Furthermore, firm quotas would also remove the possibility of shifting quotas on to successful farms in order to let them make up for the shortcomings of their neighbours.[17] This would reduce the possibility of fulfilling the raion plan, and thus create problems for the obkom, that would find it more difficult to meet the oblast plan. Consequently, these officials might also be expected to resist change.

The root of the problem, of course, is that the whole system is built on the principle of forcing farms to engage in operations that are not profitable, or at least less profitable than available alternatives. If fulfilment of procurement quotas were a profitable undertaking, there would be no need to supervise. From this follow two problems.

First, since the whole rationale of party control is that of compulsion, it is not possible to construct a set of incentives that coincide for the two players. Were the kolkhoz to be granted self-determination, the role of the raikom would also largely be over. Secondly, there is a very tangible problem that is not related to vested party interests. If constant supervision were to cease, with no other change, the farms would be given greater leeway to engage in their common practice of deceit and concealment. This in turn would mean that output of favourably priced products would gradually increase and that of unfavourably priced ones decrease. Given the inflexibility of the Soviet system, it would be very difficult to deal with such changes, and certain products might disappear more or less completely.

It is difficult to see how a penalty/reward system should be constructed, short of a reform of the price system, which would prevent the kolkhoz from deviating from the plan in order to maximise its own profit. For this reason we may suspect that the top leadership as well – which does not have the same personal vested interests in detailed party control – will be loath to curb the activities of local party officials.

It is impossible to predict the likely turn of developments on this issue. However, such a prediction is crucial for any attempt to speculate around future development in general, and we shall thus return to it below. Let us first, however, examine the remaining links in our chain.

Marketing

One area where the problem of an ambivalent party attitude is given ample illustration is that of the role of the kolkhoz markets. As we have seen above, these markets compete with the official distribution network for the favour of the customers, and the odds are very uneven.

The quality of food found in official stores is perhaps best illustrated in a *Pravda* cartoon, which shows a man posting a sign that reads: 'Today fresh vegetables'. The man is wearing a gas mask.[18] The continued existence of the official distribution network can only be explained by the persistent shortages and by the practice of 'conditional sales', whereby the customer is compelled to buy, say, some rather old herring, in order to acquire the right to buy some new chairs.[19]

It is against this background that the kolkhoz markets should be viewed. People gladly pay higher prices in order to get good-quality produce, and yet these prices are unnecessarily high. The ambivalent policy towards the markets has had two important consequences. On the one hand investment has been neglected, with a resultant lack of storage space, sanitary facilities and other installations, and on the other, it has been impossible to exploit economies of scale, mainly due to the prohibition against middlemen.

There is thus a firm link in the chain, in terms of the prohibition against private trade, but there are also weaker links. One obvious improvement would be increased investment in the infrastructure of the markets. While this on the one hand would compete with a long list of other pressing investment needs, and as such is not very interesting for our purposes, it also forms a link in our chain, in that increased efficiency in private marketing might not be a desirable outcome from the local party point of view.

A similar problem is posed by the buro torgovlya, the 'trade bureaus' which exist in some markets. Increased reliance on their services would lead to major savings in peasant time, increased efficiency in marketing and thus lower prices for the consumer. Again, however, this might not be desirable, and then it becomes 'impossible'.

The common denominator is that of party attitudes. There is an increasing pressure for improved efficiency, and a large article in *Pravda* in 1982 calls for a 'new attitude to the private markets'.[20] Yet we have also seen ample documentation to the point that local party officials are hostile to such developments. Thus, the extent to which our 'weak links' will yield is again dependent on the future development of party attitudes.

The Labour Problem

The kolkhoz labour problem has two dimensions, that of a deficient aggregate supply, and that of a poor utilisation of existing resources. In practice these will have the same manifestation, and thus be inseparable, but since they have different causes and thus different cures, they will be discussed separately here.

The problem of a *deficient aggregate supply* of labour is probably the easiest to understand, but also the hardest to cure. There are many reasons why people leave rural areas at a rate faster than can be compensated for by productivity gains. The most obvious one is that of rural-urban differentials in living standards. Rural pay is lower, pensions and other transfers poorer, the supply of consumer goods less varied, schools and cultural activities further between, etc., all of which creates a desire to abandon 'the idiocy of rural life'.[21]

Another, more subtle, cause concerns employment opportunities, and in a recent article in *Sovetskaya Rossiya* T. I. Perevedentsev discusses their impact on migration out of rural areas.[22] He claims that women are particularly hard hit, since machinery used on the farms is normally so large and unwieldy that they are excluded from all forms of skilled labour. What remains is office work or work as dairy maids.

The general picture is that possibilities of promotion are extremely limited. Chairmen and senior staff are normally appointed from without, and it thus becomes necessary to leave the kolkhoz for a number of years in order to accumulate the necessary (party) merits. The structure of the kolkhoz is such that substantial losses of manpower can be predicted. Difficult working conditions, low pay and no prospects of promotion hardly encourage people to stay on, and it is quite common for people who are sent away for training at the expense of the kolkhoz simply to break their contracts and refuse to return.[23]

While the traditional cure for these problems has simply been to prohibit mobility via the passport system, this is no longer so. Soviet policy is today clearly aimed at reducing rural-urban differentials. Kolkhozniks have been given pensions and passports, pay has been increased, etc., and there are substantial provisions in the Food Programme for increased investment in the rural infrastructure.

What remains to be seen is how much can be gained in this way. On the one hand, it is a tall order to make up for decades of a policy that has been aimed at reducing the countryside to the state of an exploited colony, economically as well as psychologically, and on the other, it would take more than increased investment to solve the structural problem of employment opportunities. Nevertheless, the problem has been recognised and a solution set in motion, which will no doubt be good in the long run.

Even if the problem of aggregate supply of labour to agriculture were solved, there would still remain the problems of low productivity within the farm and of mobility between farms. As we have seen above, these problems lead to the creation of vicious spirals of losses of labour and falling productivity. It is thus not a question of allocating more funds to agriculture. Something has to be done about the underlying structural problem, and it is here that we find perhaps the most interesting contribution of the Food Programme.

As we have seen above, the main problems with regard to the utilisation of labour, are the low level of remuneration for collective work and the absence of a direct link between effort and reward. Low pay discourages people from supplying hours and the form of remuneration discourages them from supplying effort. Something that would remove both these problems at one stroke is the beznaryadnoe zveno, the 'unassigned link'. In Chapter 4 we saw that the most important features of this form of labour organisation were (a) a long-term assignment of land and equipment to the group, (b) self-determination in production, and (c) pay according to results.

The most interesting point in Brezhnev's speech at the May 1982 plenum was that it contained the first public endorsement, from a high-ranking official, for the zveno. This might be taken as an indication that long experimentation is now to be followed by a wide-scale application.

If so, the zveno would re-establish the missing link between efforts and reward, it would raise the remuneration for labour by raising its productivity, and it would create incentives for soil improvement and care and maintenance of equipment, simply because the future income of the group would depend on these factors.

In one sweep, all the problems discussed above in relation to labour would thus be removed. Needless to say, other problems would come instead. However, before we go into these, let us investigate the impact on the kolkhoz of an introduction of the zveno.

The first consequence of such a change would obviously be the removal of compulsion. The household would again be free to choose according to the strategy that was outlined in Chapter 4. However, there would be one important difference. With a zveno there would no longer be any fixed pay for collective work. Peasants working together in a zveno would sell their output to the kolkhoz at previously fixed prices,[24] and the strategy would now imply equalling the marginal income from the plot to the marginal income from the zveno, instead of to the previously fixed piece-rate for collective work.

Two important differences between plot and zveno production should be noted. First, while labour in the zveno is better endowed with land and capital, and thus should be more productive, we assume initially that this is compensated for by a higher supply of effort per hour in plot production. Secondly, while the plot utilises household labour only, the zveno still retains a communal form, bringing together several kolkhoz members in the same group. For the moment we shall assume that all zveno members are identical, that they supply identical amounts of labour and effort to the zveno, and that they share the proceeds equally. Given the respective earnings possibilities, the household will now make a labour-leisure decision, and then allocate the *given* labour hours between the two types of work, according to the condition that the remuneration for the last hour worked in each sector should be equal. From this position we can investigate the really crucial features of zveno production.[25]

By establishing a direct link between effort and reward, it should lead to an increased supply of effort per hour worked in the zveno. By providing for self-determination in the organisation of work, it should lead to a more efficient utilisation of labour, and by providing for indirect property rights in land, in the form of long-term tenure, it should create incentives for soil improvement. All of these factors taken together will lead to an increased output per hour worked.

The outcome of this will be a reallocation of labour from the private plot to the zveno, and at this juncture the first problem emerges. With zveno productivity increasing, pay for zveno work will also increase, and this change in earnings opportunities will in turn affect the household's labour-leisure decision. It will now be possible to enjoy more leisure at an unchanged income, more income at an unchanged amount of leisure, or some combination. The effect on the *total* number of hours worked will thus be indeterminate, but judging from our presentation above, the latter option would seem the more likely. Given the arduous nature of work on the plot and the limited availability of consumer goods, the household's marginal valuation of an increase in income versus a reduction in work ought to be strongly in favour of the leisure. If this is the case, the reduction in hours worked on the plot will be larger than the increase in hours worked in the zveno, since there is a reduction in total work.

Furthermore, if it was the case under the quota system that the household chose to minimise the effort spent in collective work, then an introduction of the zveno will cause the household to increase the effort spent on the collective fields, and thus to reduce that spent on the plot, which will further increase the squeeze on the latter.

The long-run consequences of a wide-scale introduction of the zveno might thus be quite far-reaching. On the one hand private plot production would be considerably reduced, under the dual pressure of reductions in hours and in effort, and might eventually be crowded out entirely. This, of course, is most likely in the 'Tambov' case, where the plot was not initially very successful. Moreover, 'socialised' production would also be crowded out by zveno production, and a Soviet kolkhoz under these arrangements would present a very different picture indeed. With production taking place in zveno groups under self-determination, it would be reduced to a mere umbrella organisation, responsible for the purchase of inputs and the sale of output.[26] In essence, this would mean nothing short of the reintroduction of private small-scale farming, in the guise of collective production. Pehaps this is the Soviet leadership's way of severing the Gordian Knot.[27]

However, there are several important qualifications to such a development. The highly positive results that have been quoted for zveno experiments[28] might be seriously biased. Proponents who attempt zveno production will probably allocate superior resources to it, in terms of land and equipment as well as labour, which will not be possible on a wider application.

Furthermore, we have quoted above observations by Soviet authors that the zveno might lead to serious problems in terms of widening income differentials and an aggravation of the seasonal unemployment problem.[29] Finally, it is important to note that the zveno is still a form of communal production. Thus, even if productivity increases, and resultant increases in pay make this form of labour competitive with plot production, there might still arise a Prisoner's Dilemma situation. The long-standing hostility towards work on the communal fields and the deeply engrained practice of shirking might not be easily overcome.

It is thus far from certain that the zveno actually will be introduced on a wide scale. The Politburo spokesman on agriculture, M. Gorbachev, did not even mention the zveno in a long article on agriculture shortly after the May 1982 plenum, which might be taken as an indication that there is still some political opposition.[30]

Furthermore, it should also be noted that we have implicitly assumed that productivity on the private plot would remain constant. However, if there were any changes in the restrictions on plot production, productivity here might also increase, and this would counteract the effect of the zveno.

In spite of all these qualifications, it is important that the real root of the labour problem has been widely recognised, and even if it does encounter difficulties, the introduction of the zveno on a wider scale will surely have positive effects in terms of *output*. What remains to be seen is to what extent it will be *allowed* to expand, both with regard to the more tangible problems discussed above, and in terms of party interference, i.e. it remains to be seen how 'weak' this link is.

Other Inputs

Although the problems of non-labour inputs are by no means smaller than those of labour, we shall not have much to say here on that topic. As we have seen in previous chapters, the causes of these problems lie largely outside the kolkhoz proper, and indeed outside agriculture altogether. A thorough analysis would necessitate discussing, amongst other things, radical reforms in industrial planning, which lies slightly outside the scope for our presentation. Let us therefore very briefly review the main problems.

The problem of *land utilisation* was seen to lie in a lack of mobility, and on this point change is highly unlikely. The removal of land from the market goes back to the very first night after the storming of the Winter Palace, and this would thus appear to be perhaps the firmest link in our chain. Of course, there are weaker links as well, such as making vacant land available for pensioners from the cities, and maybe even allowing a minor expansion of the private plots, but these are relatively unimportant. The basic inflexibility of land as a factor of production will most likely remain, between farms as well as between plots and communal fields.

The problem of *capital utilisation* was seen to have two essentially different dimensions. On the one hand, investment was sadly neglected during the first decades of Bolshevik policy, which produced an infrastructure that is seriously underdeveloped today. The resultant losses are massive, and the cure is obvious. More investment in areas like roads and storage facilities would surely yield high returns. The problem is that these investment objects compete with a long list of equally neglected areas, where returns might be just as high. It thus reduces to a simple selection problem, which we shall not explore here.

The real problem is that of rapidly falling returns to investment, and as we saw in Chapter 6, this is largely the result of a failure of the 'partners' of the kolkhozy to take farm interests into account when devising production plans. The Food Programme does recognise this problem and calls for a scheme of bonuses to make enterprises and administrations cater to the needs of their customers. Since the problem lies at the very root of the nature of industrial planning, however, it is unlikely that this scheme will have any greater impact. More likely is that it will be just another patch on the already existing mosaic of bonuses and indicators.

Furthermore, it is unlikely that official pressure on those who are responsible for imbalances, delays, substandard quality and sometimes outright fraud is going to help. Such pressure has been applied for years, in the form of letters of complaint in the press, but to little avail — even when culprits have been directly named.[31] The cause is simply that if they were to improve along the indicated lines, they themselves would suffer instead. Their plans are such that they have to engage in some of the criticised activities in order to achieve the all-important plan fulfilment.

Finally, given the unwieldy Soviet bureaucracy, they have excellent opportunities of defending themselves against such change by simply stalling. Change is obviously 'possible' in one sense of the word, but maybe not in the other. Although there has been a considerable Soviet interest, particularly in the reforms in Hungary,[32] no definite recommendations have been made for the Soviet economy. It rather appears that the present problems will continue and perhaps even deteriorate.

Conclusion

The situation facing the leadership under Andropov can hardly be said to be encouraging. Four consecutive harvests have failed. Massive imports of grain are draining precious foreign exchange reserves. Reductions in livestock herds threaten the politically sensitive meat supply. Formal rationing is being introduced on top of the 'traditional' shortages. Labour productivity is falling. Returns to capital are falling, etc., etc. The chain is being subjected to a strain that it can hardly be able to take for much longer.

Our ambition in this presentation has been to portray the present crisis as mainly a politico-economic problem, and it is against this background that we shall now try to assess possible future development.

Scenarios

One possible outcome would simply be to close the 'scissors' of consumer and producer prices by drastically increasing the former. As we have seen above, one cause of the food crisis is that over the past two decades wages have doubled while most prices have remained virtually constant. Closing this gap would mean rationing via the wallet, instead of via long lines ouside the shops.

At the same time, this would also attack the very basis of legitimacy for the Soviet regime. Although price increases would not reduce actual availability, it would bring home very forcefully the real level of living standards.When rationing is by standing in line, at least there is an illusion of a higher living standard (what could be afforded if it could only be found) and a form of equality (first come, first served).

The argument that price increases would be inequitable, in that they would favour the rich, is not very relevant. These are already provided for via special privileges, special shops, etc., and would not be greatly affected by price increases in the regular outlets. The likelihood of a forceful popular reaction to such a measure has also been indicated on several occasions above. Although it cannot be completely ruled out,[33] this development would appear unlikely.

Another perspective is that of 'business as usual'. By simply ignoring the crisis, the regime can avoid making unpleasant alterations and concessions. However, the bulk of our account above has been aimed at showing that a continuation of present policy will not be possible for much longer, simply because it would have equally unpleasant political implications as a 'reform solution'.

On the one hand, further deteriorations in the food situation would lead to civil unrest, and to cope with this, the authorities would have to resort to even tighter repression. Given that the external situation for the Soviet Union is rather difficult at present, it can hardly be desirable to see the internal situation deteriorate as well.

On the other hand, a continuation of present policy would probably also be blocked by influential groups in the Soviet Union which are presently suffering from the increased priorities given agriculture in the allocation of resources. Representatives of the 'military-industrial complex', for example, can hardly be expected quietly to accept budget cuts in order to increase further the flow of resources into the 'Black Hole' of the agricultural sector.[34] While such intervention might equally well demand more repression as more concessions, we shall maintain that a tougher stance is not a likely course of development. It thus remains to investigate what the ingredients might be in a 'possible' solution.

Reform

'Reform' in the Soviet context is a rather difficult concept. While in the West, governments might legislate on changes in the political and economic structure, and expect results (even if not the desired ones), in the Soviet case this is not necessarily so. The regime might legislate on far-reaching reforms, only to find the bureaucracy stalling and nothing really happening. The most outstanding example of this are the 'Liberman proposals' in the 1960s, which were to change basic principles of industrial planning, but which in practice came to nothing.[35]

The present situation in agriculture is precisely of this nature. If we return to our 'chain', we have seen that many of the links — those that we have termed 'weak' — have in practice already broken. Short of a major overhaul of the entire politico-economic system — the 'firm' links — all the ingredients necessary for quite substantial change are already there.

In the socialised sector, the labour problem could be mitigated by an application of the zveno; party interference and the shifting of procurement quotas are already illegal; and the recent provision for the kolkhoz to count sales on the free market against its procurement quotas might in the end lead to a disappearance of the entire procurement system. The problem of land rent could be mitigated via differentiation of prices and/or taxes, a major strain could be taken of the transport and storage system by allowing on-farm storage, etc. All of these are quite legal. They are not contrary to any of the 'firm' links in the chain, and yet very little seems to happen. Why?

Precisely the same situation holds with respect to the private sector. Productivity could be increased by providing small-scale mechanised implements, by lifting restrictions on private livestock holdings, and by expanding plot sizes. There are prototypes for minitractors, but they are not produced. There are provisions for expanding private livestock, but only in experiments.[36] Private marketing could be made more efficient, but instead we find harassment. All these measures would have beneficial effects on production. They would not break any of the 'firm' links. Yet they are not widely adopted. Why?

Constraints

At this point it would be all too easy to say that none of the above-mentioned measures are adopted simply because of ideological restrictions, because they are too market oriented, i.e. because 'the Rabbi does not eat ham'. Yet this would be a simplistic explanation. To explore the implications of ideological constraints further, we shall need to differ between top level *policy makers* and local-level *policy implementers*. Their respective behaviours will be seen to differ considerably.

In the former case, considerations of ideology frequently conflict with considerations of economic performance and it would be wrong to say that one dominates the other. Ideological constraints are probably best seen as something that complicates potential debate. If you are not convinced that certain changes will have desired outcomes, it is always possible to invoke ideological arguments in order to avoid a serious debate. Once you are convinced, however, ideology can always be reinterpreted to lend support.[37]

The obstacle to change is of this kind. The debate around marginal cost pricing, for example, was much complicated by the need for all involved to reconcile their arguments with the labour theory of value. The reason that nothing actually came out of the debate, however, should probably be sought in a failure to convince top leaders that the proposed changes would actually work. The Soviets normally claim that reform is difficult to undertake in their case (as compared to other eastern bloc economies) because their country is so large. This is obviously nothing but a manifestation of risk aversion, and of not knowing what the real consequences would be, if reform were attempted.

The best example of this is probably the long debate around the zveno. Although there has been plenty of evidence to the point that these small groups are superior in terms of productivity, we have seen that there are very real economic problems involved as well, which should lead to a questioning of the reform, irrespective of ideological overtones.

The top leadership should thus be viewed as pragmatic politicians, paying lip-service to ideology, and sometimes using it to further their own interests in the struggle for power, but not as idealists, willing to sacrifice economic gain for ideological principles. The future of 'reform' will thus depend to a larger extent on whether top leaders can be convinced that it will work than on whether it has unpleasant ideological consequences.

If we turn to local officials, on the other hand, their situation is completely different. They are not charged with responsibility for long-run development. As long as they fulfil the plan, everything is fine, and as we have seen above, they can sometimes go to quite some lengths in order to do so. The problem with change in this context is that these local officials will frequently have vested interests in the present structure, and will thus block any attempt at reform.

In agriculture in particular, most of the reform proposals have been aimed at increased self-determination and increased reliance on the market mechanism. For local party bureaucrats, such reforms pose a threat to their own very existence, since their function of control and interference would be replaced by markets and self-determination. Consequently they can be expected to fight tooth and nail to block any such reform, and they have considerable power to do so, simply by stalling. During the latter half of the 1970s in particular, Brezhnev frequently showed signs of exasperation at his inability to 'push' desired changes through an uncooperative *apparat* (bureaucracy).

In summary, there can be said to be two horns to the dilemma of 'reform'. On the one hand it will be necessary to convince top leaders that a given proposals will actually work, which might be a tall order, given traditional risk aversion. On the other hand, even if top leaders are convinced, it will still remain for them to push the reform through the apparat, which might be an even taller order. Is it then possible that anything will actually happen in the near future, or will things simply continue, in a sort of 'permanent crisis'?

Prospects

At this point, we shall have to disappoint a reader who had expected any form of drastic change, either in the form of harsh repression or in the form of far-reaching reforms. Neither of these seem likely developments, judging from present indications. Yet we shall maintain our hypothesis that it is on the one hand impossible to continue present policy, and on the other equally impossible to undertake change. On both counts 'impossible' is viewed in the political framework that has been used above. Obviously there must then be a 'third way', and it is this that we shall now, by way of conclusion, attempt to outline.

The situation at the beginning of the 1980s is in one important respect similar to that in 1921 and in 1930. An increasingly dissatisfied peasantry is cutting back production at a time when continued increases are badly needed. Admittedly, the analogy might be a bit far-fetched. On previous occasions the crisis was in terms of outright starvation, while today it is more in terms of frustrated expectations. Yet the present Soviet population has a vastly different set of expectations from those prevailing in the 1920s and the 1930s, which makes the political importance of fulfilling expectations a matter of considerable importance.

Most importantly, however, the *principle* is the same. *Within* the given system there is no solution to the crisis. In 1921 Lenin retreated and allowed more or less free play for the market forces. In 1930 Stalin backed down briefly and then applied unprecedented repression. Both these are examples of scenarios that we have deemed 'impossible', the former representing 'reform' and the latter 'continuation'. What then is the third way that will steer the economy between the Scylla of Lenin and the Charybdis of Stalin?

Given that the crisis today is less serious and the economy more stable, the pressure is not such that drastic measures will be necessary. Andropov will have more leeway, but the question remains as to what can actually be done. In the short run, his hands will be tied, partly by the current Five-Year Plan and partly by the overall priorities outlined in the Food Programme. Yet the pressure will continue to increase and the only likely outcome will be a gradual yielding of the 'weak' links in our chain.

The interesting moment will materialise when there is actually scope for some manoeuvre. The earliest possible such date will be in 1985, when the current Five-Year Plan expires, but work on the coming plan is probably so far progressed that little can be done at that point. This would leave us with 1990, which is also the expiration date for the Food Programme. What will happen then hinges crucially on the distinction we made above between *policy makers* and *policy implementers*.

Should it be the case that the leadership at that date has decided that important changes must be made in the agricultural structure, in order to accommodate the post-Stalinist policy of creating incentives rather than relying on compulsion alone, then it will still remain for them to 'push' the desired changes through the apparat, whose members would stand to lose personally from such reforms. The choice of roads should thus not be seen simply in terms of the top leadership making up its mind. It will still remain to be seen what power they actually have to overcome an uncooperative bureaucracy.

What will happen at that date will to a large extent depend on events in coming years. What we have termed the 'third way' is not really a third *option* as such. A gradual yielding of the 'weak' links in the chain will only serve to stave off the worst *manifestations* of the crisis. At the same time, however, the pressure on the remaining 'firm' links will increase. The longer a real decision is postponed, the further the economy will be moving down the road towards 'reform'. While it might be inferred that this should be a relatively painless way of making real changes in a gradual way, two important facts must be pointed out.

First, further 'patchwork' will not lead to any substantial improvement in agricultural performance,but will only ease the problem somewhat. Thus, pressure on the government will remain in terms of a continued food problem. Secondly, with a gradual yielding of the 'weaker' links, expectations for further concessions will be rising, and consequently any decision to restore 'order' will entail more and more repression (cf. the drastic measures undertaken by Stalin to restore order after the NEP period).

Simply postponing a decision will thus aggravate the problem in political terms, and eventually one road or the other must be chosen. It only remains for us to conclude by hoping that the leadership at that time will not prove equal to Stalin in 1930.

Notes

1. Khachaturov (1982), p. 56, finds with frustration that 'Higher organs continue their practice of sending the farm detailed plans on sowings as well as on types, numbers and productivity of livestock. This leads to the suppression of economic initiative and any form of independent decision making is effectively curtailed.'

2. The May 1982 plenum was followed by lively activity in the press and journals. See Gorbachev (1982), Tikhonov (1982a) and Tikhonov (1982b), for some more influential contributions. The coverage since has faded somewhat, but is still active. See for example Chernichenko (1983).

3. Tikhonov (1982a), p. 4.

4. The increasing priorities given to agriculture will obviously constrain progress in other major undertakings, such as Siberian development.

5. *Kommunist*, no. 11 (1982)

6. *Pravda*, 25 May 1982. See also Chapter 1 above.
7. See further the account in Chapter 3 above.
8. Ibid.
9. This point is underlined by provisions in the Food Programme for increased in-kind payments of wages.
10. In Alec Nove's words, this is the dilemma facing a Rabbi who 'cannot' eat ham. Nove (1977), p. 361.
11. Gray (1981), p. 44.
12. Ibid., p. 50.
13. Ibid., p. 51.
14. Khachaturov (1982), p. 75.
15. Gray (1981), p. 46.
16. *Selskaya Zhizn*, 7 August 1982. While this concession is limited to 10 per cent of the procurement targets and to above-plan deliveries, it is an important erosion of a very basic principle – that of a state monopoly in trade (recall the decree on Food Dictatorship).
17. Recall the fate of chairman Openkin in Valentin Ovechkin's story.
18. *Pravda*, 19 August 1982.
19. Nove (1977), p. 187.
20. *Pravda*, 23 August 1982.
21. Marx and Engels (1977), p. 40.
22. *Sovetskaya Rossiya*, 24 August 1982.
23. Ibid., 10 June 1982, complains about skilled people refusing to return from the cities.
24. *Ekonomicheskaya Gazeta*, no. 4 (1982), has an important supplement with detailed information on this system.
25. See further Hedlund and Lundahl (forthcoming).
26. For curiosity's sake we might note that this was Lenin's concept of co-operation, as expressed in one of his final pamphlets. See Lewin (1974a), p. 95.
27. In 1970, Dmitry Pospielovsky writes: 'In fact it is possible that the more empirically minded Soviet experts and even party functionaries foresee this development of links as a quiet and relatively painless return to a form of functional private farming, without the reconversion of land into a private market commodity.' Pospielovsky (1970), p. 429.
28. See for example *Ekonomicheskaya Gazeta*, no. 44 (1981).
29. *Literaturnaya Gazeta*, 7 August and 13 November 1968.
30. *Kommunist*, no. 11 (1982).
31. *Pravda*, 7 January 1982.
32. See for example Buzdalov and Bukh (1982) and Otsason (1983).
33. It may be of some importance that, in his speech at the May 1982 plenum, Brezhnev failed to repeat the customary promise of low food prices.
34. The Red Army newspaper *Krasnaya Zvezda* recently (7 May 1982) carried a highly critical article on present agricultural policy.
35. These have later been referred to as 'the reform that never was'.
36. *Selskaya Zhizn*, 18 January 1981.
37. A typical example of this is the reinterpretation of the controversial zveno as 'the only true school of communism', since it makes people work closely together and depend on each other. Pospielovsky (1970), p. 420.

REFERENCES

Aage, Hans (1980) 'Labor Allocation in the Soviet Kolkhoz', *Economics of Planning, 16* (3)

Abramov, Fedor (1963) 'Vokrug do okolo', *Neva* (January)

Abramsky, C. and Williams, B. (eds.) (1974) *Essays in Honor of E.H. Carr*, London

Ames, Edward (1965) *Soviet Economic Processes*, Homewood, Ill.

Amosov, A. and Marunchenko, Yu (1978) 'Avtomobilnye dorogi v strukture agropromyshlennogo kompleksa', *Voprosy Ekonomiki, 49* (3) (March)

Beerman, R. (1967) 'The Grain Problem and Anti-Speculation Laws', *Soviet Studies, 19* (1) (July)

Belov, Fedor (1956) *The History of a Soviet Collective Farm*, London

Bergson, Abram and Kuznets, Simon (eds.) (1963) *Economic Trends in the Soviet Union*, Cambridge, Mass.

Berman, M.D. (1977) 'Short-run Efficiency in the Labor-managed Firm', *Journal of Comparative Economics, 1* (3) (September)

Bonin, J.P. (1977) 'Work Incentives and Uncertainty on a Collective Farm', *Journal of Comparative Economics, 1* (1) (March)

Bornstein, Morris (1962) 'The Soviet Price System', *American Economic Review, 52* (1) (March)

—— (1963) 'The 1963 Soviet Industrial Price Revision', *Soviet Studies, 15* (1) (July)

—— (1969) 'The Soviet Debate on Agricultural Price and Procurement Reforms', *Soviet Studies, 21* (1) (July)

—— (1970) 'Soviet Price Theory and Policy' in Bornstein and Fusfeld

—— and Fusfeld, Daniel (eds.) (1970) *The Soviet Economy*, Homewood, Ill.

Bradley, M.E. (1971) 'Incentives and Labor Supply on Soviet Collective Farms', *Canadian Journal of Economics, 4* (3) (August)

—— and Clark, M.G. (1972) 'Supervision and Efficiency in Socialized Agriculture', *Soviet Studies, 23* (3) (January)

—— (1973) 'Incentives and Labor Supply on Soviet Collective Farms: Reply', *Canadian Journal of Economics, 6* (3) (August)

Brandt, Kondrad, Schiller, Otto and Ahlgrimm, Franz (1953) *Management of Agriculture and Food in the German-occupied and Other Areas of Fortress Europe*, Stanford

Bush, Keith (1966) 'Agricultural Reforms Since Khrushchev' in US Congress (1966)
—— (1975) 'Soviet Agriculture: Ten Years Under New Management', *Radio Liberty Research Supplement*, 25 May
Buzdalov, I. (1979) 'Sovershenstvovanie upravleniya selskim khozyaistvom', *Voprosy Ekonomiki, 50* (9) (September)
—— and Bukh, M. (1982) 'Khozyaistvennyi mekhanism agropromyshlennoi sfery', *Voprosy Ekonomiki, 53* (3) (March)
Cameron, N.E. (1973a) 'Incentives and Labor Supply in Cooperative Enterprises', *Canadian Journal of Economics, 6* (1) (February)
—— (1973b) 'Incentives and Labor Supply on Soviet Collective Farms: Rejoinder', *Canadian Journal of Economics, 6* (3) (August)
Carey, David W. and Havelka, Joseph F. (1979) 'Soviet Agriculture: Prospects and Problems' in US Congress (1979)
Carr, E.H. *A History of Soviet Russia:*
(1950) *The Bolshevik Revolution*, London, vol. I
(1952) *The Bolshevik Revolution*, London, vol. II
(1953) *The Bolshevik Revolution*, London, vol. III
(1954) *The Interregnum*, London
(1958) *Socialism in One Country*, London, vol. I
(1959) *Socialism in One Country*, London, vol. II
(1964) *Socialism in One Country*, London, vol. III, pt. 1
(1964) *Socialism in One Country*, London, vol. III, pt. 2
(1969) *Foundations of a Planned Economy* (with R.W. Davis), London, vol. I, pt. 1
(1969) *Foundations of a Planned Economy* (with R.W. Davis), London, vol. I, pt. 2
(1971) *Foundations of a Planned Economy*, London, vol. II
(1976) *Foundations of a Planned Economy*, London, vol. III, pt. 1
(1976) *Foundations of a Planned Economy*, London, vol. III, pt. 2
(1978) *Foundations of a Planned Economy*, London, vol. III, pt. 3.
Chernichenko, Yu (1965) 'Russkaya pshennitsa', *Novyi Mir, 41* (11) (November)
—— (1983) 'Kombain kosit i molotit', *Novyi Mir, 58* (3) (March)
CIA (Central Intelligence Agency) (1974) *USSR Agricultural Atlas*, Washington, DC
—— (1979) 'USSR — Long Term Outlook for Grain Imports', *ER 7910057* (January)
Cohen, Stephen, F. (1980) *Bukharin and the Bolshevik Revolution*, Oxford
Conquest, Robert (1961) *Power and Policy in the Kremlin*, London

Dallin, Alexander (1957) *German Rule in Russia 1941-45*, London

Dalrymple, Dana (1964) 'The Soviet Famine of 1932-34', *Soviet Studies, 15* (3) (January)

—— (1965) 'The Soviet Famine of 1932-34. Some Further Reference', *Soviet Studies, 16* (4) (April)

Davis, R.W. (1970) 'A Note on Grain Statistics', *Soviet Studies, 21* (3) (January)

—— (1980) *The Socialist Offensive*, London: vol. I (1980a) *The Industrialisation of Soviet Russia*, vol. II (1980b) *The Soviet Collective Farm*

Desai, Padma (1981) *Estimates of Soviet Grain Imports in 1980-85: Alternative Approaches*, International Food Policy Research Institute, Research Report no. 22, Washington, DC (February)

Deutscher, Isaac (1949) *Stalin*, Oxford

Diamond, Douglas B. (1966) 'Trends in Output, Inputs and Factor Productivity in Soviet Agriculture' in US Congress (1966)

—— and Davis, W. Lee (1979) 'Comparative Growth in Output and Productivity in US and USSR Agriculture' in US Congress (1979)

Dobb, Maurice (1966) *Soviet Economic Development Since 1917*, London

Domar, Evsey (1966) 'The Soviet Collective Farm as a Producer Cooperative', *American Economic Review, 56* (4) (September)

Dorosh, Efim (1962) 'Raigorod v fevrale', *Novyi Mir, 38* (10) (October)

—— (1964) 'Dozhd popolam solntsem', *Novyi Mir, 40* (6) (June)

Durgin, Frank A. (1960) 'Toward the Abolition of the RTS', *Soviet Studies, 12* (1) (July)

—— (1962) 'The Virgin Lands Program 1956-60', *Soviet Studies, 13* (3) (January)

—— (1964) 'Monetization and Policy in Soviet Agriculture since 1952', *Soviet Studies, 15* (4) (April)

Emelyanov, A.M. (1979) 'Problemy i perspektivy razvitiya selskogo khozyaistva SSSR v svete reshenii iyulskogo (1978) plenuma TsKKPSS', *Vestnik moskovskogo universiteta, seriya ekonomiki* (January)

—— (1982) 'Razvitie agropromyshlennogo kompleksa SSSR. Razrabotka i osuschestvlenie prodovolstvennoi programme', *Ekonomicheskie Nauki* (1)

Emmons, Terence (1968) *The Russian Landed Gentry and the Peasant Emancipation of 1861*, London

Erlich, Alexander (1960) *The Soviet Industrialization Debate*, Cambridge, Mass.

Fainsod, Merle (1958) *Smolensk Under Soviet Rule*, London
—— (1963) *How Russia is Ruled*, Cambridge, Mass.
Fisher, H.H. (1927) *The Famine in Soviet Russia*, New York
Garbuzov, V. (1978) 'Zadachi dalneischego ukrepleniya ekonomiki i finansov kolkhozov i sovkhozov', *Planovoe Khozyaistvo, 54* (10) (October)
Georgescu-Roegen, N. (1960) 'Economic Theory and Agrarian Economics', *Oxford Economic Papers, 12* (1) (February)
Gorbachev, M. (1982) 'Prodovolstvennaya programma i sadachi ee realisatsia', *Kommunist, 58* (10) (July)
Gray, K.R. (1981) 'Soviet Agricultural Prices, Rent and Land Cadastres', *Journal of Comparative Economics, 5* (1) (March)
Gregory, Paul R. and Stuart, Robert C. (1974) *Soviet Economic Structure and Performance*, New York
Grossman, Philip (1968) 'A Note on Agricultural Employment in the USSR', *Soviet Studies, 19* (3) (January)
Gsovski, Vladimir (1949) *Soviet Civil Law*, vols. I-II, Ann Arbor, Mich.
Gumerov, R. (1979) 'Zakupochnye tseny i stimulirovanie selskokhozyaistvennogo proizvodstva', *Planovoe Khozyaistvo, 55* (3) (March)
Gustafson, Thane (1981) *Reform in Soviet Politics: Lessons of Recent Policies on Land and Water*, Cambridge
Hedlund, Stefan and Lundahl, Mats (forthcoming) 'Linking Efforts and Rewards: The "Zveno" System of Collective Farming', *Economics of Planning*
Hill, Ian (1975) 'The Private Plot in Soviet Agriculture', *The Journal of Peasant Studies, 2* (4) (July)
Hopkins, Mark W. (1970) *Mass Media in the Soviet Union*, New York
Hough, Jerry (1965) 'The Soviet Concept of the Relationship Between the Lower Party Organs and State Administration', *Slavic Review, 24* (2) (June)
—— (1969) *The Soviet Prefects. Local Party Organizations in Industrial Decision Making*, Cambridge, Mass.
—— (1971) 'The Changing Nature of the Kolkhoz Chairman' in Millar (1971b)
Hutchings, Raymond (1971) *Soviet Economic Development*, Oxford
Ilychev, A. (1978) 'O roli avtomobilnykh dorog v strukture agropromyshlennogo kompleksa', *Voprosy Ekonomiki, 49* (11) (November)
Ireland, N.J. and Law, P.J. (1981) 'Efficiency, Incentives and Individual Labor Supply in the Labor-managed Firm', *Journal of Comparative Economics, 5* (1) (March)
Israelsen, Dwight (1980) 'Collectives, Communes and Incentives',

Journal of Comparative Economics, 14 (4)

Ivannikov, I. (1978) 'Kapitalnye vlozhenya v selskoe khozyaistvo — effektivnoe napravlenie', *Planovoe Khozyaistvo, 54* (10) (October)

Ivanov, Leonid (1963) 'V rodnykh mestakh', *Novyi Mir, 39* (3) (March)

Jasny, Naum (1949) *The Socialized Agriculture of the USSR*, Stanford

—— (1961) *Soviet Industrialization, 1928-52*, Chicago

—— (1968) *Khrushchev's Crop Policy*, Glasgow

Joravsky, David (1967) 'Ideology and Progress in Crop Rotation' in Karcz (1967a)

—— (1970) *The Lysenko Affair*, Cambridge, Mass.

Kahan, Arcadius (1963) 'Soviet Statistics of Agricultural Output' in Laird (1963)

Kalinkin, A. (1982) 'Razvitie lichnogo podsobnogo khozyaistva', *Ekonomika Selskogo Khozyaistva, 62* (4) (April)

Karcz, Jerzy (1957) 'Soviet Agricultural Marketings and Prices 1928-54', *RAND, RM-1930*, Santa Monica, Calif.

—— (1964a) 'Quantitative Analysis of the Collective Farm Market', *American Economic Review, 54* (4) (June)

—— and Timoshenko, V.P. (1964b) 'Soviet Agricultural Policy 1953-62', *Food Research Institute Studies, 4* (2)

—— (1965) 'The New Soviet Agricultural Program', *Soviet Studies, 17* (2) (October)

—— (1966) 'Seven Years on the Farm: Retrospect and Prospects' in US Congress (1966)

—— ed. (1967a) *Soviet and East European Agriculture*, Berkeley, Calif.

—— (1967b) 'Thoughts on the Grain Problem', *Soviet Studies, 18* (4) (April)

—— (1968) 'Soviet Agriculture: A Balance Sheet' in Treml and Farrell (1968)

—— (1970) 'Back on the Grain Front', *Soviet Studies, 22* (2) (October)

—— (1971) 'From Stalin to Brezhnev: Soviet Agricultural Policy in a Historical Perspective' in Millar (1971b)

—— (1979a) 'Agriculture and the Economics of Soviet Development' in Wright (1979)

—— (1979b) 'Indexes of Soviet Farm Marketings 1925/26 — 40' in Wright (1979)

Kerblay, Basile (1968) *Les Marches Paysans en URSS*, Paris

Khachaturov, T.S. (1982) 'Puti realisatsii prodovolstvennoi programmi', *Voprosy Ekonomiki, 53* (11) (November)

Kleimyshev, P. (1982) 'Effektivnost ispolzovania proizvodstvennykh resursov selskogo khozyaistva', *Voprosy Ekonomiki, 53* (3) (March)

Krylov, Constantin (1979) *The Soviet Economy*, Lexington, Mass.

Kuznets, Simon (1963) 'A Comparative Appraisal' in Bergson and Kuznets (1963).

Laird, Roy D. (1958) *Collective Farming in Russia*, Lawrence, Kan.

—— (ed.) (1963) *Soviet Agricultural and Peasant Affairs*, Lawrence, Kan.

—— and Crowley, Edward (eds.) (1965) *Soviet Agriculture: The Permanent Crisis*, New York

Lange, Oscar (1938) *On the Economic Theory of Socialism*, New York

Lazutin, V. (1981) 'Razvitie lichnogo podsobnogo khozyaistva trudyaschiesha', *Planovoe Khozyaistvo, 5* (8) (August)

Lerner, Abba (1944) *The Economics of Control*, New York

Lewin, Moshe (1965) 'The Immediate Background of Soviet Collectivization', *Soviet Studies, 17* (2) (October)

—— (1966) 'Who Was the Soviet Kulak?', *Soviet Studies, 18* (2) (October)

—— (1968) *Russian Peasants and Soviet Power*, London

—— (1974a) *Political Undercurrents in Soviet Economic Debates*, Princeton

—— (1974b) 'Taking Grain' in Abramsky and Williams (1974)

Lokshin, P. (1981) 'Stoimost i struktura roznichnogo tovarooborota', *Voprosy Ekonomiki, 52* (10) (October)

Makarova, I. (1979) 'Razvitie lichnogo podsobnogo khozyaistva', *Ekonomika Selskogo Khozyaistva, 59* (1) (January)

Malafeev, A.N. *(1964) Istoria Tsenoobrasovania v SSSR*, Moscow

Male, D.J. (1971) *Russian Peasant Organization Before Collectivization*, Cambridge

Manevich, E. (1981) 'Ratsionalnoe ispolzovanie rabochei sily', *Voprosy Ekonomiki, 52* (9) (September)

Marx, Karl and Engels, Friedrich (1977) *Manifesto of the Communist Party*, Moscow

Maynard, Sir John (1962a) *The Russian Peasant*, New York

—— (1962b) *Russia in Flux*, New York

McCauley, Alastair (1982) 'Sources on Earnings Inequality: A Comment on A. Nove's Income Distribution in the USSR', *Soviet Studies, 34* (3) (July)

McCauley, Martin (1976) *Khrushchev and the Development of Soviet Agriculture*, New York

Meiendorf, A. (1982) 'Obshchestvenno neobkhodimye zatraty i zakupochnye tseny v selskom khozyaistve', *Voprosy Ekonomiki, 53* (3) (March)

Millar, James (1970) 'Soviet Rapid Development and the Agricultural

Surplus Hypothesis', *Soviet Studies, 22* (1) (July)

—— (1971a) 'The Agricultural Surplus Hypothesis. A Reply to Nove', *Soviet Studies, 23* (2) (October)

—— (ed.) (1971b) *The Soviet Rural Community*, Urbana, Ill.

—— (1974) 'Mass Collectivization and the Contribution of Soviet Agriculture', *Slavic Review, 33* (4) (December)

Miller, Robert F. (1966) 'The Politotdel', *Slavic Review, 25* (3) (September)

—— (1970) *One Hundred Thousand Tractors*, Cambridge, Mass.

—— (1971) 'Continuity and Change in the Administration of Soviet Agriculture Since Stalin', in Millar (1971b)

Mills, Richard (1970) 'The Formation of the Virgin Lands Policy', *Slavic Review, 29* (1) (March)

Mints, A.A. (1972) *Ekonomicheskaya otsenka estestvennykh resursov: Nauchnometodicheskie problemy ucheta geograficheskikh nalichii v effektivnosti ispolzovaniya*, Moscow

Movshovich, G.M. (1977) *Prognozirovanie v pishevoi promyshlennosti*, Moscow

Mozhin, V.P. and Krylatykh, E.N. (1982) 'O razrabotke prodovolstvennoi programme', *Ekonomika i Organizatsia Promyshlennogo Proizvodstva* (6) (June)

Narkhoz (*Narodnoe Khozyaistvo SSSR*) (*Statistical Yearbook*), Moscow

Narkiewicz, Olga (1966) 'Stalin, War Communism and Collectivization', *Soviet Studies, 18* (1) (July)

Nicolayevsky, Boris (1966) *Power and the Soviet Elite*, London

Nimitz, Nancy (1959) 'Soviet Agricultural Prices and Costs' in US Congress (1959)

Nove, Alec (1958) 'The Problem of Success Indicators in Soviet Industry', *Economica, 25* (1) (February)

—— (1962) 'Was Stalin Really Necessary?', *Encounter* (April)

—— (1963) 'Incentives for Peasants and Administrators' in Laird (1963)

—— (1964a) 'The Uses and Abuses of Kremlinology', *Survey* (January)

—— (1964b) 'The Peasants in Soviet Literature Since Stalin' in *Was Stalin Really Necessary?*, London

—— (1967) 'Peasants and Officials' in Karcz (1967a)

—— (1969) *An Economic History of the USSR*, London

—— (1970) 'Soviet Agriculture under Brezhnev', *Slavic Review, 29* (3) (September)

—— (1971a) 'The Agricultural Surplus Hypothesis: A Comment on James Millar's Article', *Soviet Studies, 22* (3) (January)

—— (1971b) 'A Reply to the Reply', *Soviet Studies, 23* (2) (October)

—— (1974) 'Some Observations on Bukharin and his Ideas' in Abramsky and Williams (1974)

—— (1977) *The Soviet Economic System*, London

—— (1982a) 'Soviet Agriculture: New Data', *Soviet Studies, 34* (1) (January)

—— (1982b) 'Income Distribution in the USSR: A Possible Explanation of Some Recent Data', *Soviet Studies, 34* (2) (April)

OECD (Organization for Economic Cooperation and Development) (1979) *Prospects for Soviet Agricultural Production in 1980 and 1985*, Paris

Oi, Walter and Clayton, Elizabeth (1968) 'A Peasant's View of a Soviet Collective Farm', *American Economic Review, 58* (1) (March)

Otsason, P. (1983) 'Upravlenie selskokhozyaistvennymi predpriyatiyami v Vengrii', *Voprosy Ekonomiki, 54* (1) (January)

Ovechkin, Valentin (1952) 'Raionnye budni', *Novyi Mir, 27* (9) (September)

de Pauw, John (1968) 'Measures of Agricultural Employment in the USSR: 1950-66', *US Bureau of the Census. Foreign Demographic Analysis Division* (October)

Perevedentsev, V.I. (1975) *Metody izucheniya migratsii naseleniya*, Moscow

Ploss, Sidney (1965) *Conflict and Decision-making in Soviet Russia*, Princeton

Pospielovsky, Dmitry (1970) 'The "Link System" in Soviet Agriculture', *Soviet Studies, 21* (4) (April)

Prodovolstvennaya Programma SSSR na period do 1990 goda i mery po ee realizatsia (1982) Moscow

Protsenko, V. (1971) 'Osobennosti raschetov s byudzhetom predpriyati myasnoi i molochnoi promyshlennosti', *Finansy SSSR, 5* (May)

Putterman, L. (1980) 'Voluntary Collectivization: A Model of Producer's Institutional Choice', *Journal of Comparative Economics, 4* (2) (June)

Roberts, Paul Craig (1970) 'War Communism: A Reexamination', *Slavic Review, 29* (2) (June)

Robinson, Geroid T. (1961) *Rural Russia under the Old Regime*, New York

Rush, Myron (1958) *The Rise of Khrushchev*, Washington, DC

Scherer, John L. (1981) *USSR, Facts and Figures Annual*, Gulf Breeze, Fla.

Schlesinger, Rudolph (1945) *Soviet Legal Theory*, London

—— (1949) 'The Biology Discussion: A Commentary', *Soviet Studies, 1* (2) (October)

—— (1951) 'Some Problems of Present Kolkhoz Organization', *Soviet Studies, 2* (4) (April)

Schoonover, David M. (1979) 'Soviet Agricultural Policies' in US Congress (1979)

Schroeder, Gertrude (1969) 'The 1966-67 Soviet Industrial Price Reform: A Study in Complications', *Soviet Studies, 20* (4) (April)

Selskoe Khozyaistvo SSSR (1971) Moscow

Sen, Amartya (1966) 'Labor Allocation in a Collective Enterprise', *Review of Economic Studies, 33* (4) (October)

Sharov, A. (1965) 'Zametki o genetiki', *Znamya, 35* (4) (April)

Shmelev, G. (1979) 'Kolkhoznyi rynok', *Trud*, 6 January

—— (1981) 'Obschestvennoe proizvodstvo i lichnoe podsobnoe khozyaistvo', *Voprosy Ekonomiki, 52* (5) (May)

Sholokhov, Mikhail (1934) *Virgin Soil Upturned*, London

Simms, James (1977) 'The Crisis in Russian Agriculture at the End of the Nineteenth Century', *Slavic Review, 36* (3) (September)

Sinyuva, M.I. (1980) *Nechernozemnaya zona RSFSR. Ekonomicheskie problemy razvitia selskogo khozyaistva*, Moscow

Slepov, Lazar (1951) 'O bolshevistskom metode rukovodstva khozyaistvennymi organami', *Bolshevik* (2) (January)

—— (1958) *Vysshie i mestnye organy partii*, Moscow

Smith, R.E.F. (1968) *The Enserfment of the Russian Peasantry*, Cambridge

Solzhenitsyn, Alexander (1962) 'Odin den Ivana Denisovicha', *Novyi Mir, 37* (11) (November)

Spravochnik predsdatelya kolkhoza (1972) Moscow

Stuart, Robert F. (1972) *The Collective Farm in Soviet Agriculture*, Lexington, Mass.

Susiluoto, Ilmari (1982) *The Origins and Development of Systems Thinking in the Soviet Union*, Helsinki

Suslov, I. (1982) 'Kolkhozy v sisteme narodnogo khozyaistva', *Voprosy Ekonomiki, 53* (12) (December)

Swearer, Howard R. (1963) 'Agricultural Administration under Khrushchev' in Laird (1963)

Szamuely, Laszlo (1974) *First Models of the Socialist-Economic System*, Budapest

Talbott, Strobe (1971) *Khrushchev Remembers*, London

Taniuchi, Yuzuru (1968) *The Village Gathering in Russia in the Mid-1920s*, Birmingham

—— (1981) 'A Note on the Ural-Siberian Method', *Soviet Studies, 33* (4) (October)

Tarschys, Daniel (1978) *Sovjetunionens Politiska System*, Stockholm

Tatu, Michel (1969) *Power in the Kremlin*, London

Tendriakov, V. (1965) 'Podenka — vek koroktii', *Novyi Mir, 41* (5) (May)

Tikhonov, I. (1982a) 'Edinyi narodnokhozyaistvennyi kompleks mnogonatsionalnoe sovetskogo gosudarstva', *Kommunist, 58* (11) (July)

Tikhonov, V. (1982b) 'Prodovolstvennaya programma SSSR', *Voprosy Ekonomiki, 53* (7) (August)

Treml, Vladimir G. and Farrell, Robert (1968) *The Development of the Soviet Economy*, New York

US Congress (1959) Joint Economic Committee, *Comparison of the United States and The Soviet Economies*, Government Printing Office, Washington, DC

—— (1966) Subcommittee on Foreign Economic Policy, *New Directions in the Soviet Economy*, Government Printing Office, Washington, DC

—— (1979) Joint Economic Committee, *Soviet Economy in a Time of Change*, Government Printing Office, Washington, DC

USDA (US Department of Agriculture) (1981) *Agricultural Situation: USSR*, Supplement to WAS-24, Government Printing Office, Washington, DC (April)

Vanek, Jaroslav (1970) *The General Theory of Labor Managed Market Economies*, Ithaca, NY

Vlasov, V.A. and Studentkin, S.S. (1950) *Sovetskoe Administrativnoe Pravo*, Moscow

Volin, Lazar (1970) *A Century of Russian Agriculture*, Cambridge, Mass.

Voronin, V. (1980) 'Lichnye podsobnye khozyaistva i torgovlya', *Voprosy Ekonomiki, 51* (6) (June)

Voslensky, Michail (1980) *Nomenklatura*, Vienna

Vucinich, Wayne (1968) *The Peasant in Nineteenth-Century Russia*, Stanford

Wädekin, Karl-Eugen (1967) *Privatproduzenten in der Sowjetischen Landwirtschaft*, Cologne

—— (1973) *The Private Sector in Soviet Agriculture*, Berkeley, Calif.

Ward, Benjamin (1958) 'The Firm in Illyria: Market Syndicalism', *American Economic Review*, 48 (4) (September)

Wesson, Robert (1962) 'The Soviet Communes', *Soviet Studies*, 13 (4) (April)

———(1963) *Soviet Communes*, New Brunswick, NJ

Wickman, Kurt (1981) 'Brott eller Kontinuitet?', *Historisk Tidskrift* (4)

Wright, Arthur (ed.) (1979) *Jerzy F. Karcz. The Economics of Communist Agriculture. Selected Papers*, Institute of Development Studies, Bloomington, Ind.

Wronski, Henri (1957) 'Remuneration et Niveau de Vie dans les Kolkhoz. Le Troudoden' in *Observation Economique XIII*, Ecole Pratique des Hautes Etudes, Paris

Yaney, George (1964) 'The Stolypin Reform', *Slavic Review, 23* (2) (June)

Zaslavskaya, T.I. and Korel, L.U. (1981) 'Migratsia naselenia mezhdu gorodom i selom', *Sotsiologicheskie Issledovania, 8* (3) (January-March)

Zinovjev, Alexander (1980) *The Yawning Heights*, London

Zoerb, Carl (1965) 'The Virgin Lands Territory: Plans, Performance, Prospects' in Laird and Crowley (1965)

INDEX